ENCYCLOPAEDIA OF
INDIA, PAKISTAN AND BANGLADESH

ENCYCLOPAEDIA OF

INDIA, PAKISTAN AND BANGLADESH

(In 9 Volumes)

(Volume 5)

OM GUPTA

ISHA

ISHA BOOKS

Delhi-110033

Encyclopaedia of India, Pakistan and Bangladesh
(In 9 Volumes)

ISBN : 81-8205-389-7 (Set)
ISBN : 81-8205-394-3 (Vol. 5)

Rs. 6300 (Set)

Published in 2006 in India by
Isha Books
D-43, Prithviraj Road,
Adarsh Nagar, Delhi - 110033
e-mail : ishabooks@hotmail.com

Laser Typesetting : Vinayak Printers, Delhi
Printed at : Salasar Imaging Systam, Delhi

Preface

According to Oxford dictionary Encyclopaedia is a book or aset of books that gives information on many subjects or many aspect of one subject. This encyclopaedia does that on India, Pakistan and Bangladesh. It is the first work of its kind. There have been anthologies on India but there is no compendium of information in an alphabetical order. Even Britannica could go as far as four-volume encyclopaedia on Indian history.

Encyclopaedia is an extension of a dictionary. The latter gives you meanings of words while the former gives facts about people, places and events. No one can claim to compile all the facts and that of a sub-continent called India. But then it is the prerogative of the editor to pick up his entries that he considers would be useful to his reader. Generally we soon find our comfort levels in a language. And rarely consults a dictionary and lesser an encyclopaedia. But those who dare, find the experience worth it. It can be easily compared to a human body. In our daily life we tend to be our own quacks and medicate on the basis of common sense. If we refer to a doctor we come to know the actual cause of the symptom and get relieved on knowing the gravity of the situation or the absence of it. One would realize that encyclopaedia reveals the fundamentals of any situation, person or the event and we feel at home with that information.

A dictionary and an encyclopaedia can easily enlarge the process of learning even to an uninitiated person. It is truer in case of humanities. Popular myth about encyclopaedia is that it is meant to be referred to in a library only. The librarians, the world over keep encyclopaedia in such zealously guarded protection that the generally refrain from asking for it. Since the advent of internet in our life, the bulkiness of encyclopaedias has disappeared. That is why we have divided this enterprise in nine volumes. Encyclopaedias are generally global in its expanse. Even subject-related encyclopaedias give the global perspective.That is why country-specific encylopaedias have never been seriousy attempted. We hope that this effort will fill that volume. Traditionally encyclopaedias don't deal with factual data e.g. Indian exports, population figures, GDP. That is the job of annual reference books. They are also different from alamans in as much as that they don't give dated entries. That will become texts on history. Encyclopaedias need to be updated. A country is alive and kicking. People and events continue to play role in various aspects of life. Hence they need to be added. That is why either annual supplements or updation needs to be done in encyclopaedias. We would strive for that.

Regarding its contents only those entries have been included that continue to influence the life of a nation. There are historical figures who might have played a significant role in their times but if those deeds have no relevance to the present they have been excluded. Another example is literary awards. They always create controversies because their selection at times is subjective. Hence only universally accepted meritorious work has found place in these volumes. In this context a debatable point need to be stated. Who is more important book or the author. Conventionally work is an end product and only that is a measure of the author's importance but then a prolic writer might have produced a large body of creations. Hence to save space the author is entered with all his important work.That is also an international practice.

Lastly, why India, Pakistan and Bangladesh have been clubbed together. Before India's independence they were one nation. They share a common heritage and composite culture. Their post-independence history is different but 22their foundation is undivided. In order to appreciate the historical context better it is necessary to cross-refer and that was possible when they are juxtaposed.

Om Gupta

J

Jabalpur : Jabalpur is a city in Madhya Pradesh state of India. It is located in Mahakoshal region in the geographic center of India. Jabalpur is the administrative headquarters of Jabalpur District and Jabalpur Division. The city is considered to be a Sanskardhani, literally meaning a "cultural centerplace". The numerous gorges in the neighboring rocks have been taken advantage of to surround the city with a series of lakes, which, shaded by fine trees and bordered by fantastic crags, add much beauty to the suburbs. However many of these lakes now have been encroached for the fishing purpose or for building works, although greenery still exists.

The city itself dates from the nineteenth century, and is laid out in wide and regular streets. It has a beautiful collection of marble rocks called bhera-ghat surrounding the holy Narmada River. Many visitors every year come to visit Jabalpur because of this major attraction. Jabalpur is an important junction for the Indian Railways. Jabalpur also has a big Defence and Military Center—HQ of the MPBO Area, the headquarters of West Central Railway Zone, the Madhya Pradesh State Electricity Board, and the Madhya Pradesh High Courts. It is also known for giving to the world, philosophers like Maharishi Mahesh Yogi of Transcendental Meditation fame and Bhagwaan Rajneesh (Osho).

Jabro : This dance form is peculiar to Chang- Thang and Rong areas of Ladakh region in Kahsmir. Both males and females face each other forming rows or circles and dance leaping hand in hand forwards and backwards reciting melodious songs.

Jacobabad : Jacobabad is a city in the Sindh province of Pakistan, located at lat. 28°16′37.32"N, long. 68°27′05.04"E. The city is crossed by the Pakistan Western Railway and many main roads of the province. The town was founded near the village of Khangarh in 1847 by General John Jacob, for many years commandant of the Sindh Horse. Jacob who died and was buried there in 1858, and left a marvellous Victoria Tower in his remembrance in the heart of the city.

Jadeshwar : Jadeshwar is a temple having a 'Swayambhu linga' built by Vadodara's Vithoba Diwan at the beginning of Nineteenth century AD. This temple runs Anna—Kshetra & Dharmashala to stay over-night. One can enjoy breathtaking scenic beauty with serpentine curves & a lake on the way.

Jaffarabad : The Jaffarabad district lies in the southeast of the Pakistani province of Balochistan. The district is named after Mir Jaffar Khan Jamali, a Muslim League veteran from Balochistan and a close friend of Quaid-e-Azam Mohammad Ali Jinnah. The district comprises two sub-divisions (Usta Mohammad and Jhat Pat) containing four tehsils - Usta Mohammad, Jhatpat, Gandakha and Suhbat Pur. There are no Levy Thanas and ten police stations.

Jagatsinghpur : Jagatsinghpur is a district of Orissa, India. Notable areas include Port of Paradip. Jagatsinghpur is also famous for the Sarala Temple and is well-known as the cultural heart of Orissa. The district (smallest in size among the 30 districts in Orissa) has produced some of the most famous names in Oriya and Indian literature: Sarala Das, Birakishore, Gopal Chhotaray, and Bibhuti Pattnaik, for example. Jagatsinghpur was the worst hit district in the super cyclone in October 1999 in which thousands of people died.

Jharsuguda is a district in Orissa, India. The district once had an airport during World War II. The district is rich in coal and several other mineral reserves. Of late, iron and steel industries are coming up marking the sunshine days of the district in the times to come!

Jagdalpur : Jagdalpur is a city in Chhattisgarh state of central India. The city is located on the south bank of the Indravati River, and has a population of approximately 150,000. It is the administrative headquarters of Bastar District and Bastar Division, and was the capital of the erstwhile princely state of Bastar.

Jagdish Chandra Bose : Jagadish Chandra Bose was one of the pioneers of modern science in India. His research was on the properties of electro-magnetic waves. His major achievement was to demonstrate the similarity of responses to stimulation among the living and the nonliving as well as the fundamental similarity of responses in plant and animal tissues. The British Government knighted him in 1917. He founded the 'Bose Research Institute' in Kolkatta in 1917.

Bose was not only a biologist, but also a physicist. Bose believed that by focusing on the boundaries between different physical and biological sciences, he would be able to demonstrate the underlying unity of all things. Bose's biological researches were founded initially by the discovery that an electric receiver seems to show science of fatigue after continued use. He can rightly be called the inventor of wireless telegraphy. Bose was the first in the world to fabricate and demonstrate in public (1985) the device that generated microwaves-radio waves of very short wave length. But his invention was not patented before Guglielmo Marconi (1896) who became internationally recognised as the inventor. After completing his studies in London, Bose return to Kolkatta and was appointed Professor at Presidency College in Kolkatta. Then he became the director of the institute he founded and remained in the post till his death on 23rd November 1937.

Jagjit Singh : Jagjit Singh is a popular singer of ghazals in Hindi/Urdu and Punjabi, a composer and also a playback singer in Bollywood. He was born in Ganganagar (also called "SriGanganager"), Rajasthan.

In 2003, he was awarded the Padma Bhushan.

Jagjit Singh Aurora : Lt-Gen Jagjit Singh Aurora (February 13, 1916—May 3, 2005) was the Indian commander whose comprehensive defeat of Pakistan in 1971 led to the creation of Bangladesh. He was born in Jhelum, Pakistan and died in New Delhi, India. He was born the son of an engineer in Jhelum, in what is now Pakistan. He was commissioned into the 2nd Punjab Regiment in 1939 after his graduation from the Indian Military Academy, and went on to command it during the 1947-1948 hosilities with Pakistan in Kashmir. He had reached the rank of brigadier by the time he was involved in border hostilities with Chinese troops in 1961.

In 1971, Aurora was made commander of Indian forces in the east, and he was responsible for hostilities in East Pakistan. Aurora had helped to oversee the logistical preparations for the coming battles, including the improvement of roads, communications and bridges, as well as the movement of 30,000 tons of supplies close to the border of East Pakistan. On December 16, 1971, Aurora accepted the surrender of Pakistani forces led by General

Niazi. The signing of the document ended the war, and led to the formation of Bangla Desh.

Jagrata Muslim Janata Bangladesh : Jagrata Muslim Janata Bangladesh (Awakened Muslim Masses of Bangladesh), also known by the acronym JMJB, is a Islamist, terrorist organisation based in Bangladesh, especially around the country's north-western region. It is reported to be affiliated with al-Qaeda. The organisation was the feature of a January 2005 New York Times article based upon the rise of Islamic radicalism in Bangladesh. It was also responsible for a series of suicide bombings in Bangladesh.

The group is led by Siddiqur Rahman, also known as "Bangla Bhai", and Shaykh Abdur Rahman. Both of them are wanted by the Bangladesh Government for terrorism. Several lesser leaders, for example, the head of the military branch, have been captured. Formed in the late 1990s, JMJB came into spotlight through its murder spree in the North-western region of Bangladesh. Soon after, in 2004 the organisation was banned by the ruling Bangladesh Nationalist Party-led government and measures were taken to eradicate its missions and presence. Many of JMJB's members and leaders were former Mujahedin who fought in Afghanistan and who personally knew Osama bin Laden. Its captured activists have stated that they were trained and hoped to join their Jihadist comrades in Afghanistan and Iraq in fighting against the U.S.-led coalition and the democratic political establishments in place within those countries.

Their leaders include Bangla Bhai, Shaykh Abdur Rahman, Shaykh Abd as-Samad as-Salafee and Dr. Asadullah al-Ghalib. The JMJB is extremely critical of the Jamaat-e-Islami Bangladesh, which it deems as heretical due to the latter's participation in the Bangladeshi political establishment and patronisation of secularism and sacrilege of Islamic values and principles.

Jahanara Imam : Jahanara Imam (1929–1994) was a Bangladeshi writer and political activist. She is most widely remembered for her endeavor to bring war criminals of the Bangladesh Liberation War to trial. Jahanara Imam was born in a conservative Muslim family in Murshidabad, now in West Bengal, India. She, however, received higher education and studied in Carmichael College in Rangpur and institutions in Kolkata. After the partition of India, her family moved to Mymensingh. Imam joined them after completing her studies from Kolkata and strted teaching at a local girl's school. In 1947, she married Shariful Alam Imam Ahmed. They moved to Dhaka after a few years, and Jahanara Imam started teaching at Siddheswari Girl's School, of which she became the Headmistress later. After taking training in education in Dhaka, she went to USA as a Fullbright scholar in 1964-65 to get further training in education. Jahanara Imam later got a Masters degree in Bangla literature from Dhaka University.

In 1971, the Bangladesh Liberation War broke out. Jahanara Imam's eldest son, Rumi, joined the Mukti Bahini to fight the Pakistani forces. Bottled in Dhaka with no information about her son, Jahanara kept a diary to express her thoughts. Rumi never returned from the war, and Shariful Imam died following an interrogation by the Pakistan army. After Bangladesh achieved independence, Imam stareted a literary career, and her most notable publication was that of her diary. In 1981 she was diagnosed with mouth cancer. In nineties, Jahanara Imam became the central figure of a political movement to try the 1971 war criminals. Imam died of cancer in 1994.

Jahangir : Nuruddin Jahangir (August 31, 1569 – October 28, 1627) was the ruler of the Mughal Empire from 1605 until 1627. He signed a treaty with the British East India Company promising their merchants preferential treatment, opening the Indian subcontinent to Britain for the first time. He is also the person known to history as Shehzada Salim of Anarkali fame, immortalized in the famous Urdu film Mughal-e-Azam. Prince Salim's personal nickname was Shaikhoo. The name Jahangir is from Persian, meaning "Conqueror of the World", "World-Conqueror", or "Dominant over the World". Alternative spellings of the name include Jehangir, and Cihangir (in Turkish).

He was born as Prince Muhammad Salim in August 1569, the eldest son of the Mughal Emperor Akbar. Akbar ensured that his son received the best education possible. Salim started his studies at the age of four and was taught Persian, Turkish, Arabic, Urdu, history, arithmetic, geography and other sciences by important tutors like Abdur Rahim Khan-i-Khahan.

Prince Salim succeeded to the throne on the eighth day after his father's death. He took the name Jahangir and began his 22-year reign at the age of 36. Having seized power, he had to fend off his own son Prince Khusraw's claim to the throne. Khusraw was defeated and as a punishment, his eyes were taken out. Jahangir started his reign with several popular acts. He released prisoners of war, promised to protect Islam and granted general amnesty to his opponents. He set up a "Chain of Justice" outside his palace. Anyone in trouble could simply pull the chain and receive a hearing from the Emperor.

Jahangir married his twentieth and last wife, the extremely beautiful and intelligent Mehr-un-Nisa, in May 1611. She was the widow of Sher Afghan, one of Jahangir's lords, who died under questionable circumstances. Mehr-un-Nisa was given the title of Nur Jehan on her marriage to Jahangir. Jahangir was fond of ease and comfort. He was an alcoholic and could be found day and night with wine goblets in his hands. He was also susceptible to the influence of others, a weakness exploited by many. Because of his constantly inebriated state, Nur Jehan became the actual power behind the throne. He died in 1627 and was buried in Shahdra, a suburb of Lahore, Punjab, Pakistan.

Jahangir Nagar : Jahangir Nagar is the former name of Dhaka, Bangladesh. It was named after Mughal Emperor Jahangir.

Jahangirnagar University : Jahangirnagar University is a public university in Bangladesh. The university was established in 1970 by the Jahangirnagar Muslim University Ordinance, 1970 (later amended as Jahangirnagar University Act, 1973), During the two preceding years, it operated as a project, Its first Vice-Chancellor took up office on September 24, 1970. The first batch of students, a total of 150, was enrolled in four departments: Economics, Geography, Mathematics and Statistics. Its formal inauguration was delayed until January 12, 1971, when the university was formally launched by Vice Admiral S. M. Ahsan, the then Chancellor.

Jahaniyan Mosque : Jahaniyan Mosque is the latest of all the surviving monuments of the Sultanate period in Gaur. It is also called Jan-Jan Miyan's Mosque or Jhanjhania Mosque. From an inscription over its doorway it is known to have been built by Bibi Malti, probably a lady of the court, in 1535 AD, during the reign of Sultan Ghiyasuddin Mahmud Shah, son of Alauddin Husain Shah. The nomenclature 'Jahaniyan Mosque' is rather obscure. It is believed that it might have been a corruption of a saint's name, Jahaniyan Jahangasht.

Jaijaidin : Jaijaidin is a major Bangla weekly published from Dhaka, Bangladesh. It shot into fame during the 1980 due to its stance against the military ruler Hossain

Mohammad Ershad, and was banned by him. It started republication after democracy was restored in 1991.

Jain Temples : On hill crests around Rajgir in Bihar, far in the distances one can see about 26 Jain temples. They are difficult to approach for the untrained, but make exciting trekking for those in form.

Jainal Hazari : Jainal Hazari is the infamous Don of the underworld of Dhaka. At over 6'8 and supposedly weighing over 300lbs, the man is known by many as the 'Tower of Terror'. Or, in Bangla, Shontrasher Choora. He was a gangster turned MP who terrorised many villages and got away with it. Jainal is currently serving a sentence in jail, thanks to the new governement in Bangladesh. Jainal, (sometimes spelt Joynal or Zoynol)

Jainism : Jainism is primarily an Indian religion. There are more than 3 million Jains in India, forming almost the smaller sections among the various religious groups. In spite of its small number, the Jain community has a strong influence on the Indian life. Jains belong chiefly to the mercantile class, spread mainly over central, northern and southern India. Splendid Jain temples and statues can be found almost in all parts of the country. The Jains have also set up many trusts and charitable institutions in the country.

The theme of self-conquest, common to all religions is supremely important to the Jains. The very word Jaina is derived from 'Jina' conqueror. Carrying the idea of self-conquest to its extreme, Jainism has become the worlds most rigourously ascetic faith. God has no place in this system. The popular god's of Hinduism are accepted, but they are placed lower than the Jains who are regarded as the true recipients of worship.

Vardhamana better known by his title Mahavira (great Hero) was an elder contemporary of the Buddha. He cannot be called the founder of Jainism but rather its reformer. He is said to be the last of a line of 24 Jains. The Ist Rsabha whose name is detected in the Vedas and hence Jainism can be claimed to be of great antiquity. The 22nd prophet 'Neminatha' (or Austanemi) who came from Kathiawar is very popular in Gujarat. He is supposed to be a kinsman of Lord Krishna, the Hindu god. Jainism belongs to mythology rather than history till the period of this prophet.

The 23rd prophet Parsvanatha belonged to 8th century BC has been considered by the researchers and was therefore a historical personage. He was the son of Asvasena, the king of Benares. He laid a normal life till the age of thirty and thereafter renounced all his worldly possessions, devoting himself to meditation and asceticism and attained supreme knowledge. When he was 70 he retired to a mountain now known as Parsanath near Bihar and went into meditation. He lived till 100 and died after a rigorous fast of one month. He had many followers. Mahavira was converted when he encountered a disciple of Parsvanatha and it is he who completed the doctrine. Therefore Jainism in its complete forms is not the work of one prophet, but Mahavira is held in the highest esteem as he completed the work and really set its principles and was also responsible for its growth.

Vardhamana was born in 599BC at Kundagrama near Vaishali, about 27 miles north of Patna, in Bihar. He was born to an aristocratic parents of the Naya Clan. When he was about 30, his parents passed away and with his brothers permission, he distributed his worldly possessions and left house.

Mahavira imposed upon himself the life of a religious mendicant. After 3 months in the severe cold he renounced wearing cloths. He meditated for 2 years, undertook several fasts and began his journeys for 12 years across

Magadh up to the western boundary of Bengal. He perfected his knowledge and elaborated the fundamental principles of the religious life which he preached later on. He attained Nirvana (omniscience) on a summer night of Vaisabha Sukla Dashmi under a Sal tree on the bank of the river Riyvalia near Jrmbhika grama. After leading the life of an ascetic for 42 years, Mahavira died or attained Nirvana at the age of 72, at Pavapuri near the present Patna.

Mahavira had 11 disciples, each entrusted with a band of about 300 to 500 monks to preach the religion. Bhadrabahu, contemporary of the great Mauryan king Chandragupta was the greatest propagator of faith. After Bhadrabahu's death, serious differences began to arise among the Jain community. The group led by him migrated towards the west coast and Deccan, while others remained in the north. The group which remained in the north were chiefly led by Sthulabhadra, the last of the omniscient. The final break between the two groups came around AD 79. Jains divided into Digambaras (sky /air as their cloth). i.e., naked who follow Mahavira and Swetambaras (wearers of white clothes), who follow Parshvanatha. Most famous among the disciples were Gautama, Indrabhuti and Sudharman and they are said to have attained omniscience (knowing everything).

Mahavira is said to have preached in Ardhamgadhi language. A fixed form was given to the Jain Canon is the 5th century AD at Valabhi which consists of 45 works of varied content. Digambaras did not accept, this canon. They believed mostly on the oral teachings of the monks and that liberation is impossible unless one renounced clothes, in the foot steps of Mahavira. They contest that Mahavira was married. Women can attain liberation and the omniscients can take ordinary nourishment. Finely they believe that the ancient texts have definitely been lost and do not believe in the authenticity of the scriptures which constitute the canon of Swetambaras. The Swetambara canon is called 'Agama' or 'Sidhanta' or even 'Gampidaha'. The other important Jain religious texts are 'Devadashangas'; 'Upangas' and 'Mulashatras'.

Jains have made valuable contributions in many areas of Indian culture: philosophy, literature, painting, sculpture and architecture. Their poetry is often excessively didactic. Their sculpture is of a high quality and some of the images of Tirthankaras are technically perfect. Their faces are however devoid of any expression, as they are supposed to have transcended all human emotions. The greatest glory of Jaina religious art lies in temple architecture, particularly at Ginar, Palitana and Mount Abu. These temples reveal a breadth of aesthetic sensitivity and a feeling for ornamentation reminiscent of the finest specimen of classical Hindu and Buddhist architecture.

Jaintia Hills : Jaintia Hills is an administrative district in the state of Meghalaya in India. The present district was created in 22 February 1972 and occupies an area of 3819 km^2. It has a population of 295,692 (as of 2001), of which a vast majority is rural. The district headquarters are located at Jowai. The district is part of the Meghalaya subtropical forests ecoregion. For the tribal division into twelve elaka (provinces), each under a dolloi, tributary to the Raja of Jaintiapur. Agriculture and mining are the dominant economic activities. The district has large reserves of coal and is the largest producer of coal within Meghalaya.

Jaintia Kingdom : The Jaintia kingdom from eastern Shillong plateau extended to the plains south of it and to the north of the Barak river valley in Assam. Jaintia is derived from Synteng, the collective name of different tribal groups from the region. The Syntengs are Mon-Khmer languages that are close to Khasi. The Jaintia hills is part of Meghalaya. What is today the Sylhet region was at one time under the jurisdiction of the Jaintia king. The origin of the Jaintia kingdom is not known. But the Synteng people follow a megalith culture that first found expression in the Shillong plateau in prehistoric times, which indicates that they are indeed settlers from very old times. After the 17th century invasion by the Kachari king Satrudaman, the Jaintia kingdom came under increasing Kachari and Ahom influence.

Jaipur : Jaipur, also popularly known as the Pink City, historically sometimes rendered as Jeypore, is the capital of Rajasthan state, India. Jaipur is also the capital of Jaipur District. Jaipur is the former capital of a princely state of the same name. The city was founded in 1728 by Maharaja Sawai Jai Singh, the ruler of Amber. The population in 2003 was approximately 2.7 million. The city was built of pink stucco in imitation of sandstone, and is remarkable among pre-modern Indian cities for the width and regularity of its streets. The city is laid out into six quarters, separated by broad streets 111 ft (34 m) wide. The urban quarters are further divided by networks of gridded streets. Five quarters wrap around the east, south, and west sides of a central palace quarter, with a sixth quarter immediately to the east. The Palace quarter encloses a sprawling palace complex (the Hawa Mahal, or palace of winds), formal gardens, and a small lake. A fort crowns the hill in the northwest corner of the old city. Another noteworthy building is Jai Singh's observatory, Jantar Mantar. Jaipur, with its rich and colourful past, resplendent with tales of valour and bravery is now one of the most important heritage cities in India, and is a must-see for tourists coming to India.

Jaisalmer : Jaisalmer is a town in the Indian state of Rajasthan. It lies in the heart of the Thar Desert and has a population of about 78,000. It is the administrative headquarters of Jaisalmer District. Jaisalmer's is said to have once been a halting point along a traditional trade route traversed by the camel caravans of Indian and Asian merchants. Any possible remnant of that era was finally extinguished upon the partition of India in 1947, which rendered the town a drought-prone desert backwater on the international border. Ironically, skirmishes between India and Pakistan gave Jaisalmer a strategic importance and made it servicable as an army supply depot. Later, the Rajasthan Canal served to revive the surrounding desert areas. Roads and railroads were then built, knitting the hitherto remote town with the rest of Rajasthan.

Jaishankar Prasad : Jaishankar Prasad (1889—1937) was one of the most famous figures in modern Hindi literature. He was a dramatist, novelist, poet and story-writer. Prasad belonged to the Chhayavaadi school of Hindi poetry. His most famous work is Kamayani, which is considered the best of the Hindi poetry, next only to Tulsidas' Ramacharitamanas. Kamayani tells of the Flood and the central characters of the epic poem is Manu (a male) and Shradha (a female). Manu is representative of the human psyche and Shradha represents love. Another female character is Ida, who represents rationality. Some critics surmise that the three lead characters of Kamayani symbolizes a synthesis of knowledge, action and desires in human life.

Jaladurga Kalyanotsavam : Kolletikola in Kaikalur taluk of Krishna district is a place of historical significance. This district is in Andhra Pradesh. There was a temple dedicated to Jaladurga in Kolletikola. The festival of this deity is celebrated for sixteen days from the first day of the month of phalguna. The tenth, eleventh and twelfth are important festive days. On the eleventh day the wedding of Jaladurga and Gokarmeswara swami is celebrated. About ten thousands fowls, five hundred goats, and a thousand sheep are sacrificed to the deity. The sacrifices are conducted behind the fort, far away from the temple. Coconuts, plantains, saffron and kumkum are also offered to the deity. About one lakh persons from neighbouring districts congregate during the festival. A fair is held in front of the temple.

Jalalia : Jalalia is a village located in the Attock District in Punjab, Pakistan. It's approximately 4-5 miles east of the city of Hazro. Jalalia is bordered on the southeast and south by the town of Ghourghusti, on the southwest by the village of Shinka, on the west by the village of Momen Pur, on the north by the Indus River, and on the east by the village of Shakh Chur. Jalalia is approximately 15-20 miles west of Tarbela Dam.

Jalal-ud-din Firuz Khilji : Jalal-ud-din Firuz Khilji (d. 1296), first Indian ruler from the Khilji dynasty from 1290-1296. He was regarded as a foreign intruder and a barbarian, he did not show himself in his own capital of Delhi. He built another capital at Kilokhri a few miles from the city and ruled from there for six years. In 1292, a horde of more than 100,000 Mongols invaded the country. Successes in battle and smart negotiation caused a partial retreat on the part of the Mongols. They rose again five years later when his nephew and son-in-law Ala ud din Khilji was on the throne. Ala-ud-din was also responsible for a successful raid in to Deccan as Governor of Kara under his uncle, the king, Jalal-ud-din. While Ala-ud-din was returning from there with the spoils of victory, Jalal-ud-din hurried to Kara to meet him. He was murdered by his nephew when he arrived

Jalan Museum : Jalan museum in Bihar holds the private collection of jade, Chinese paintings and silver filigree work of the Mughal period. It is constructed at the site of Sher Shah's fort.

Jalandhar : Jalandhar is an ancient city in the state of Punjab, India. It was the capital of Trigarttas (people living in the "land between three rivers": Ravi, Beas and Sutlej) in the times of Mahabharata war. It has an urban population of almost a million, and another million live in the rural areas outside the city. The city is located almost 375 km from Delhi, and about 90 km from Amritsar. Jalandhar is named after Jaldhar, a demon king who lived in water as his name suggests. If the name is divided in two parts JAL & DHAR. JAL means water and DHAR means to live in. It was the capital of Punjab until 1953, when it was replaced by Chandigarh.

The city is the media and mass communication hub of the region having the regional headquarters of the national television and radio channels. The city is well known for its production of sports equipment and leather goods. Many major sports equipment manufacturers such as BDM, Cosco, JJ Jonex, Spartan and F.C. Sondhi group are based here. In sports goods the worlds best footballs, cricket and hockey equipment are made in Jalandhar, major sports giants such as Adidas, Reebok, and Mitre outsource from jalandhar. Jalandhar offers a large selection of hotels for travellers. One of the leading hotels in the city is The Regent Park Hotel. In ancient time, the district or Kingdom of Jalandhar comprised the whole of the Upper Doabas from the Ravi to the Satluj. According to the Padama Purana, as quoted by General Conningham the country takes its name from the great Daitya King Danava Jalandhara the son of the Ganga by Ocean

Jalandhar is the world's biggest manufacturer of leather tool pouches and aprons with major USA and European customers buying from factories in Jalandhar. Jalandhar is also famous for its surgical tool industry. Jalandhar produce a large number of surgical tools. Big companies like Camlin outsource its production here.A place called basti sheikh has got many cottage projects which run without any help of the Punjab government which has turned enemy of the Industry. Jalandhar also has the biggest printing industry in India. With major publishing and advertising companies like, mbd, aay bee advertisers having their main offices in Jalandhar.

Jalaun : Jalaun is a city in Jalaun District of Uttar Pradesh state, in northern India. The town was formerly the residence of a Maratha governor, but never the headquarters of the district, which are at Orai. In early times Jalaun seems to have been the home of two Rajput clans, the Chandelas in the east and the Kachwahas in the west. The town of Kalpi on the Yamuna was conquered by the armies of Muhammad of Ghor in 1196. Early in the 14th century the Bundelas occupied the greater part of Jalaun, and even succeeded in holding the fortified post of Kalpi. That important possession was soon recovered by the Delhi Sultanate, and passed under the way of the Mughal Empire.

Jalaun was the scene of much violence during the Revolt of 1857. When the news of the rising at Kanpur reached Kalpi, the men of the 53rd Native Infantry deserted their officers, and in June the Jhansi rebels reached the district, and began their murder of Europeans. It was not until September 1858 that the rebels were finally defeated. In the later 19th century, the district suffered much from the invasive kans grass (Saccharum spontaneum), owing to the spread of which many villages were abandoned and their land thrown out of cultivation. The population of the district was 399,726 in 1901, and the two largest towns are Kunch and Kalpi (pop. 10,139 in 1901). The district was traversed by the line of the Indian Midland railway from Jhansi to Kanpur.

Jalaun District : Jalaun District is a district of Uttar Pradesh state of India. The district is named for the town of Jalaun, which was the former headquarters of a Maratha governor, but not the administrative headquarters of the district, which are at Orai. Other large towns in the district are Kalpi, Konch, and Madhogarh. Jalaun District is a part of Jhansi Division. The district lies entirely within the level plain of Bundelkhand, north of the hill country, and is almost surrounded by the Yamuna River, which forms the northern boundary of the district, and its tributaries the Betwa, which forms the southern boundary of the district, and the Pahuj, which forms the western boundary. The central region thus enclosed is a dead level of cultivated land, almost destitute of trees, and dotted with villages. The southern portion presents an almost unbroken sheet of cultivation. The Non River flows through the centre of the district, which it drains by innumerable small ravines. The districts of Etawah and Kanpur lie to the north across the Yamuna, while Hamirpur District lies to the east and southeast, Jhansi District lies to the southeast, and Bhind District of Madhya Pradesh lies to the west cross the Pahuj.

Jaldhaka : A river originating in the eastern Himalayas.It is a trans-boundary river. originates from the himalayas of southeast Sikkim and flows over Jalpaiguri and Cooch Behar. The river enters Bangladesh through Lalmonirhat District. After entering Bangladesh, the river joins with the dharla and flows as Dharla before debouching into the brahmaputra near kurigram. The total length of the Jaldhaka is about 192 km of which a little part lies within Bangladesh.

Jaldhaka River : Jaldhaka river is one of the trans-boundary rivers, originates from the Himalayas of southeast Sikkim and flows over Jalpaiguri and Kuchbihar. The river enters Bangladesh through Lalmonirhat district. After entering Bangladesh, the river joins with the Dharla and flows as Dharla before debouching into the

Brahmaputra near Kurigram. The total length of the Jaldhaka is about 192 km of which a little part lies within Bangladesh.

Jalebi : Jalebi is a sweet common in India. It's hawked all over city streets. It is easy to make, consisting of deep-fried, syrup-soaked batter in large, chaotic pretzel shapes.

Jalebis are mostly bright orange in colour but are also available in white and best served warm and dripping. Jalebis when served cold have a minor chewy texture, with a crystalised sugar "crunch".

Jalgaon : Jalgaon is a city in western India, in northern Maharashtra state, Jalgaon District on the northern Deccan Plateau. Located within the productive, irrigated agricultural region of Kandesh, Jalgaon is a significant collection and distribution center of agricultural goods. The leading products are jowar and raw cotton; the region's rich volcanic soil is particularly well-suited to cotton production. Jalgaon is an important center for cotton-textile and vegetable-oil mills, particularly groundnut-oil and hydrogenation plants. Jalgaon is also well known for bananas production. The city is also famous for its gold market which has reputation of being pure.

Modern Jalgaon is now boasts of vast industrial area, educational institutes and good hospitals. The railway junctions serve routes to Mumbai, Nagpur, Delhi and Surat. The city is well developed with good roads, shopping centres, residential areas, with good infrastructure in communication and transport.

Jallian Wala Bagh : This place noted for its most notorious massacre under British rule. It is 400 meters north of the Golden Temple. The British General Dyer was the Lieutenant Governor of the province in 1919. He banned all meetings and demonstrations led by Indians against the economical set back by World War I.

On 13 April 1919, pilgrim spoured into Amritsar to celebrate the Baisakhi festival, a holiday in the Sikh calendar. In the afternoon thousands of people gathered at Jallian Wala Bagh to celebrate the Baisakhi. This ground surrounded by high walls on all sides has only a narrow alley for access. General Dyer personally led the troops to the sight and ordered his men to open fire without any warning. It resulted in the death of 379 and injured more than 1200. India was outraged by Dyer's massacre. Gandhiji, called for a nation wide strike and started the Non-cooperation Movement, which became an important mile stone in the struggle for India's Independence.

Today this ground has been changed to a park and it has a pleasant garden. There is a narrow path between the houses which leads to the lawn of the park. At the entrance there is a memorial plaque which recounts the history.

There is a well on the north side in which many people who tried to escape from the bullets were drowned, and remnants of walls have been preserved to show the bullet holes. At the east end of the garden there is a large memorial built in memory of those who died here.

Jalpaiguri : Jalpaiguri is a town in the state of West Bengal, India. It is the headquarters of Jalpaiguri district, and the divisional headquarters of the North Bengal region. Jalpaiguri was initially founded as a trading centre, as the origins of its name suggests. The name Jalpaiguri comes from the Bhutanese term je-le-pe-go-ri, which means 'a place where warm clothes are bought and sold'. Some people attribute the name to the more common Bengali term jalpai, which means Olives and thus the name meaning the town of Olives.

The town was part of the Duars area of the old Kamarupa and later the Bhutanese kingdoms, which was later annexed by the British in 1864. They divided the captured area into two parts and merged the eastern half into the Goalpara district (now in Assam) and converted the western half into a new district of Western Duars and then in 1869, it was reorganised and renamed to Jalpaiguri, with Jalpaiguri town becoming the district headquarters.

Jama Masjid : The Masjid-i-Jahan Numa, commonly known as Jama Masjid is the principal mosque of Old Delhi. Commissioned by the Mughal Emperor Shah Jahan and completed in the year 1656 AD, it is one of the largest and best known mosques in India. Masjid-i-Jahan Numa means "the mosque commanding a view of the world", and the name Jama Masjid is a reference to the weekly congregation observed on Friday at the mosque.

The courtyard of the mosque can hold upto twenty-five thousand worshippers. The mosque also houses several relics in a closet in the north gate, including a copy of the Quran written on deerskin, a red beard-hair and a pair of sandals said to belong to the prophet Muhammad and his footprint embedded in a marble slab.

Jamaat-e-Islami : Jamaat-e-Islami (JI) was an Islamic political movement founded in South Asia by Syed Ab'ul Ala Maududi in 1941. Today it is one of the largest components of the coalition of religious parties, the Muttahida Majlis-e-Amal, in Pakistan. Members are often referred to, usually by others, as Jamaatis. The latter is also used as an adjective for certain political viewpoint or attitude.

Jamaat-e-Islami Bangladesh : Jamaat-e-Islami Bangladesh a political party advocating for incorporating Islamic ideology into state system. From the early 1930s an attempt was made to float a political party under the leadership of Maulana Sayyid Abul Ala Maududi with an object of launching Islamic movement in India. Activities to that end began from 1932 through a monthly journal Tarjuman al-Quran. Maulana Maududi expressed his difference of opinion with the Muslim League's ideology in his lecture on 'Way to Establish Islamic Hukumat' delivered at Aligarh University in September 1940. In February 1941, a programme was undertaken to hold a convention for launching a new political party. Accordingly, in a meeting held in Lahore on 25 August 1941, the Jamaat-e-Islami was established with Maulana Maududi as its ameer or chairman.

The first convention of the party on all-India basis was held on 19-21 April 1945 at Pathankot in the Punjab. After the partition of India in 1947 the party was divided into Jamaat-e-Islami Hind with headquarters in Delhi and Jamaat-e-Islami Pakistan with its central office in Lahore. The central leadership of the All Pakistan Jamaat-e-Islami was vested upon Maulana Sayyid Abul Ala Maududi, the founder-ameer of the party.

Jamaat-ul-Mujahideen : Jamaat-ul-Mujahideen is a banned Bangladeshi Islamist organisation which calls for the establishment of an Islamic state in Bangladesh, governed by Islamic shari'a. It favours violent methods in its attempt to implement such laws and government. They have claimed responsibility for several violent attacks and bombing, including the August 17, 2005 Dhaka bombings and are also believed to have been involved in an explosion of seven bombs on February 13, 2003 at one of its hideouts, having been preparing to explode them in northern Bangladeshi towns during International Mother Language Day.

The group had until their capture by RAB secirity authorities in March 2006, been led by Siddiqul Islam a.k.a. "Banglabhai" and Shaykh Abdur Rahman. In addition, several captured members of the group have claimed that their targets include traditional Bangladeshi cultural and non-government organisations such as BRAC, Proshika, and Grameen Bank.

Jamashedji Tata : Jamshedji Tata is considered to be the path-finder of modern industrial builders. He is known as the grand father of Indian Industry for his acumen and enthusiasm. Jamshedji's father Nasarvanji Tata used to trade in jute with China and Britain. He started export from India. Jamshedji started a cloth mill in Nagpur more than hundred years ago. At that time almost all the cloth used to come from England.

Jamshedji Tata was the main person behind the idea to start an Iron and steel Factory. But his dreams was fulfilled by his sons, when they started the Tata Iron and Steel Factory in 1907 first three years after his death. He established the Indian Institute of Science Bangalore (IISc). Then Hydro -electric Project at Bombay is an example of his foresightedness. The Taj Hotel in Bombay was also built by Tata, which ranks as one of the best hotels in the world.

Jamdani : Jamdani is a kind of fine cloth made in Bangladesh. Though mostly used for saris, Jamdani is also used for scarves, handkerchiefs etc. Jamdani is believed to be a fusion of the ancient cloth-making techniques of Bengal (perhaps 2000 years old) with the Middle Eastern influence of muslin brought by the Muslims starting from the 1300s.

Jamia Mosque : The first mosque ever built in Multan was the Jamia Mosque, which was constructed on the orders of Mohammad Bin Qasim. Ruins of this mosque were visible till 1954 at Qasim Bella which have now been washed away by the repeated floods of the river Chenab.

Jamiat Ulema-e-Islam : The Jamiat Ulema-e-Islam (Assembly of Islamic Clergy) is a political party in Pakistan. It is part of the islam-fundamentalist Muttahida Majlis-e-Amal, that won at the last legislative elections, 20 October 2002, 11.3% of the popular vote and 53 out of 272 elected members. It is a Deobandi organisation, and the post-partition Pakistani successor to the colonial-era Indian Deobandi Islamic organisation. It has close relations with the Taliban, another Deobandi-inclined movement. Currently in Pakistan, it has two wings : that of Maulana Samiul Haq and that of Maulana Fazlur Rehman. Both are members of the national assembly and part of the MMA coalition.

Jamiat Ulema-e-Pakistan : The Jamiat Ulema-e-Pakistan (Assembly of Pakistani Clergy) is a political party in Pakistan. It is part of the Islamic fundamentalist Muttahida Majlis-e-Amal, that won at the last legislative elections, 20 October 2002, 11.3 of the popular vote and 53 out of 272 elected members. It is of barelvi Islamic thinking and was founded and headed until 2004 by the late Shah Noorani saheb.

Jamini Prakash Gangopadhyaya : Jamini Prakash Gangopadhyaya was a Bengali artist and sculptor. A nephew of Rabindranath Tagore, Jamini Prakash, in his early life, was a student of British painter CL Palmer. Later he joined the Calcutta Government Art School, where he came in contact with an eminent artist Pulin Kunda, and as his associate he became adept in the western style of painting.

The paintings of Jamini Prakash pervade a sense of serenity. Like most of his contemporaries he used to select religious themes from Indian epics as his subject of paintings. Besides, he drew portraits and landscapes. An unparalleled artist of the early nineteenth century, Jamini Prakash excelled in portraiture and landscape. He drew numerous paintings of views of the Himalayas and the Kanchanjangha. He also painted scenes of fishing boats and fleet of merchants' boats with bloated sail floating on the estuary of rivers. Each of his paintings displayed novelty in composition and was mystic and colourful, reminiscent of European Impressionistic style, where fleeting light on play of color are noticeable.

Jamiruddan Sircar : Jamiruddan Sircar (born 1931) is a politician from Bangladesh. He is a member of the Bangladesh Nationalist Party. He was speaker of the parilament when, on June 21, 2002, he became acting president because of the resignation of A.Q.M. Badruddoza Chowdhury. He remained acting president until a new president was elected on September 6, 2002.

Jamkhandi : Jamkhandi was one of the princely states of British India, under the Bombay Presidency, and later the Deccan States Agency. It was one of the southern Mahratta Jagirs. Its Hindu rulers were of the Pathwardhan dynasty and used the title "Raja" or "Raja Sahib". The Patwardhan family also ruled several other nearby princely states including Sangli, Miraj and Kurundwad and chiefs of Budhgaon and Tasgaon, all of whose ruling families claimed descent from a common ancestor, Hari Patwardhan. The state gained prestige after it defeated Tipu Sultan in a battle. The Raja's descendants now live in nearby Kolhapur.

Jamkhandi state covered an area of 1357 square kilometers, and had a population of 103,375 in 1901, while the population of the town itself was 13,029 in that year. In 1911, the state enjoyed a revenue estimated at Rs.91,163/- and paid a tribute to the British Raj of Rs.1,300/-. Its flag was an orange rectangle, containing the royal coat-of-arms. The state was founded by Shri Shankarji Narayan in the year 1811, and was acceded to Dominion of India on February 19, 1948. It is currently a part of Bagalkot district in Karnataka state. Modern Jamkhandi is famous for producing sugarcane.

Jammu : Jammu is one of the three regions comprising the Indian state of Jammu and Kashmir. Jammu borders Kashmir valley to the north, Ladakh to the east, Himachal Pradesh to the south and Pakistan occupied Kashmir to the west. Jammu city is the winter capital of Jammu and Kashmir.

Jammu and Kashmir : Jammu and Kashmir is the northern-most state of Republic of India, lying mostly in the Himalayan mountains. Jammu and Kashmir shares a border with Himachal Pradesh to the south, Pakistan to the west and People's Republic of China to the north and the east. Srinagar is the capital of Jammu and Kashmir. Jammu and Kashmir consists of three divisions: Jammu, the Kashmir Valley and Ladakh. Srinagar is its summer capital, and Jammu its winter capital. Kashmir is known for its pristine natural beauty and rich cuisine. The state is India's only Muslim majority state. Minority religions in the state include Hinduism, Buddhism and Sikhism.

Jammu and Kashmir lies at the heart of a bitter territorial dispute between India, Pakistan and the People's Republic of China. India considers the entire state as its sovereign territory, but has control of only half the area. The territory under its control is administered as the state of Jammu and Kashmir, and it enjoys special provisions under Article 370 of the Indian Constitution. India's claim to the entire state is disputed by Pakistan, which controls a third of Kashmir. Aksai Chin, an arid region in the east, is claimed by India but administered by China. Since the 1990s, the state has long been hit by terrorism and violence, which has resulted in the deaths of thousands of people. In the recent past, however, due to increased vigilance by the Indian Armed Forces the violence has decreased, leading to a level of normalcy in the state and the return of domestic and foreign tourists. The Indian army maintains a significant deployment of troops to maintain the law and order in the state.

Jammu and Kashmir People's Democratic Party : The Jammu and Kashmir People's Democratic Party is a political party in Jammu and Kashmir, India. Since 2004 it has one member each in the Lok Sabha and in the Rajya Sabha.

Jamnagar : Jamnagar is a city in the western Indian state of Gujarat, and serves as the capital of the Jamnagar District. Its population in 1991 was roughly 326,000 people. The city was built up substantially by Maharaja Kumar Shri Ranjitsinhji in the 1920s, when the district was known as Nawangar. The district lies just to the south of the Gulf of Kutch.

Most residents of Jamnagar are Gujarati and speak the Gujarati language. A small percentage speak the Kachchi language, which is written in the Gujarati script but is not mutually intelligible with Gujarati. Jamnagar has recently shot to prominence as Reliance Industries has established the world's largest refinery there. Marine National Park, the only marine sanctuary of India is near Jamnagar—on the coral reef island of Pirotan.

Jamnagar is well-known for its four marble Jain temples: Vardhman Shah's Temple, Raisi Shah's Temple, Sheth's Temple, and Vasupujya Swami's Temple. All were built between 1574 and 1622.

Jamrud : Jamrud, is a town located in the North-West Frontier Province of Pakistan. The town is the doorway to the Khyber pass, part of the Hindu Kush range. The town has road and rail linkages with Peshawar city of Pakistan, and a pass connects it with Landi Kotal, located near the borders of Afghanistan.

Jamrud, lying in the close proximity to the Khyber pass, has remained a location on the trade route between central Asia and the South Asia and a strategic military location.

Jamsehdpur : A city founded by the late Jamshedji Nusserwanji Tata, Jamsehdpur, India, then known as Sakchi was home to the first private Iron and Steel company of India. The areas surrounding Jamshedpur are rich in minerals, including iron ore, coal, manganese, lime. Some of these areas are Jamadoba, Noamundi and West Bokaro.

The city recently won international acclaim when it was selected for the 2004 Global Compact City award from the UN in India, beating other contenders such as Bangalore, Pune, Chandigarh, amongst others. A true testimony indeed to it's robust infrastructure, cosmopolitan outlook and strong industry

Jamshoro : Jamshoro is a city in the province of Sindh, Pakistan, It is on the right bank of Indus River, approximately 18 kilometers from the city of Hyderabad and 150 kilometers from provincial capital Karachi. It is virtually the gate-way to the Indus Valley, world famous for its civilization and rich cultural heritage. The Arnica Fort is located 40 km. to its north, in the northward continuation of the same hilly track which become Laki Ranges, merging with the Khirthars northwards

Jamuna Bridge : Jamuna Bridge, more correctly called the Jamuna Multi-purpose Bridge, opened in June 1998, is the longest bridge in Bangladesh as well as in South Asia, and the 11th longest bridge in the world. It was constructed over the Jamuna River, mightiest of the three major rivers of Bangladesh, and fifth largest in the world in terms of volumetric discharge.

The bridge established a strategic link between the eastern and western parts of Bangladesh. It generates multifarious benefits for the people and especially, promotes inter-regional trade in the country. Apart from quick movement of goods and passenger traffic by road and rail, it facilitated transmission of electricity and natural gas, and integration of telecommunication links. The bridge, stretching from Tangail to Sirajganj is located on the Asian Highway and the Trans-Asian Railway which, when fully developed, will provide uninterrupted international road and railway links from South-east Asia to North-west Europe.

Jamuna River : Jamuna River is one of the three main rivers of Bangladesh. It is called Brahmaputra River in India and its origin is Tibet, China. It meets the Padma River near Goalondo and flows as Padma until it meets the Meghna River near Chandpur. After that, it flows into the Bay of Bengal as the Meghna River.Jamuna river was a barrier in establishing a direct road link between capital Dhaka and northern part of Bangladesh better known as Rajshahi Division till 1996, but Jamuna Multi-purpose bridge which is the 11th largest bridge of the world was inagurated in 1996 to remove that barrier.

Jana Gana Mana : Jana Gana Mana (Thou Art the Ruler of the Minds of All People) is the national anthem of India. It is the first of five stanzas of a poem by Nobel laureate Rabindranath Tagore, written in formal Bengali language. A formal rendition of the national anthem takes approximately 52 seconds. A short version consisting only the first and last lines takes about 20 seconds and is also played occasionally.

Janamashtami : Janamashtami is celebrated India as the birth anniversary of Krishna, the incarnation of Lord Vishnu. The temples witness an extravagant and colorful celebration on this occasion. Raslila is performed to recreate incidents from the life of Krishna and to commemorate his love for Radha. The image of the infant Krishna is bathed at midnight and is placed in a cradle. Devotional songs and dances mark the celebration of this festive occasion all over Northern India.

Janapada : Term "Janapada" literally means the foothold of a tribe. The derivative meaning of Janapada from Jana points to an early stage of land-taking by the Jana (tribe) for a settled way of life. This process of first settlement on land had completed its final stage prior to the times of Buddha and Panini. The Pre-Buddhist North-west region of Indian sub-continent was divided into several Janapadas demarcated from each other by boundaries. In Panini, Janapada stands for country and Janapadin for its citizenry. These Janapadas were named after the tribes or the Janas who had settled in them. By circa 600 BCE, many of these Janapadas had further evolved into larger political entities by the process of land-grabbing which eventually led to the formation of kingdoms known in Buddhist traditions as the Mahajanapadas or the great nations.

Janardhan Temple : This temple in Assam is situated on the hillock Suklesvar in the heart of the city. The temple consecrated in the 10th century was rebuilt in the 17th century. Located near Suklesvar Ghat of the Brahmaputra river, the temple has an image of the Lord Buddha, which is a unique blend of Hinduism and Buddhism.

Janata Dal : Janata Dal is an Indian political party which was formed through the merger one of the major Janata Party factions, the Lok Dal and a group of Congressmen led by V.P. Singh. It first came to power in 1989, after allegations of corruption, known as the Bofors affair, caused Rajiv Gandhi's Congress (I) to lose the elections. The National Front coalition that was formed consisted of the Janata Dal and a few smaller parties in the government, and had outside support from the Bharatiya Janata Party and the Communists. V. P. Singh was the Prime Minister. In November 1990, this coalition collapsed, and a new government headed by Chandra Shekhar which had the support of the Congress (I) and a faction of the Janata Dal came to power. This coalition fell shortly causing new elections in June 1991 which brought the Congress back to power.

Its second spell of power started in 1996, when the Janata Dal-led United Front coalition came to power, with outside support from the Congress, choosing H. D. Deve Gowda as their Prime Minister. Congress (I) withdrew their support in less than a year, hoping to gain power with the support of various United Front constituent groups, and Inder Kumar Gujral became the next Janata Dal Prime Minister. His government fell in a few months, and in February 1998, the Janata Dal-led coalition lost power to the Bharatiya Janata Party.

This party has had several splits. Amongst the larger splinter groups include the Rashtriya Janata Dal (which ruled the state of Bihar), Samajwadi Party (a major force in Uttar Pradesh), Biju Janata Dal (governing Orissa), Janata Dal (Secular) (governing Karnataka) and the Janata Dal (United), whose leader George Fernandes was the Defense Minister of India. Several smaller splinter groups also exist, including Lok Janshakti Party.

Janata Dal (United) : Janata Dal (United) is a political party in India with political presence mainly in Bihar and Karnataka. It is led by George Fernandes. The current party was formed by the merger of the erstwhile Janata Dal (United) with the Samata Party on October 30, 2003. The uniting force is beleived to be common opposition to Rashtriya Janata Dal in Bihar especially after the RJD welcomed Samata Party rebels like Raghunath Jha and

Brahmananad Mandal into the party. Janata Dal (United) is a constituent of the National Democratic Alliance. The Janata Dal (United) and the Rashtriya Janata Dal -ironically bitter political opponents today—originate from the same Janata Dal and Jayaprakash Narayan's Total Revolution movement of 1974. Currently, the JD(U) heads the government in Bihar. The JD(U) along with its alliance partner, the BJP overthrew the RJD-led UPA government in Bihar in November, 2005. The government is headed by JD(U) leader, Nitish Kumar.

Janjgir-Champa : The district Janjgir-Champa is situated in the center of Chhatisgarh and so it is considered as the Heart of Chhattisgarh. The District Head Quarter Janjgir of the district Janjgir-Champa is the city of Maharaja Jaajawalya Dev of Kulchury dynasty. The Janjgir-Champa district is a major producer of Food Grains in the state Chhattisgarh. The Vishnu Mandir of Janjgir district reflects the golden past of this district. The Vishnu Mandir is an ancient artistic sample of Vaishnav community.

The Hasdeobango project has been considered as life supporting canal for the district Janjgir-Champa. Under this project 3/4th area of the district will be covered for irrigation. The District Head Quarter of Janjgir-Champa is in Janjgir , which is situated on National Highway 200. Janjgir is 65 KM. away from Bilaspur and 175 KM from State capital Raipur through road route. District head quarter Janjgir is also connected with Rail Line of South-Eastern Railway. It is situated on Hawarah-Mumbai main line. State capital Raipur is 152 KM. from Janjgir through Rail route. The railway station of district Janjgir is Naila and Champa.

Janjua Rajput : The Janjua Rajput are a prominent tribe of Punjab (both Pakistani and Indian Punjab). They have a history that spans centuries through various notable rulers, tribal chiefs, princes and kings since the time of the Mahabharat to the present age through Generals such as General Asif Nawaz Khan Janjua (other Generals are also mentioned below). They were amongst the earliest Rajput converts to Islam and established their own Riyasats (kingdoms) during the 12th century which up until the early 19th century remained in their respective control. Janjuas rebelled against the Delhi Sultanate in the early 13th century and also later aided the Mughal conqueror Babur's route into India with other allied mountain tribes and served in the Mughal army in their conquests of India. Many forts within Punjab are still remnant of their royal past, such as the Kusak fort, Sohava fort, Garjaak fort in Makhiala Jhelum, Malot fort in Chakwal District, Nagi fort, Dalowal fort, Dhandot fort, Kath Saghral and Masral fort, Dhak Janjua fort, Akrand fort and many more. They have played a major part in Punjabi history in their regions through their alliances and rebellions with invaders and other mountainous warrior tribes.

Jantar Mantar (Observatory) : The Yantra Mandir (also known as the Jantar Mantar) is an equinoctial dial, consisting a gigantic triangular gnomon with the hypotenuse parallel to the Earth's axis. It is literally known as 'Instruments for measuring the harmony of the heavens. It was built between 1728 to 1734 by Jai Singh. Each instrument of this observatory is used for a particular function and gives an accurate reading.

The Samrat Yantra is a large sundial (the triangular structure) marked with hours and minutes. The arc at the left side will show the time from sunrise to midday and the right side will show the time from midday to sunset. The time is read, where the shadow is sharpest. The sundials are constructed on latitude 270 North. To adjust the reading to Indian standard Time (IST), between 1 minute 15 seconds to 32 minutes must be added according to the time of year and solar position.

Jarag Fair : This fair is held in Jarag, a village in tehsil pail. It is held in Chet (March-April) in honor of the goddess Seetla. It is also known as the Baheria fair. Sweet gurgulas (jaggery cakes fried in oil) are prepared one day earlier and then given in offering to the goddess and thereafter to the donkey who is her favourite. After propitiating the goddess, the family members eat the remaining Savoury gurgulas with great relish. This festival is observed in Malwa and Powad, but the fair is held only in Jarag. There is a pond where the devotees of Seetla gather. They scoop the earth and raise a small hillock which is accorded the status of the goddess's shrine. Potters specially bring their donkeys decked in colored blankets. Some even put bells or conch shells and beads round their necks. In many folksongs of the Punjab, there is a reference to the fair of Jarag.

Jari Dance : This dance accompanies jari singing and is usually performed by shi'ah Muslims. It is organised during muharram and recounts the mournful death of Imam Hossain at Karbala. About 8-10 youths form a jari dance group. The leader of the group is called ustad and the others dohar. The dancers wear everyday garments but tie red handkerchiefs round their wrists and brows. In some areas they also wear strings of bells round their ankles. The ustad plays the chati and sometimes the dohars play the jharni, made of bamboo, to maintain the rhythm and keep up the beat. In some places the beat is maintained by clapping. The ustad stands in the centre and sings. The dohars move in a circle round him, singing the refrain of the song. The dancers express their grief by the movements of their heads, hands and feet. Jari dance performances start with the sighting of the Muharram moon. Jari groups go around different houses of the village. They are paid cash or given some food for their performances. On ashura the various dance groups assemble at a place designated as Karbala for a final performance.

Jarnail Singh Bhindranwale : Jarnail Singh Bhindranwale or Jarnail Singh Brar was the leader of Damdami Taksal, a Sikh organisation based in India. Jarnail Singh Bhindranwale (Feb 12, 1947 – June 6, 1984).

Jarnail Singh was born in the village of Rode, Faridkot district, Punjab, India. His father Joginder Singh, was a local Sikh leader. Jarnail Singh was the seventh of eight brothers. As a child he was hyperactive and anti-social, once described by a BBC journalist as 'not being very intelligent' and with such acute learning disabilities he failed to attain any education and dropped out of school at an early age. Being unable to read, write or speak any English, his only career option was to enter religious politics and eventually made a career by becoming a controversial firebrand cleric.

Bhindranwale was widely perceived to be a supporter for the creation of Khalistan, a proposed theocratic state. However, in a BBC he revealed some ambiguity in an interview where he stated that if the government agreed to the creation of Khalistan, he would not refuse. In 1978, it was alleged he was involved in a confrontation at with the Nirankari Sikhs. It was during this confrontation, that firing by the Nirankari Sikhs and retaliation by Orthodox Sikhs led to the death of 3 Nirankaris and 12 Akhand Kirtini Jatha members.

On June 1, 1984. Indian Prime Minister Indira Gandhi initiated Operation Bluestar and ordered the Indian Army to surround the Golden Temple complex to flush out militants. It was widely reported that Bhindranwale did not survive the operation and is thus regarded as a "martyr" by his followers.

Jarrals : The Jarrals Rajputs are a prominent tribe of Azad Kashmir and Punjab of Pakistan. They are well known for being the last longest ruling dynasty of Rajaur in Kashmir which only ended in the mid 19th century with the advent of the British Raj. They hold the title of Raja which is their ancestral royal title since the times of the Mahabharata as well as the title of Mirza, which was conferred by the Mughal emperor of India Shah Jahaan. They ruled Rajaur through various successive rulers and also played a major part in the development of the region of Rajaur even until the modern day.

Jashpur : The district of Jashpur in India is divided in two parts as per the geographical point of views. The hilly belt,the northern part, running from Loroghat kastura, Narayanpur, Bagicha up to the Surguja district. This belt having forest area. It has a reserve forest also. It covers the Sanna, Bagicha and narayanpur. This pat area is called upper ghat. Upper ghat is climbed through Loroghat. Loroghat is about 4 km in length and there are three turnings of very dangerous. And the remaining southern part is called nichghat. In Jashpur raigarh road, there are two more ghats, Jhanda bhat before Kansabel and Belaghat after Kansabel. Both are of climbing.

Jasimuddin : Jasimuddin (full name Jasimuddin Mollah) (1903-1976)was a renowned Bengali poet. He is commonly known in Bangladesh as Polli Kobi, the Rural Poet.

Jat : The Jat or Jatt people live in northern India, in the states of Haryana, Punjab and Rajasthan, and are also scattered throughout Delhi, Uttar Pradesh, Gujarat and Kashmir. The Jats also have a strong military tradition, and many Jats were recruited into the British India army during World War I. Large number of Jats serve in the Indian Army, including the Jat Regiment, Rajputana Rifles, Sikh Regiment and the Grenadiers, among others. The Jat regions in India are among the most prosperous on a per-capita basis (Haryana, Punjab, and Gujarat are among the wealthiest of Indian provinces). Historically, the Maharajas (kings) of the cities of Bharatpur and Dholpur in Rajasthan were Jats, as were the Ranas (kings) of the town of Gohad in Madhya Pradesh. They ruled the Malwa plateau.

Jat Regiment : The Jat Regiment is an infantry regiment of the Indian Army. It claims its origins from the Calcutta Native Militia raised in 1795, which later became an infantry battalion of the Bengal Army. After 1860, there was a substantial increase in the recruitment of Jats in the Indian Army, however the Class Regiment, The Jats, was initially created as infantry units in 1897 from old battalions of the Bengal Army. In January 1922, at the time of the grouping of the Class Regiments of the Indian Army, the IX Jat Regiment was formed by bringing under a single regiment, four active and one training battalion.

Jataka Tales : The Jataka is a voluminous body of folklore and mythic literature, primarily associated with the Theravada Buddhist tradition, as written in the Pali language (from about the 3rd century, A.D.); however, the stories found in the Jataka have been found in numerous other languages and media — many of them being translations from the Pali versions, but others are instead derived from vernacular traditions prior to the Pali compositions. Sanskrit and Tibetan Jataka stories tend to maintain the Buddhist morality of their Pali equivalents, but re-tellings of the stories in Persian and other languages sometimes contain significant amendments to suit their respective cultures.

Jatakarmam : It is meant for the development of the intellect of the child. When the male child is born, the ritual connected with birth is performed immediately in Kerala. A small portion of a mixture of honey and ghee is given to the new born infant. This rite symbolises good fortune.

Jataru Kayang : This is a popular dance at festivals. In this dance songs connected with the festival are sung. As the musician play upon their instruments the leader of the dance, dances with a traditional Chamar in his hands The chamar becomes a great source of resentment and leads to fights among the dancers. The Ghure who is the leader of the dance has to deposit a small fee at the temple of the deity for using the chamar.

Jatiya Party : It is a state-sponsored centrist party floated on 1 January 1986 under the chairmanship of Lt General HM Ershad. In the parliamentary election held in May 1986 and thereafter in March 1988, it won easily, although both the elections were said to have been rigged heavily. The movement for restoration of democracy waged by the opposition parties and students forced Ershad to resign on 6 December 1990, and he was imprisoned. The election to the 5th Sangsad was held in 1991 under a neutral caretaker government and JP secured 35 seats and emerged as the 3rd largest party. JP has now fragmented into JP (Ershad), JP (Anwar Hossain Manju) and JP (Naziur Rahman Manju).

Jatiya Party (Ershad) : The Jatiya Party (Ershad) (National Party (Ershad)) is a political party in Bangladesh. It is a faction of the original Jatiya Party, that was founded by the military dictator Hossain Mohammad Ershad. Other factions are the Jatiya Party (Naziur) and Jatiya Party (Manju). Currently the Jatiya Party (Ershad) is the fourth largest party in Parliament; with 14 seats out of 300 available; and got a 7.5% share of the vote at the 2001 general election.

Jatiya Party (Manju) : Jatiya Party (Manju) (National Party (Manju)) is a political party in Bangladesh. It is a faction of the original Jatiya Party, that was founded by the military dictator Hossain Mohammad Ershad. Other factions are the Jatiya Party (Naziur) and Jatiya Party (Ershad).

Jatiya Party (Naziur) : The Jatiya Party (Naziur) (National Party (Naziur)) is a political party in Bangladesh. It is a faction of the original Jatiya Party, that was founded by the military dictator Hossain Mohammad Ershad. Other factions are the Jatiya Party (Ershad) and Jatiya Party (Manju).

Jatiya Samajtantric Dal (JSD) : Jatiya Samajtantric Dal (JSD) The party emerged as a major leftist party after the emergence of Bangladesh. Its origin can be traced to the division within the Bangladesh Students League, a student front of AL. The leftist group led by Sirajul Alam Khan and ASM Abdur Rab steered the formation of the new party on 31 October 1972 with Abdur Rab and (Major) ma jalil as joint convenors. Its motto was scientific socialism and it sought to establish through revolution a classless society, free of exploitation, under the leadership of peasants and workers. The party vehemently opposed the Awami League in power from 1972 to 1975. It organised a people's militia to topple the AL government. It organised strong anti-government agitation during 1974 and 1975. JSD also established clandestine cells in the army under the rubric of people's revolutionary army.

Following the coup of 15 August 1975 and a counter coup, JSD is said to have organised a revolution on 7 November 1975 under the leadership of Lt. Colonel (retd) Abu Taher. The government undertook strong measures against the party, and many of its leaders and workers were arrested. A faction of JSD led by Khaliquzzaman Bhuiyan left it and established Bangladesh Samajtrantik Dal (BSD) which claimed to be the true Marxist-Leninist party. In 1982, BSD fragmented into two parties, one led by

Khaliquzzaman Bhuiyan and another by AFM Mahbubul Haq. JSD also split into three groups in 1984, JSD (Rab), JSD (Siraj), JSD (Jalil) over the issue of whether to participate or not in the upazila election, which was held in 1984. In 1986, JSD (Siraj) again broke into two: JSD (Inu) and JSD (Siraj). There was a further break-up in which JSD (Raja) turned into a separate party, which joined Awami League in 1991.

Jatiya Sangsad : The Parliament of the People's Republic of Bangladesh is called Jatiya Sangsad. Jatiya Sangsad is vested with the legislative powers of the Republic. Jatiya Sangsad consists of 300 members elected in accordance with law from single territorial constituencies by direct election. The members of Jatiya Sangsad are designated as Members of Parliament (MPs).

Members of parliament are elected for five years. Unless dissolved earlier constitutionally by the president, Sangsad stands dissolved on the expiry of the period from the date of its first meeting. Of course President can dissolve the Sangsad anytime under special circumstances. The term of the Sangsad can be extended for a maximum period of one year in a state of war. If after the expiry of the term of the Sangsad and before the holding of the next general elections, the President is satisfied that owing to the existence of a state of war in which the Republic is engaged it is necessary to recall the Sangsad, he shall summon the Sangsad to meet and that is to be done in consultation with the Prime Minister. In addition to 300 members, there were 30 seats exclusively reserved for women members to be elected by elected members of the Sangsad. But the term for provision of reserved seats for women expired in December 2001, and the provision for reserved seats was not renewed. Women can, however, contest in general seats. A member of Sangsad is required to make the oath of affirmation with the Speaker after the election.

Jatiyo Sangsad Bhaban : Jatiyo Sangsad Bhaban is the National Assembly Building of Bangladesh, located in the capital Dhaka.

It is an architectural masterpiece created by Louis I. Kahn and one of the largest legislative complexes in the world. It houses all parliamentary activities of Bangladesh.

Jatiyo Smriti Soudho : Jatiyo Smriti Soudho or National Martyrs' Memorial is a monument in Bangladesh. It is the symbol of the valour and the sacrifice of the martyrs of the Bangladesh Liberation War of 1971, which brought the independence of Bangladesh from Pakistani rule. The monument is located in Savar, about 35 Kilometres north-west of the capital, Dhaka.

Plans for the monument were initiated right after the independence, in 1972. Following the site selection, road and land development, a nation-wide design competition was held in June, 1978. Following evaluation of the 57 submissions, Syed Mainul Hossain's design was chosen. The main structure and the artificial lake and other facilities were completed in 1982. The monument is composed of 7 isosceles triangular pyramid shaped structures, with the middle one being the tallest. The highest point of the monument is 150 feet. There is an artificial lake, and several mass graves in front of the main monument.

Jatra : Jatra (literally 'going' or 'journey') is a form of folk drama of Bengal, combining acting, songs, music, dance, characterised by stylised delivery and exaggerated gestures and orations. Jatra is believed to have developed from ceremonial functions held before starting on a journey. Other explanations are that it developed from processions brought out in honour of different gods and goddesses. These processions often included songs and dances. rathayatra, for example, is a festival of this kind.

Jatra was an important form of entertainment in the past. Nowadays it has been replaced by many modern forms. The tastes of audiences have also changed. Thus the demand for jatra has diminished to a great extent. Jatra performances are therefore being modified. Social and contemporary subjects juxtapose historical and mythological stories. Modern stage techniques are also modifying the manner of speaking, costumes, musical instruments, make up, stage, lights etc. At the same time, contemporary Bangla theatre is drawing upon the indigenous jatra. In place of western, text-based drama, the mixture of dance-song-performance of the jatra is lending a unique strength to contemporary Bangla drama

Jaunpur : Jaunpur is a city in Jaunpur District in Uttar Pradesh state of India. Demographically, Jaunpur resembles the rest of the Purvanchal area in which it is located a primarily rural agricultural population with high illiteracy and low human development. Jaunpur's notable history dates from 1388, during which period the Sultan of Delhi Feroz Shah Tughlaq appointed Malik Sarwar, a eunuch, as governor of the region. The Sultanate was weakened by the 1398 sacking of Delhi by the Mongols under Timur, and Malik Sarwar then declared independence. He and his adopted son founded what came to be known as the Sharqi dynasty. During the Sharqi period the Jaunpur Sultanate was a strong military power in Northern India, and on several occasions threatened the Delhi Sultanate.

Jaunpur was then a major center of Urdu and Sufi knowledge and culture. The Sharqi dynasty was known for its excellent communal relations between Muslims and Hindus, perhaps stemming from the fact that the Sharqis themselves were originally indigenous converts to Islam, as opposed to descendants of Persians or Afghans. Jaunpur's independence came to an end in 1480, when the city was conquered by Sikander Lodi, the Sultan of Delhi.

The Sharqi kings attempted for several years to retake the city, but ultimately failed.

Although many of the Sharqi monuments were destroyed when the Lodis took the city, several important mosques remain, most notably the Atala Masjid, Jama Masjid and the Lal Darwaza Masjid. The Jaunpur mosques display a unique architectural style, combining traditional Hindu and Muslim motifs with purely original elements. The old bridge over the Gomti River in Jaunpur dates from 1564, the era of the Mughal emperor Akbar. The Jaunpur Quila, a fortress from the Tughlaq era, also remains in ruined form. Jaunpur district was annexed into British India based on the Permanent settlement of 1779, and thus was subject to the Zamindari system of land revenue collection. During the Revolt of 1857 the Sikh troops in Jaunpur joined the Indian rebels. The district was eventually reconquered for the British by Gurkha troops from Nepal. Jaunpur then became a district administrative center.

Javed Ahmad Ghamidi : Javed Ahmad Ghamidi (1951—) is a well-known Pakistani scholar, exegete, and educationist.

He is the president of Al-Mawrid, Institute of Islamic Sciences, Lahore, and the chief editor of two monthly journals published from Lahore, Renaissance and Ishraq.

Javed Miandad : Mohammad Javed Miandad Khan (born June 12, 1957), known in the Cricketing World as Javed Miandad, was born in Karachi, Pakistan.

He had a long career as an international cricketer for Pakistan between 1975 and 1996, and had 3 mildly successful but controversial coaching runs with the team as well.

Jawahar Tunnel : Jawahar Tunnel is built at Banihal at a height of 2194.56 metres above sea level. There are two tubes each one of which is about 2825 metres long. It is the longest tunnel in Asia. Before the construction of this tunnel the distance between Jammu and Kashmir was 328 Kms, but now it has been reduced to 300 Kms. only.

Jawaharlal Nehru : Nehru was born in Allahabad (UP). His father Motilal Nehru was a famous Lawyer and a great Patriot. Nehru was educated in England. As an architect of modern India and a doughty champion of world peace, Jawaharlal Nehru is immortalized in history. Nehru came to be respected as a world statesman for his policies of peace, secularism and non- interference in any country's internal affairs.

He was elected as the President of Indian National Congress five times and it was under the President ship of Nehru that Congress adopted the famous resolution of Complete independence at its Lahore session in 1929. When the country gained freedom in 1947, Nehru became its first Prime Minister. Under Nehru India made Technical and Industrial advances.

Nehru was a man of letters. His most famous books are his 'Autobiography', 'Glimpses of world History' and 'Discovery of India'. Nehru loved Children a great-deal. Every year his birthday is celebrated as 'Children's day'.

Jawaharlal Nehru State Museum : The ground floor covers the images of tribal people. Collections include art, musical instruments, religious articles and wood carvings. The first floor contains the archaeological finds from Itafort, Noksaparbat and Malinithan in Lower Siang district. The textiles, weapons, ornaments are also kept on this floor. There is also a library and a handicraft centre which specialises in traditional Cane manufacture.

Jawan Sawar Muhammad Hussain Shaheed : Born 18th June 1949 in Dhok Pir Baksh (now Dhok Mohammad

Husain Janjua). Enlisted as a driver on 3 September 1966. Although only a driver in the 20th Lancers, when war broke out in 1971, Sowar Mohammad Hussein took an active part in every battle in which his unit was engaged unmindful of any danger, no matter how grave.

When he spotted the enemy digging in along a minefield near the village of Harar Khurd in December 1971 on his own initiative he directed accurate fire at the enemy resulting in the destruction of sixteen enemy tanks. But while directing fire from recoilless rifles, he was hit in the chest by a burst of machine-gun fire and died on 10 December 1971 at the age of 22.

Jawara : It is performed in the Bundelkhand area and is essentially a harvest dance, reflecting the gaiety and pleasure of the peasants who have reaped a good harvest.

Jaya TV : Jaya TV is one of the major Tamil language satellite television channels based in Chennai, India. Owned by AIADMK supremo, and the current Chief Minister of Tamil Nadu, J. Jayalalitha, the channel is sometimes criticised for its pro AIADMK approach in news and other programs.

Jayadeva Goswami : Jayadeva Goswami was a composer of Hindu hymns and poetic works, including especially the Sanskrit work, the Gita Govinda, a now-famous work on the divine love of the Hindu god Krishna. Two of his hymns are also part of the Guru Granth Sahib of the Sikhs.

Jayadeva was born near Puri in Orissa. His life can be dated to 12th century kings of Orissa.

Jayanti of Manikya Prabhu : The Jayanti of Manikya Prabhu in Andhra, the incarnation of Dattatreya, is celebrated for five days in a month of Margasira on a grand scale. It attracts devotees from the neighbouring states of Maharashtra and Karnataka.

Jayaprakash Narayan : Jayaprakash Narayan (October 11, 1902—ctober 8, 1979), widely known as JP, was an Indian freedom fighter and political leader. He was one of the few leaders of modern India who fought for its independence and took part in active politics for a long time after it became independent.

Narayan, Jaya Prakash, 1902–79. Indian political leader. He was a founder (1934) of the Congress Socialist party and later (1952) the Indian Socialist party. He was an opponent of Indira Gandhi and formed the coalition Janata party which successfully opposed her Congress party's bid to retain power (1977), although he did not accept political office.

Jayendra Saraswathi Swamigal : Sri Jayendra Saraswathi Swamigal (born July 18, 1935 as Subramanyam Mahadeva Iyer) is the 69th Shankaracharya (guru and head of the Kanchi Kamakoti Peetham), a Hindu religious order. Subramanyam Mahadeva Iyer was nominated by his predecessor, Sri Chandrasekarendra Saraswati as his successor and was given the title Sri Jayendra Saraswathi on March 22, 1954. He is one of the leading religious figures in Hinduism today.

As the head of the order, he has taken an active role in the promotion of education and social welfare. He was instrumental in establishing many schools and educational institutions to cater to the needs of poor. He established many hospitals including the Shankara Nethralaya in Chennai and Guwahati, Assam, and the Children's Hospital, Hindu Mission Hospital and the Tamilnadu Hospital. These provide free and low cost medical care for the poor and needy.

He involved himself in the removal of caste based differences in Hindu society, he was the first Shankaracharya to visit the homes of "lower" caste Hindus.

He has also attempted to mediate in the resolution of the Ram Janmabhoomi issue. He has also publicly opposed proselytization practised by Christian missionaries in India, which later resulted in the Jayalalithaa government in Tamil Nadu enacting a law to ban religious conversion by force or inducement. The Tamil Nadu government also started to enforce the a preexisting ban on animal sacrifice in temples, echoing concerns raised by Jayendra Saraswathi.

He was arrested on November 11, 2004 and charged by state prosecutors of conspiring in the murder of a temple manager, Sankararaman. On January 10, 2005, the Supreme Court of India granted him bail, after finding that there was no prima facie case made out against him.

Jazzy B : Jazzy B (aka "The Crown Prince of Bhangra" and "The Original Folksta"), born on April 1, 1975 as Jaswinder Singh Bains in Nawanshahr, Punjab, India, is a popular Bhangra artist who is easily recognized by fans of the genre with his spiky hair, stylish clothes, and the range and depth of his vocals.

He moved to Vancouver, Canada at the age of five and now resides in Birmingham, England. He has worldwide appeal as he often tours Canada, England, India, the United States, and many other parts of the world where there is a large Punjabi population.

Jehangir Karamat : General Jehangir Karamat is currently (2005) the Ambassador of Pakistan to the United States of America. He presented his credentials December 9, 2004. He is also one of very few Chiefs of Army Staff to have resigned over a disagreement with his civilian superiors.

General Karamat is a graduate of the National Defence College, the Command and Staff College, and the U.S. Army Command and General Staff College at Fort

Leavenworth, U.S.A. He has a Masters degree in International Relations. He retired as Chairman, Joint Chiefs of Staff, and as Chief of Army Staff in October 1998. His assignments have included being Director General of Military Operations (DGMO) and Chief of General Staff. He has also commanded troops in Saudi Arabia. Since his retirement, General Karamat has been a visiting fellow at CISAC Stanford University, and the Brookings Institution, Washington D.C. He was part of a U.N.-sponsored study on Afghanistan, and is Chairman of the Board of Governors of the Islamabad Policy Research Institute. He has been Colonel Commandant and Colonel-in-Chief of the Pakistan Armored Corps. He was also President of the Pakistan Polo Association. His parent cavalry regiment is the 13th Lancers. General Karamat's name was first mentioned as a replacement for Ambassador Ashraf Jehangir Qazi around the end of September 2004, when Mr Qazi was appointed by Kofi Annan, the Secretary General of the United Nations, to be his Special Representative to Iraq.

Jehangir Mahal : Built by Raja Bir Singh Ju Deo in the 17 th century. Its strong lines are counterbalanced by delicate chhatris and trellis work, the whole conveying an effect of extraordinary richness.

Jehangir Ratanji Dadabhoy Tata : Jehangir Ratanji Dadabhoy Tata (July 29, 1904–November 29, 1993) was a pioneer aviator and important businessman of India.

J.R.D. Tata was born in Paris, France, the son of Ratanji Dadabhoy Tata, an Indian of Parsi (Persian) descent, and his French wife Sooni nee Suzanne Briere. His father was a first cousin of Jamshetji Tata, a pioneer industrialist in India. 'Jeh', or 'JRD' as he was commonly known, came to be regarded as the most famous industrial pioneer in modern India. As his mother was French, he spent much of his childhood in France and as a result, French was his first language.

J.R.D. Tata was inspired early by aviation pioneer Louis Bleriot, and took to flying. In 1929 Tata got the first pilot licence issued in India. He later came to be known as the father of Indian civil aviation. He founded India's first commercial airline, Tata Airlines, in 1932, which in 1946 became Air India, now India's national airline.

For decades, Tata directed the huge Tata Group of Companies, with major interests in many industries in India, including steel, engineering, hospitality and electrical companies. He was famous for succeeding in business while maintaining high ethical standards—refusing to bribe politicians or use the black market. His contributions to founding many famous institutions of higher learning in India are also well recognised. Among a host of awards, he received the Padma Vibhushan in 1957 on the eve of silver jubilee of Air India. He was awarded the Bharat Ratna in 1992 for his service to industry and nation building. He also received the Guggenheim Medal for aviation in 1988. He died in Geneva, Switzerland in 1993 at age of 89. J. R. D. Tata was a Zoroastrian of Parsee (Persian) descent.

Jehlum River : Jehlum River or Jhelum River is the largest and most western of the five rivers of Punjab, and passes through Jhelum City. It is a tributary of the Indus River.

The river Jhelum was called Vitasta by the ancient Indians in Vedic period and Hydaspes by the ancient Greeks. The river was regarded as a god by the ancient Greeks, as were most mountains and streams; the poet Nonnus in the Dionysiaca makes the Hydaspes a titan-descended god, the son of the sea-god Thaumas and the cloud-goddess Elektra. He was the brother of Iris the goddess of the rainbow, and half-brother to the harpies, the snatching winds. Since the river is in a country foreign to the ancient Greeks, it is not clear whether they named the river after the god, or whether the god Hydaspes was named after the river.

Alexander the Great crossed the Jhelum in 326 BC to defeat Porus at the Battle of the Hydaspes. According to Arrian, he built a city "on the spot whence he started to cross the river Hydaspes", which he named Bukephala (or Bucephala) to honour his famous horse Bukephalis which was buried there. It is thought that ancient Bukephala was near the site of modern Jhelum City. The waters of the Jhelum are allocated to Pakistan under the terms of the Indus Waters Treaty.

Jelepla Pass : Jelepla Pass is an all weather pass between India and Tibet. Etymologically the term Jelepla is derived from Jelep meaning lonely and La meaning pass in Tibetan. The pass is in Sikkim and the route connects Lhasa to India. The pass is at an altitude of 4,267 metres (14,300 feet) above msl and is 46 metres (150 feet) in length. On the Indian side there are two routes to Jelepla, one through Darjeeling and the other through Kalimpong. The Kalimpong route is an ancient one which was responsible for the boost in the local economy due to the trading of wool and furs early last century. The pass was closed after the Sino-Indian War in 1962. It passes through the towns of Pedong in northern West Bengal, Rhenok,and Kupup.The route from Darjeeling passes through the towns of Ari, Sendochen and Gnatong and finally to Pedong.

The route is scenic with forests of rhododendronss blooming in spring. Numerous hamlets dot the bucolic surroundings which give a traveller a sybaritic experience. On the Tibetan side the pass leads to the Chumbi Valley of the Tibetan Plateau.

The Jelepla pass was in use from early times as trade was flourishing between India and Tibet. After the appropriation of India by the British, the British started to construct roads into Sikkim around 1884. This was viewed with some apprehension among the Tibetans and in 1886 a small Tibetan militia occupied the region around the pass. In May 1888, they attacked the British but were warded off. Later in September the same year the British regained the area around the pass.

With the growing Russian influence in Tibet, a British expedition was sent via Jelepla to Lhasa in 1904 led by Colonel Younghusband. This expedition was met by hostile Tibetan forces which were defeated by the British. After India's independence in 1947, Sikkim, which was then a monarchy gave India the status of a suzerain nation. During the 1962 Sino-Indian War, there were border skirmishes between the Indian and Chinese armed forces in and around the passes of Jelepla and Nathula. After the war the two passes were closed permanently. With the recent thawing in relations between India and China, plans are afoot to reopen the two passes which will result in an economic boom for the region.

Jessore Zilla School : Jessore Zilla School, established in 1838, is one of the oldest schools in Jessore District, southwest Bangladesh. In 2000 it had some 1,450 students, running in two shifts (7-12 am and 12.20-5.35 pm). Famous educators at the school include Muhammad Shahidullah and Krishna Chandra Majumder.

Jet Airways : Jet Airways is an airline based in India, serving domestic and international routes. The airline operates over 250 flights to 44 destinations across the country, with the majority of flights operated from Chhatrapati Shivaji International Airport, Mumbai. It currently controls about 40% of India's aviation market.

Jhabua : Jhabua is a town in western Madhya Pradesh state of central India. It is the administrative headquarters of Jhabua District. Jhabua was the capital of a princely state of the British Raj's Central India, in the Bhopawar agency. Its area, with the dependency of Rutanmal, was 1336 square miles. After India's independence in 1947, its rulers acceded to India, and Jhabua became part of the newly created Madhya Bharat state, which in 1956 was merged into Madhya Pradesh.Jhabua is a tribal district and one of the most backward districts of the state. Bhil tribe inhabits the interior of the district.Bhagoria, a tribal festival, which coincides with holi is a sight to behold. The bhils celebrate it with great fervour.

Jhajhariya : Jhajhariya is a delicacy of Indian origin made of corn, milk, ghee and sugar garnished with raisins and nuts. Grated or coarsely ground fresh corn is slowly roasted in small amount of ghee for a couple of hours until it loses most of the water and assumes a dry granular form. This is a labor intensive step since it involves constant stirring and monitoring. But this preprocessing can be done once a year and the resulting material can be stored unrefrigerated.

The final prepration is done before serving; it involves heating the preprocesed stuff for about five minutes on a medium flame, then adding an equal volume of boiling water, heating for another five minutes and then adding about 3X boiling milk followed by further heating, then adding about an equal volume of sugar and raisins. It is good when served hot, but better still after refrigerating.

Jhajjar : Jhajjar is one of the nineteen districts of Haryana state, India. Jhajjar district, Haryana was carved out of Rohtak district on July 15, 1997. The district headquarter is situated in Jhajjar town at a distance of about 65 km from Delhi. The town is said to have been founded by one Chhaju and Chhajunagar was changed to

Jhajjar. It is also derived from Jharnaghar, a natural fountain. A third derivation is from Jhajjar, a water vessel, because the surface drainage of the country for miles around runs into the town as into a sink. Other towns in the district are Bahadurgarh and Beri. Bahadurgarh was founded by Rathi Jats and formerly known as Sharafabad. It is situated 29 km from Delhi and had developed into an important of industrial canter.

Jhal Magsi : Jhal Magsi district is in the center of Balochistan province of Pakistan. The district is named after the town of Jhal, seat of the Magsi tribe, thus the name. Jhal Magsi is the headquarter of the major Baloch tribe within the district. The Magsi tribe is historically branched off the early Lashar tribes. The district is divided into two sub-divisions : Gandawah and Jhal Magsi. Both sub-divisions have a separate and different administrative history. Gandawah is a historical and ancient town in Balochistan. Its oldest name was Kandabil, which was renamed Gangaaba during Arab rule. During the British colonial period this name was changed to Gandawah.

Jhalawar : Jhalawar is a city in southeastern Rajasthan. It was the capital of the former princely state of Jhalawar, and is the administrative headquarters of Jhalawar District.In old days known as Brijnagar.

The former ruling family of Jhalawar belonged to the Jhala clan of Rajputs, and their ancestors were petty chiefs of Halwad in the district of Jhalawar, in Kathiawar. About 1709 one of the younger sons of the head of the clan left his country with his son to try his fortunes at Delhi. At Kota he left his son Madhu Singh, who soon became a favorite with the maharaja, and received from him an important post, which became hereditary. On the death of one of the Kota rajas (1771), the country was left to the charge of Zalim Singh, a descendant of Madhu Singh. From that time Zalim Singh was the real ruler of Kota. He brought it to a wonderful state of prosperity, and under his administration, which lasted over forty-five years, the Kota territory was respected by all parties. In 1838 it was resolved, with the consent of the chief of Kota, to dismember the state, and to create the new principality of Jhalawar as a separate provision for the descendants of Zalim Singh. The districts then severed from Kotah were considered to represent one-third (120,000) of the income of Kotah; by treaty they acknowledged the supremacy of the British, and agreed to pay an annual tribute of Rs.8000/-. Madan Singh received the title of maharaja rana, and was placed on the same footing as the other chiefs in Rajputana. He died in 1845.

An adopted son of his successor took the name of Zalim Singh in 1875 on becoming chief of Jhalawar. He was a minor and was not invested with governing powers till 1884. Owing to his maladministration, his relations with the British government became strained, and he was finally deposed in 1896, "on account of persistent misgovernment and proved unfitness for the powers of a ruling chief." He went to live at Varanasi, on a pension of Rs.2,000/- and the administration was placed in the hands of the British resident.

After much consideration, the British resolved in 1897 to break up the state, restoring the greater part to Kota, but forming the two districts of Shahabad and the Chaumahla into a new state of area 810 square miles, which came into existence in 1899, and of which Kunwar Bhawani Singh, a descendant of the original Zalim Singh, was appointed chief

Jhang : Jhang is a Punjab district having a town with same name on the Chenab river, with 387,418 inhabitants

Jhansi : Jhansi is a city of Uttar Pradesh state of northern India. Jhansi is a major road and rail junction, and is the administrative seat of Jhansi District and Jhansi Division. The walled city grew up around its stone fort, which crowns a neighboring rock. In the 9th century, the region of Jhansi came under the rule of the Rajput Chandela dynasty of Khajuraho. The artificial reservoirs and architectural remains of the hilly region probably date from this era. The Chandelas were succeeded by their servants the Khangars, who built the nearby fort of Karar. About the fourteenth century the Bundelas poured down upon the plains from the Vindhya Range, and gradually spread themselves over the whole of the Bundelkhand region which now bears their name. The fortress of Jhansi was built by the ruler of Orchha state in 1610. Legend says that when a king of Orchha saw a shadow ('jhain' in bundelkhand) on a distant mound, he is said to have called it jhain-si (kind of shadow). Jhansi got its name from this utterance.

The Muslim governors of the Mughal empire were constantly making incursions into the Bundela country, and in 1732 Chhatrasal, the Bundela raja, called in the aid of the Hindu Marathas. They came to his assistance, and were rewarded on the raja's death in 1734 by the bequest of one-third of his dominions. The Maratha general developed the city of Jhansi, and peopled it with inhabitants from Orchha state. In 1806 British protection was promised to the Maratha chief, and in 1817 the Peshwa in Pune ceded all his rights over Bundelkhand to the British East India Company.

In 1853 the Raja of Jhansi died childless, and his territory was annexed by the Governor-General of India. The Jhansi state and the Jalaun and Chanderi districts were then formed into a superintendency. The widow of the raja, Rani Lakshmi Bai, protested the annexation because she was not allowed to adopt an heir, and because the slaughter of cattle was permitted in the Jhansi territory.

The Revolt of 1857 accordingly found Jhansi ripe for rebellion. In June a few men of the 12th native infantry seized the fort containing the treasure and magazine, and massacred the European officers of the garrison. The rani put herself at the head of the rebels, and died bravely in battle in Gwalior. It was not till November 1858 that Jhansi was brought under British control. Jhansi was given to the Maharaja of Gwalior, but came under British rule in 1886 as the result of a territorial swap. Jhansi was added to the United Provinces, which became the state of Uttar Pradesh after India's Independence in 1947.

Jhargram : It is a beautiful place situated in west Midnapore district in West Bengal. The beauty of Jhargram is still hidden to many people because it is not publicised widely. But those who really are nature lover must visit once to this place. Mainly the forest areas and a village known as Sevayatan 5Kms from Jhargram. Sevayatan is known for its beauty of Kechenda lake and surrounding forests.

Jharia : Suburts of Dhanbad, is rich colliery centre & has entensive commerce in Jharghand.

Jharkhand : Jharkhand is a state in eastern India. It was carved out of the southern part of Bihar state on 15 November 2000. Jharhkand is bordered by the states of Bihar to the north, Uttar Pradesh, Chhattisgarh to the west, Orissa to the south, and West Bengal to the east. The industrial city of Ranchi is its capital. The other major cities, all highly industrialised cities of eastern India, are Jamshedpur, Bokaro,Giridih, and Dhanbad. Jharkhand is also popularly known as Vananchal. The word Vananchal is derived from combination of two Hindi words: Vana meaning "forests", and anchal meaning "area" – thus the word "Vananchal" denotes a land mass covered with forests. Jharkhand is known for its mineral wealth and forestry products together with excellent human resources.

Jharkhand Mukti Morcha : Jharkhand Mukti Morcha is a political party in India. It has a strength of 5 in the 14th Lok Sabha. 4 of its MPs are from Jharkhand. Shibu Soren is the president of JMM.

Jhaudiya Mosque : Jhaudiya Mosque located about 21 km southwest of Kushtia town of Bangladesh is locally attributed to a saint. Adjacent to the mosque there is also a ruinous tomb. Muslims and Hindus gather there everyday, particularly on Friday, and offer special prayers for gaining the saint's grace. The identity and date of the saint are not known.

The mosque has been thoroughly repaired and a verandah added in the east. Recently the Department of Archaeology, Bangladesh has taken the monument under its protection, removed the verandah and made some minor repairs with a view to bringing it back to its original shape and design.

Jhelum : Jhelum is a city in northern Punjab Province in Pakistan (population 293,000 in 1998). Jhelum lies on the right bank of the Jhelum River. Across the river is a smaller town, Sarai Alamgir, where the Military College Jhelum (MCJ) is based. The old Grand Trunk Road passes through both towns. On the site of modern Jhelum, Alexander the Great founded the city of Alexandria Bucephalous (named after his horse Bucephalus, who died in a famous battle here, known by Greeks as the Battle of the Hydaspes).

Jhelum River : The Jhelum River is the largest and most western of the five rivers of Punjab, and passes through Jhelum City. It is a tributary of the Indus River. The river Jhelum rises from north-eastern Jammu and Kashmir and is fed by glaciers, and then passes through the Srinagar district. The Neelum River, the largest tributary of the Jhelum, joins it near Muzaffarabad, as does the next largest, the Kunhar River of the Kaghan valley. It is then joined by the Poonch river, and flows into the Mangla Dam reservoir in the district of Mirpur.

The Jhelum enters the Punjab in the Jhelum District. From there, it flows through the plains of the Punjab, forming the boundary between the Chaj and Sindh Sagar Doabs. It ends in a confluence with the Chenab at Trimmu in District Jhang. The Chenab merges with the Sutlej to form the Panjnad River which joins the Indus River at Mithankot.

Jhoori : The word means a lover or a beloved and is said to be connected with Jhoomar. Jhoomar is a female dance form in Himachal Pradesh. Both men and women sing and dance to Jhoori. It is a dance performed in the open and describes extra-marital love. It is very popular in Sirmaur and Mahasu areas and has a special rhythm of its own. Each piece has four lines and the last syllable in the first line is pronounced in a drawn-out fashion. The Jhoori songs place a great importance on the rhyming pattern within the song.

Jhumar : The Jhumar is a folk dance of the harvest season in Punjab. Although it shares many features with the Bhangra, it can be clearly distinguished from the latter on account of its thematic content and its emphasis on recreating the gaits of animals and birds. In the Bhangra, there is not attempt to show the movements of sowing and reaping the harvest; in the Jhumar all the functions of daily life are recreated and the pairs of dancers who come into the central area, often imitate the movements of the animals they rear. Two men become bullocks of the field, a third plough and the fourth a farmer. The gaits of the animals, the ploughing of the field, sowing of the seeds and harvesting are shown step by step. The crops are cut and then the dancers again rejoin into a circle and dance very much in the manner as of the Bhangra.

Jhummir (Jhumar) : It is an old dialectical folk dance form of Punjab that originated in Baluchistan in Pakistan. After Partition, the dance faded away from the Indian Punjab, except in parts of Ferozepur district, where it is practised by some Rai Sikh migrants from Pakistan. Unlike the fast-paced and vigorous Bhangra, jhummir is a slower, more rhythmic dance and is usually performed by men. Dancers circle around the drummer, and keep up a soft, sibilant chorus as they dance. The dance is accompanied by the rhythm of dhol (drum) and bolian (songs).

Jhumpa Lahiri : Jhumpa Lahiri (b.1967) (née Nilanjana Sudeshna) is a contemporary American author of Bengali descent based in New York City. Ms. Lahiri attended Barnard College, graduating in 1989 with a major in English Literature and later attended Boston University, earning Master's Degrees in both Creative Writing and Comparative Studies in Literature and the Arts, as well as a PhD in Renaissance Studies.

She also worked a short time teaching creative writing at Boston University and Rhode Island School of Design. She was awarded the 2000 Pulitzer Prize for Fiction for her debut collection of nine short stories, Interpreter of Maladies. Much of her short fiction concerns the lives of Indian-Americans and the nuances of their lives.

Jibanananda Das : Jibanananda Das (17 February 1899 - 22 October 1954) is an acclaimed Bengali poet. Literal meaning of name is Joy (ananda) of Life (Jivan). Born in Barisal, Bangladesh, Jibanananda was educated at Barisal BM College and Calcutta's Presidency College. He then worked as a teacher of English in Kolkata. In early 1930s, he was unemployed for several years, earning a meagre amount as a private tutor of school students. His relatives got him jobs in Assam and Punjab, but he refused to leave Bengal as the pursuit of literature was far more important to him than financial stability. He briefly held teaching posts in Bagerhat and Delhi before returning to Barisal. He was a teacher in the B.M. College in Barisal from 1934 to 1947. After the partition of India in 1947, he returned to Kolkata. In Kolkata again he had to face unemployment for several years before getting a post of lecturer in the Howrah Girls' College in 1953. He died in 1954 after being struck by a tram.

Jiddu Krishnamurti : Jiddu Krishnamurti (May 12, 1895 Madanapalle, India–February 17, 1986 Ojai, California), often written as J. Krishnamurti, was discovered, in 1909, as a teenager by C.W. Leadbeater in India on the private beach at the Theosophical headquarters at Adyar in Chennai. He was subsequently raised under the tutelage of Annie Besant and C.W. Leadbeater within the world-wide organization of the Theosophical Society, who believed him to be a vehicle for a prophesied World Teacher.

As a young man, Jiddu disavowed this destiny and also dissolved the Order established to support it, and eventually spent the rest of his life travelling the world as an independent speaker and educator on the workings of the human mind. At age 90 he addressed the United Nations on the subject of peace and awareness, and was awarded the 1984 UN Peace Medal. He gave his last talk a month before his death, in January 1986, in India where he had been born. His supporters, working through charitable trusts, founded several independent schools across the world—in India, England and the United States—and transcribed many of his thousands of talks, publishing them as educational philosophical books.

Jilbab : In modern day usage, jilbab refers to a long, flowing, baggy overgarment worn by some Muslim women. They believe that this fulfills the Islamic demands for modesty, or hijab. The modern jilbab covers the entire body, except for hands, feet, face, and head. The head is then covered by a scarf or wrap. Some women will also cover the hands, feet, and face.

Jim Corbett National Park : Jim Corbett National Park was India's first national park, located near Nainital in the state of Uttaranchal. It was established as a national park in 1936 under the United Provinces National Parks Act of India. It is known for its varied wildlife, and as the site for the launching of Project Tiger. The park is named after Jim Corbett, a legendary hunter-turned-conservator, best known for despatching a number of man-eating tigers and leopards in this region in the first half of the 20th century. The Corbett National Park and the adjoining Sonanadi Sanctuary form the Corbett Tiger Reserve. The wildlife found in the Corbett National Park include the tiger, elephant, chital, sambar, nilgai, gharial, King Cobra, muntjac, wild boar, hedgehog, common musk shrew, flying fox, Indian Pangolin, and nearly 600 species of birds.

Jinnah International Airport : Jinnah International Airport is Pakistan's largest international and domestic airport. It is located in Karachi, Sindh, Pakistan and has the IATA Airport Code KHI. It is known as the Jinnah Terminal as well.

Jiwani : Jiwani is the most southwesterly city of Pakistan, on the Makran coast near the Iranian border. Currently underdeveloped with a population of 20,000, it is expected to become a major commercial centre, in concert with the development of the port of Gwadar a few kilometers to the east. Jiwani is located at the eastern end of Gwadar Bay, which is shared between Iran and Pakistan. The area around the bay includes an important mangrove forest extending across the international border, and is an important habitat for a wide variety of wildlife, especially the endangered Olive Ridley and Green Turtles. Plans to grant fishing concessions and offshore drilling rights are potentially a threat to the wildlife of the area.

Jiwani holds strategic importance in the region, located immediately adjacent to the shipping lanes to and from the Persian Gulf. This is the main reason that the town hosts a small naval base and an airport with a 5,500-foot runway.

Jivajirao Scindia : Jiyajirao Scindia (1916–1961) was the last reigning Maharaja of Gwalior state in central India, and the rajpramukh (appointed governor) of the erstwhile Madhya Bharat state of independent India. Jiwajirao scindia ruled the state of Gwalior as absolute monarch until shortly after India's independence on August 15, 1947. The rulers of Indian princely states were required to accede to either of the two dominions (India and Pakistan) created by the India Independence Act 1947.

Jivajirao signed a covenant with the rulers of the adjoining princely states that united their several states form a new state within the union of India known as Madhya Bharat. This new covenanted state was to be governed by a council headed by a ruler to be known as the Rajpramukh. Madhya Bharat signed a fresh Instrument of Accession with the Indian dominion effective June 15, 1948. Jiwajirao Scindia became the first rajpramukh, or appointed governor, of the state on 28 May 1948. He served as Rajpramukh until October 31, 1956, when the state was merged into Madhya Pradesh.

Jnanpith Award : The Jnanpith Award is the highest literary honour conferred in the Republic of India. It is presented by the Jnanpith Trust, which is largely owned by the Jain family, publishers of The Times of India. The award carries a cheque for Rs. 500,000, a citation plaque and a bronze replica of Vagdevi. The award was instituted in 1961. Its first recipient was Malayalam writer G Shankara Kurup in 1965. An Indian citizen who writes in any of the official languages of India is eligible for the honour. Before 1982, the awards were given for a single work by a writer. From 1982, the award has been given for a lifetime contribution to Indian literature. So far Kannada writers have won 7 awards, which is the highest for any language. Hindi writers have won 6.

Jodhpur : Jodhpur, the second largest city in Rajasthan, India, was founded in 1459 by King Rao Jodha. It is a popular tourist destination offering palaces, forts and temples. The old city of Jodhpur is surrounded by a 10km long wall that was built 100 years after the city was founded. Jodhpur is called the blue city, due to its many blue-painted houses; it can be seen to best advantage from the Mehrangarh Fort, an old maharaja fort placed on a rock above the city. Jodhpur is also called sun city because sun can be seen shining almost in all seasons.

Jog Waterfall : The Jog waterfall (Jogada Gundi in Kannada) is the fifth highest waterfall in Asia, (after Barehipani, Dudhsagar, Nohkalikai and Nohsngihiang Falls in India), located in Shimoga District, Karnataka state, southern India. It's also called The Gerusoppe falls. It is created by the river Sharavati, falling through a height of 292 m. The falls are said to be the most beautiful in India

Jomu Festival : A religious festivals of the Monpas, this is a get together sort of festival which is observed after the completion of sowing of seeds between the 5th and 6th months of Monpa, Lunar calendar. In this festival the villagers in Arunachal Pradesh go to the Gompa in their traditional dress. The function is graced by the oldest member of the village.

Jonha Falls : Jonha is located some 40 kilometres away from Ranchi in Jharkhand in India. This falls is named after Gautam as Gautamdhara.

Jorethang : Jorethang is a major town in south Sikkim, India. The town is situated at an altitude of about 300m above sea level and has a temperate climate. Jorethang lies on the way to Pelling from Darjeeling, Siliguri and Kalimpong. The route is well connected by buses and jeeps. Jorethang lies of the Rangeet River, a tributary of the River Teesta. River rafting, trekking in the region can be undertaken at Jorethang. A few kilometres north lie the hot springs which become an added tourist attraction.

Joseph Bampfylde Fuller : Sir Joseph Bampfylde Fuller (1854-1935) was the first Lieutenant Governor of the new province of Eastern Bengal and assam, an effect of the partition of bengal, 1905. Educated at Marlborough College, Joseph Bampfylde Fuller began his Indian Civil Service career in 1885 as the Commissioner of Settlements and Agriculture, Central Provinces. He became Additional member of the Viceroy's Council in 1899 and served as Secretary to Government of India during the period 1901-2. Before his elevation to the Lieutenant Governorship of the new province of Eastern Bengal and Assam on 16 October 1905, Fuller served as Chief Commissioner of Assam (1902-1905).

Fuller is particularly noted in Bengal history for the role he played as the first Lt Governor of the new province. The nationalist Bengalis and the Congress had sharply reacted to the partition measure of lord curzon. They demanded for its immediate annulment. In realising their demand the anti-partitionists had launched a countrywide agitation. To counterbalance their agitation, Fuller tried to rouse the Muslims in favour of the partition. Due to socio-economic and cultural reasons, the Muslim community seemed to have rendered their support to the partition measure.

The Partition of Bengal thus divided the two communities of Bengal politically. In combating the nationalist resistance, which took the forms of swadeshi and Terrorism, Fuller took firm measures against the resisting elements. His measures, which sometimes amounted to excesses, made the nationalist Congress to believe that the government had created the communal division as a divide and rule policy. Fuller's actions and utterances were often very tactless and blunt. In one of his interviews, Fuller is said to have remarked that of his two wives, the Mohammedan one was the favourite. One of his extreme measures was his recommendation to central government for the cancellation of the affiliation of two schools of Sirajganj for their active involvement in anti-partition movement. The central government turned down his recommendation and, in reaction, he tendered his resignation at once on 20 August 1906. Thus ended his regime of less than a year unhappily and without any achievement.

Joshimath : The name Joshimath has been derived from "Jyotirmath". Adi Guru Shankaracharya attained enlightenment here while meditating under a tree and established a Math (hermitage) here. The temples of Narsingh and Nav Durga are located here. Orchards of peaches, apples, apricots and many citrus fruits dot the landscape.

Joy Goswami : Joy Goswami (1954–) is an Indian poet. Goswami writes in Bangla and is widely considered as one of the most important Bengali poets of his genration.

Joy Goswami was born on November 10, 1954 in Kolkata. His family moved to Ranaghat, West Bengal shortly after and he has lived there ever since. Goswami was introduced and encouraged about poetry by his father, a well known political worker in the area. He lost his father at the age of six, after which the family was sustained by his mother, a teacher. She died in 1984.

Judaism : Judaism is the religion of the Hebrews. It is a religion older than Christianity. Moses was the first prophet and law giver of the Hebrews. In order to save the Hebrews from the cruel Pharaohs of Egypt, Moses led them to the promised land of God. On the way, at Mount Sinai, Moses received the 'Ten Commandments' from Jehovah, the Supreme God. Thus around 1000BC the Hebrews established themselves in Israel. Holy Books of the Law, the Prophets and the Psalms were put together and came to be known as the 'Hebrew Bible' or 'The Old Testament'. The 'Talmud' is the collection of detailed laws for the guidance of civil, domestic and social life of the Hebrews. According to Judaism right conduct is more important than right belief. Judaism does not believe in self imposed suffering or asceticism.

In India there are two ancient indigenous Jewish communities - Malayalam speaking Cochinites and the Marathi speaking Bene Israel (children of Israel). Ancestry of Cochin Jews dates back to the period when King Solomon's merchant fleet began their trade. As per scholars the Jewish settled along Kerala's Malabar coast soon after the Babylonian conquest of Judea in 586BC. They were well received by the rulers and granted a small Principality to Joseph Rabban, a Jewish leader. Their Synagogue at Cochin is one of the oldest in India and its interior is worth visiting. Today migration to Israel and other countries has considerably reduced the Indian Jewish population. Now, only a few of them remain in Cochin.

Juhu : Juhu is a suburb of Mumbai. It is famous for its sprawling beach, the Juhu Beach. It is surrounded by Arabian Sea in the west, Santacruz and Vile Parle in the east. Juhu is one of the most posh localities of Mumbai where one can find the bungalows of the famous film personalities of Bollywood. The nearest railway stations are Santacruz and Vile Parle.

Julli : Jhulli is generally danced in the dargahs of the Muslim holy men called pirs. This dance is mostly performed in sitting posture, wearing black costumes.

Junagadh : Junagadh is a former princely state of British India. In the independence and partition of India and Pakistan in 1947, the 565 princely states were given a choice of whether to join India or Pakistan. The nawab of Junagadh (a Muslim) decided that Junagadh should become part of Pakistan, which was just across the Arabian Sea. The unsettled conditions in Junagadh had led to a cessation of all trade with India and the food position became precarious. The region was in crisis and the Nawab was forced to flee to Karachi with his family and established a provisional government. Before leaving the Nawab had emptied the state treasury of its cash and securities. The Dewan of Junagadh, Sir Shah Nawaz Bhutto, the father of the more famous Zulfiqar Ali Bhutto, now decided to invite the Government of India to intervene. A plebiscite was held on 20 February 1948, in which only 91 voters out of 190,870 who voted voted to join Pakistan. India then assumed control over the entire state of Junagadh. An Azad Fauj, or liberation army, of 20,000 men with armored cars and other modern weapons entered Junagadh and the state was secured—the ruler had already left with his family for the safer pastures in Pakistan. Officially, the action was taken on the request of the Dewan of Junagadh, who feared disorder and chaos in the state.

Junagadh District : The district of Junagadh is located on the Kathiawar peninsula in western Gujarat, with the city of Junagadh as its administrative headquarters. The district is surrounded by Rajkot District (North), Porbandar District (North-West), Amreli District (East). To the South and West is the Arabian Sea.

Porbandar, Gandhi's birthplace, was earlier a part of this district, before Porbandar district was carved out of Junagadh district. Junagadh is famous for Gir Sanctury which is the only home to Asiatic Lions. Junagadh has a mountain range called Girnar which is pilgrimage for Jainism and Hinduism.

Junaid Jamshed : Junaid Jamshed is a famous Pakistani singer born in 1964 in Islamabad, Pakistan. He was the lead singer of the Pakistani band Vital Signs (pop band).

In 1995, he went on to pursue a solo career when the group split up. When he was the lead singer, Vital Signs saw its peak and enjoyed great success, especially with their signature song Dil Dil Pakistan. He is also a popular dress designer with his many boutiques in major cities across Pakistan.

Juri River : Juri river originates from the northeastern hilly areas of Tripura (India) and enters Bangladesh through Dharmanagar of Kulaura upazila in Maulvi Bazar district. From Dharmanagar the river flows further northward along the international boundary and crosses the Kulaura upazila. It falls into the Kushiyara river after flowing through the Hakaluki Haor and turning westward. The Bangladesh reach of the Juri river is about 56 km long.

Jyoti Basu : Jyoti Basu (born July 8, 1914) is a Communist politician from West Bengal, India. Basu is a Politburo member of the Communist Party of India (Marxist), and was the Chief Minister of West Bengal from 1977-2000.

Basu became involved in trade union activties in 1944; the Communist Party of India delegated him to work with the railway labourers. When the B.N. Railway Workers Union and the B.D. Rail Road Workers Union merged, Basu became the combined union's general secretary. Basu was elected to the Bengal Legislative Assembly in 1946, contesting the Railway constituency. When the Communist Party of India split in 1964, Basu became a prominent leader of the new Communist Party of India (Marxist). In 1967 and 1969, Basu became Deputy Chief Minister of West Bengal in the United Front governments. From June 21,

1977-November 6, 2000, Jyoti Basu served as the Chief Minister of West Bengal for the Left Front government. He resigned in 2000 for health reasons, and was succeeded by fellow CPI(M) politician Buddhadeb Bhattacharya. As of 2005, Basu has been the longest-serving Chief Minister in Indian political history.

Jyotirmath : Jyotirmath, also called Jyotir Math and Joshimath, is a place and a matha in Uttaranchal, India in the Himalayas. It is the original uttaramnaya maha or northern monastry, one of the four cardinal pithas established by Adi Sankara, the others being those at Sringeri, Puri and Dwaraka. Its head is usually called the Shankaracharya. According to the tradition initiated by Adi Shankara, this matha is in charge of the Atharva Veda.

As it is close to the pilgrimage town of Badrinath, and the matha has not always been active, it is sometimes incorrectly said that the original northern matha was at Badrinath. In its most recent history, the Jyotirmath became inactive in the early 19th century. The formal occupation of the matha was restarted with the aid of the heads of some of the other mathas from about 1940 onward. However, there is an unresolved controversy over the succession to the headship of Jyotirmath. The best known of the claimants to be the current head or Shankaracharya is Svarupananda Sarasvati who is also head of the Dwaraka matha.

Jyotirmayee Gangopadhyay : Jyotirmayee Gangopadhyay (1889-1945) was a brahmo activist, educationist. She was born in Kolkata on 25 January 1889. Her father, Dwarakanath Gangopadhyay, was a reputed nationalist, journalist, social reformer and leader of the Brahmo Samaj and her mother, Kadambini Devi, was the first female medical graduate of Calcutta University. Jyotirmayee Gangopadhyay remained unmarried all her life.

Jyotirmayee joined the non-cooperation movement (1920-21). She organised the first Women's Volunteer Corps within the Congress organisation and subsequently became a member of the Bengal Provincial Congress Committee. Later, she joined the Satyagraha movement and became vice-president of the Women's Satyagraha Committee. She was sentenced to imprisonment for leading a procession of women satyagrahis on 25 June 1930 and again in 1932 on charges of involvement in the satyagraha movement. In 1933 she was elected a councillor of the calcutta corporation. She was arrested in 1942 for participating in the Quit India Movement. On 22 November 1945 she was killed while leading a procession of students protesting the death of Rameswar Bandyopadhyay.

Jyotirmayee envisaged a future India industrialised along modern lines. She played an active role in directing the activities of the Aryasthan Insurance Company as a founder-member. Her patriotism led her to work assiduously for India's political liberation. She made an important contribution in fostering national consciousness among Bengali women through her writings, speeches and extensive and untiring participation in nationalist movements. The expressive diversity of her thoughts on education, political ideals and social problems is reflected through her writings in periodicals.

Jyotirmoyee Sikdar : Jyotirmoyee Sikdar is a Member of Parliament, India representing Krishnagar constituency of West Bengal in the 14th Lok Sabha.

She is affiliated to the Communist Party of India (Marxist). She was an athlete and won the Gold medals in 800 m and 1500 m events in the 1998 Asian Games. She is a recipient of the Rajiv Gandhi Khel Ratna award for the year 1998-1999. She was awarded the Padma Shri in 2003. In August 2004, she was in the news when her husband was arrested on charges of running a sex racket in Kolkata.

Jyotisha : Jyotisha is the Hindu system of astrology, one of the six disciplines of Vedanga. The Sanskrit word derives from jyótis which means "light, brightness", but in the plural also "the heavenly bodies, planets and stars". Jyotish may thus at one level be seen to signify a "science of heavenly bodies". However, as the singular purpose of jyotish and the vedas is to dispel the darkness of ignorance, it is more commonly taken to signify the "science of light". Indeed, Jyotish has historically been part of a continuous "holistic" approach to living and to spiritual practice within the life of Hindus predominant in India.

Jyotish is often discussed as the instructional element of the Rig Veda, and as such is a Vedanga, or "body part" of the Vedas. Jyotish is called the Eye of the Veda, for its believed ability to view both phenomenal reality and wisdom itself. Part of a larger Vedic curriculum including mathematics, architecture, medical and military applications, it superficially has much in common with ancient and modern Western astrology. Jyotish has many facets, and some of its basics are clearly also cornerstones of Western astrology, such as symbolically endowed signs, houses and planets. But Jyotish has its own sophisticated reference to the noumenal: the planets are "grahas", forces that seize or act upon created beings and influence their actions and life.

K

K2 Mountain : K2 is the second highest mountain on Earth, located in the Karakoram segment of the Himalayan range. Standing at 8,611 metres, K2 takes second place only to Mount Everest. The summit of K2 forms part of the Taxkorgan Tajik Autonomous County of Xinjiang, China, and borders the Northern Areas of Pakistan(part of Pakistan Occupied Kashmir according to Indian position).

The Chinese authorities officially refer to K2 as Qogir; Chinese:, Pinyin: Qiáogeli Feng; other names include Mount Godwin-Austen, Lambha Pahar, Chogori, Kechu and Dapsang.

K6 Mountain : K6, or Baltistan Peak, is a notable peak of the Masherbrum Mountains, a subrange of the Karakoram mountain range. Despite being much lower than the nearby Eight-thousanders and high 7000m peaks, it has huge, steep faces, and great relief above the nearby valleys, making it an impressive peak.

Ka Fifai Dance-Drama : Ka Fifai Dance-Drama is a drama in Arunachal. The Ka Fifai drama is woven round the theme of the traditional belief that ghosts appear and kidnap girls or men and trouble them. The participants in the drama consist of a man, his daughter who is kidnapped, the ghost who does the kidnapping, the Ministers of the State who make preparations for war against the ghost, the King of the stage in which the girl's father is a subject, and the king's men who go out to capture the ghost.

The drama opens with a man and his daughter walking in the garden. The ghost appears and captures the girl, and immediately the man greatly aggrieved rushes to the king's court to inform him of the incident and beseech him the rescue his daughter. The king's anger is aroused at this news and he calls for his Ministers and asks them to prepare for war. The King's men go in search of the ghost and bring him before the king, who severely warns him never to do such a thing again. The ghost frightened bows before the king and with this ends the drama.

Kabal River : The Kabal River is one of the largest western tributaries of the Indus River. It flows from the Hindukush Mountains in Afghanistan and enters Pakistan in Mohmand Agency. It confluencs with River Indus near Noshera town in NWFP province of Pakistan.

Kabini River : The Kabini or Kabani is a river of southern India. It originates in Wayanad District of Kerala state, south India from the confluence of the Panamaram and Mananthavady rivers, and flows eastward to join the Kaveri River, which empties into the Bay of Bengal. It also passes through the southern part of Kodagu District of Karnataka state through the Nagarhole National Park (now called Rajiv Gandhi National Park). Close to the town of H D Kote it forms the huge Kabini Reservoir. The backwaters of the Kabini reservoir are very rich in wildlife especially in summer when the water level recedes to form rich grassy meadows.

Kabir : Kabir (1440—1518) (also known as Kabira) was an Indian mystic who preached an ideal of seeing all of humanity as one. He was known to be a weaver and later became famed for scorning religious affiliation, seen as a threat to the elite. His philosophies and ideas of loving devotion to God are expressed in metaphor and language from both the Hindu Vedanta and Bhakti streams and Muslim Sufi ideals. Kabir is also considered one of the early northern India Sants.

Kabir was initiated by Ramananda. His greatest work is the Bijak, or Seedling, an idea of the fundamental one. This collection of poems demonstrates Kabir's own universal view of spirituality. His vocabulary is constantly full of ideas regarding Brahman and Hindu ideas of karma and reincarnation, and yet he also espouses ideas that are clearly Sufi as well as Hindu Bhakti understandings of God. His Hindi was a very vernacular, straightforward kind, much like his philosophies. He often advocated leaving aside the Qur'an and Vedas and to simply follow Sahaj path, or the Simple/Natural Way to oneness in God. He believed in the Vedantic concepts of atman and yet spurned the orthodox Hindu societal caste system and worship of statues, thus showing clear belief in both bhakti and sufi ideas. The major part of Kabir's work as a Sikh Bhagat was collected by the first Sikh guru, Guru Nanak, and is published in the holy Sikh book "Guru Granth Sahib".

While many ideas reign as to who his living influences were, the only Guru of whom he ever spoke was Ramananda, a Vaishnav saint whom Kabir claimed to have taken initiation from in the form of the "Rama" mantra. His poems resonate with praise for the true guru who reveals the divine through direct experience, and denounced more usual ways of attempting god-union such as chanting, austerities etc. His verses, which being illiterate he never expressed in writing, often began with some strongly worded insult to get the attention of passers-by. Kabir has enjoyed a revival of popularity over the past half century as arguably the most acceptable and understandable of the medieval Indian 'sants', with an especial influence over spiritual traditions such as that of Sant Mat and Radha Soami. Prem Rawat ('Maharaji') also refers frequently to Kabir's songs and poems as the embodiment of deep wisdom.

Kabru : Kabru is a mountain peak in the Himalayas in India and Nepal located south of Kangchenjunga. The peak is 7394 meters high (24,259 feet) and has not yet been successfully climbed. In 2004, a group of Serbian climbers unsuccessfully attempted the mountain. A series of avalanches forced the group to give up from their goal.

Kabul River : Kabul River or Kabal River is a river that rises in the Sanglakh Range of Afghanistan, separated from the watershed of the Helmand by the Unai Pass. It flows 700km before joining the Indus River in Pakistan. It passess through the cities of Kabul, Chaharbagh, Jalalabad, and Nowshera. The major tributaries of the Kabul River are the Logar, Panjshir, Kunar and Alingar rivers. The Kabul river itself is little more than a trickle for most of the year, but swells in summer due to melting snows. Its largest tributary is the Kunar, which starts out as the Mastuj River, flowing from the Chiantar glacier in Chitral, Pakistan and once it flows south into Afghanistan it is met by the Bashgal river flowing from Nurestan. The Kunar meets the Kabul near Jalalabad. In spite of the Kunar carrying more water than the Kabul, the river continues as Kabul River after this confluence, mainly for the political and historical significance of the name. This river is attested in the Rig Veda, the earliest scripture of Hinduism, under the name Kubha. The Sanskrit word later changed to Kabul.

Kabutarkhana : Kabutarkhana is a beautiful small island in the Dal Lake in Kashmir. There is a Rest House built on the island.

Kachari Kingdom : The Kachari kingdom was a powerful and advanced kingdom in medieval Assam. The rulers belonged to the greater Bodo-Kachari group. The Kachari kingdom and others (Kamata, Chutiya), led by chieftains of indigenous tribes, developed in the wake of the Kamarupa kingdom. Remnant of the Kachari kingdom existed till the advent of the British, and this kingdom gave its name to two present districts in Assam: Cachar and North Cachar Hills.

The origin of the Kachari kingdom is not clear. Some historians speculate that they are the remnants of the Mlechchha dynasty of Kamarupa kingdom. By the 13th century the Kachari kingdom extended along southern Brahmaputra, from Dikhu to Kallang and included the valley of Dhansiri and present North Cachar Hills district. According to tradition, the Kachari settlements to the east of Dhansiri withdrew before the Ahom advance. The Chutiya kingdom existed further east and the Kamata kingdom to its west.

Kachi Ghodi : This is a dance performed on dummy horses. Men in elaborate costumes ride well-decorated dummy horses, holding naked swords and dance to the rhythm of the beating of drums.

Kachwaha : The Kachwaha (also Kachhwaha or Kuchhwaha from the Sanskrit Kacchapaghata) are a Kshatriya/ Rajput clan which formerly ruled the State of Jaipur in Rajasthan, India. The Kachwahas are Suryavanshs and claim descent from Rama, ancient king of Ayodhya, hero of the Ramayana. Prior to their establishment in the area of the former Jaipur state, the Kachwahas, known during time as the Kacchapaghatas, ruled from the ancient kingdom of Narwar in Madhya Pradesh. It was the Kachwaha prince Suraj (Surya) Sen, whom founded the city of Gwalior and laid down the foundation of its fort. In 1128, they shifted their capital to the Dhundhar region of

Rajasthan and absorbed/drove out the local Mina chiefs. The original capital of the state was Dausa prior to the shift to Ramgarth, Amber and Jaipur respectively.

Kadamba Transport Corporation : Kadamba Transport Corporation is a Government of Goa road transport undertaking. It was created to provide cheap, cost-effective, safe, timely and comprehensive transportation services for Goa's multitude. To a large extent, it has accomplished this objective, although the cost for providing this service has been substantial. It is heavily subsidized by the government and is reportedly in the red, like most of India's state run road transport undertakings. The KTC operates the bus stands (main bus stops or station) in almost all of Goa's cities and towns. Their services cover the length and breadth of Goa today. The ticket prices are very reasonable and for intra Goa travel are purchased on the bus itself from the on board "bus conductor". They are packed with passengers during peak hours and there are some non-stop services as well. They have special rates for children, students and senior citizens. It functions as the school bus during school hours.

Kader Siddique : Kader Siddique is one of the most famous fighters and organizers of the Bangladesh Liberation War. Often hailed as Bagha (Tiger) Kader or Bongo Bir (Hero of Bengal), Siddique is the only civilian to be decorated as Bir Uttom (Great Hero) by the government of Bangladesh. He organized and fought with an estimated 50,000-strong army of civilians in the Tangail region against the Pakistan Army. This army was called Kaderia Bahini (Kader's Army). This group carried out many successful guerrilla operations in Tangail. Siddique was wounded at the Makrar battle near Balla village. Kaderia Bahini is notable for the capture of a Pakistani ship with large quantities of arms and ammunitions at Bhuapur. At the end of the war, on December 16,

Siddique's forces entered Dhaka along with the Indian forces, signalling the end of the war.

Kadiyapulanka Rajahmundry : Kadiyapulanka Rajahmundry is located 8 kms from Rajahmundry. It is a small, Picturesque village. This nature lover's delight is the centre of flourishing floriculture and horticulture trade.

Kadri Gopalnath : Kadri Gopalnath (b. 1950) is an Indian saxophonist and one of the pioneers of Carnatic music on the saxophone. Kadri Gopalnath was born in Dakshina Kannada district, Karnataka. He acquired a taste for music from his father Thaniappa, a nadhaswaram vidwan. Young Gopalnath once saw the saxophone being played in the Mysore palace band set. Thrilled on hearing the vibrant tone of the saxophone, Gopalnath decided to master it. It took him nearly 20 years for him to conquer the complex western wind instrument and he was eventually crowned as the "Saxophone Chakravarthy".

His achievement is remarkable since Gopalnath had to make certain modifications to the conventional instrument to play Carnatic music. So successful has this adaptation been that the great musician Semmangudi Srinivasa Iyer, the doyen of Carnatic music, has acknowledged Kadri Gopalnath as a true Carnatic music genius.

He has cut many albums and has recorded a number of cassettes and CDs. His production called 'East-West' is an audio-video presentation that, as the title suggests, is a fusion of Western and Indian music. This album took 6 months to produce and has compositions from Saint Tyagaraja, Beethoven and the likes. Identifying his talents, noted film director, K. Balachandar used Gopalnath's services in his Tamil film 'Duet', which put Gopalnath on a new pedestal. Titles and honors have come his way, the most cherished being the Asthana Vidwan of Sri Kanchi Kamakoti Peetam and the Shringerei Sharada Peetam. He was awarded the Padma Shri in 2004.

Kafeel Bhai Ghotki Walay : Kafeel Bhai Ghotki walay or Kafeel Bhai Ghotkiwala (Kafeel Bhai from Ghotki) is a former Pakistani artist who gained fame, when he moved to Karachi and started painting colorful designs on Pakistani busses, trucks and rikshaws as a hobby. He signed off every work of his as "Kafeel bhai ghotki walay" meaning, "Kafeel Bhai (brother) from Ghotki". He gained further fame when he became the first individual in the world to do left arm and right arm spin bowling, while playing cricket. He had reporters flocking in from Australia to see this wonder. He has moved back to Ghotki and works in the field of carperntary. He weaves cloth or nylon strings to make chairs now. People who know him claim that he has reluctance accepting money from people and never demands money for his goods or services, people usually have to give it to him themselves. He often refuses to take the money in his hands and asks the buyer to just place it in his pocket.

Kaghan Valley : The Kaghan valley is a valley in the Mansehra District of the North-West Frontier Province of Pakistan. It has a reputation as a place of great natural beauty. A holiday in the Kaghan Valley, the Himalayan hide-away, located north-east of the Hazara district of Pakistan's North West Frontier Province, is an unforgettable experience.

The Kaghan valley is named for the town of Kaghan rather than for the Kunhar River which flows to the length of the valley. The Valley extends for 155 kms rising from an elevation of 2,134 metres to its highest point, the Babusar Pass, at 4,173 metres. The local population is friendly and easygoing and speaks Hindko(a language spoken by the hill people in Hazara), Pushto, and/or Urdu. The region is Alpine in geography and climate, with forests and meadows dominating the landscape below peaks that reach over 17,000 feet.

Kailasagiri Visakhapatnam : Kailasagiri Visakhapatnam is a charming hill on the northern side of the city in Andhra Pradesh, Kailasagiri offers a spectacular view of the long shoreline.

Kaimur : Kaimur is an administrative district in the state of Bihar in India. The district headquarters are located at Bhabua. The district occupies an area of 3363 km^2 and has a population of 1,284,575 (as of 2001). A very large hilly and forest area, currently infested by bandits.

Kairali TV : Kairali TV is a Malayalam television channel in India. It is the first public limited channel in India. This channel is known for its support over a major political party in Kerala- CPM. Currently, Mammootty, a major actor in Malayalam, holds the post of MD at Kairali. Kairali's vision is to create programmes that meet international standards of creativity and production excellence. And Kairali's mission is to rule the airwaves as the channel with the cutting edge; namely the cutting edge of News breaking, programming and technical perfection. Today Kairali TV has emerged as the most preferred channel of Malayalees deeply entrenched in the minds of Keralites the worldover.

Kaithal : Kaithal is a town in north India, formerly a part of the Karnal District it became part of the Kaithal District of Haryana on 1st November, 1989. It is said to have been founded by the mythical hero Yudisthira, and is connected by tradition with the monkey-god Hanuman. In 1767 it fell into the hands of the Sikh chieftain, Bhai Desu Singh, whose descendants, the bhais of Kaithal, ranked among the most powerful Cis-Sutlej states. Their territories lapsed to the British in 1843. There remain the fort of the bhais, and several Muslim tombs of the 13th century and later.

Kajri : It is a peasant dance offered as thanks giving after a bumper crop.

Kaju Barfi : Kaju Barfi is an Indian dessert. Kaju literally means Cashewnuts and Barfi means a plate full of cashewnut paste and kept for setting. It is made with cashewnuts soaked in water overnight and grinded next day and then sugar, saffron and other dried fruits are added.

Kakadu National Park : Kakadu National Park is in the Northern Territory of Australia, 171 km east of Darwin. The name 'Kakadu' comes from an aboriginal floodplain language called Kakadu or Gaagudju, which was one of the languages spoken in the north of the park at the beginning of the twentieth century. Gagudju is no longer regularly spoken but descendants of this language group still live in Kakadu. The park has two seasons, 'wet' and 'dry'. In the wet (October to April) many of the attractions are impossible to get to so that the dry season (May to September) is the peak period for visitors.

Kakatiya Dynasty : The Kakatiya Dynasty was a South Indian dynasty that ruled parts of what is now Andhra Pradesh, India from 1083 to 1323. They were one of the few Telugu kingdoms that lasted for centuries.

During the 10th and 11th centuries though the Deccan came under the declining rule of chalukyas, the kakatiya clan wielded the actual power. This was cemented by the 12th century when one of the feudal chieftans of the Western Chalukyas of Kalyana, Prola II declared independence. This was the emergence of the Kakatiya dynasty in its own right.

The most prominent ruler in this dynasty was Rani Rudramma Devi, one of the few queens in Indian history. The queen was succeeded by her grandson Prataparudra Prataparudra expanded borders towards the west. However, the empire was under threat from the Delhi Sultan Alauddin Khilji. Prataparudra was captured by

Ulugh Khan (later known as Muhammad bin Tughluq) and died en route to Delhi. The Kakatiya dynasty ended and resulted in confusion and anarchy under alien rulers for sometime.

Kakatiya Dynasty : The Kakatiya Dynasty was a South Indian dynasty that ruled parts of what is now Andhra Pradesh, India from 1083 to 1323. They were one of the few Telugu kingdoms that lasted for centuries.

During the 10th and 11th centuries though the Deccan came under the declining rule of chalukyas, the kakatiya clan wielded the actual power. This was cemented by the 12th century when one of the feudal chieftans of the Western Chalukyas of Kalyana, Prola II declared independence. This was the emergence of the Kakatiya dynasty in its own right. Initially ruling over a small territory near Warangal, Prola II (1083 - 1158), gradually extended his sway to the south.

Kakinada : Kakinada is the headquarters of the East Godavari district in the state of Andhra Pradesh in India. This coastal town has a population of 289,920 (agglomeration 368,672) (2001 census) and is witnessing rapid growth thanks to the recently granted Special Economic Zone status. It was recently elevated to a municipal corporation. The city also has a deep-water port which is expanding rapidly

Kaksar Dance : The dance of the Hill Marias of the Abujhmar in MP mountains is quite different. In one of their dance-forms they carry dummy horses on their shoulders and move slowly into a wide circle. Kaksar is a festival dance, performed by the Abhujmaria of Bastar. Prior to the rains, the Maria cultivators in every village worship the deity for reaping a rich harvest. To invoke the blessing of the deity, Kaksar, a group dance, in which young boys and girls take part, is performed. Boys put on a peculiar costume of a long white robe while girls are clad in all their finery. The dance presents to both girls and boys, a unique opportunity to choose their life partners, and marriage is enthusiastically celebrated afterwards. There is a rhythm and melody in this dance. The melodious music, the tinkling of the bells combine to create an atmosphere of spell and enchantment.

Kakul : Kakul or Kakul Valley is a town 5 km north of Abbottabad city near Thandiani Hills, NWFP, Pakistan. Pakistan Military Academy is located in the eastarn side of the valley. The cadets from all around Pakistan reside in the town. The little town is a clean and beautiful area, with pine trees and green meadows. The population of the place is around 30,000 people.

Kala Pani : Kala Pani is the place of origin of river Kali near Gunji in Pithoragarh district of Uttaranchal, India.It is situated on Kailash Mansarover trek.It is situated at an altitude of 3600 mts.It is said that at this place the Great Sage Vyasa meditated and the valley is called Vyasa valley. A temple of Goddess Kali is also located here. This is a place adorned with Pine, Bhojpatra and Juniper forests and surrounded by snow clapped peaks.

Kalabagh : Kalabagh is situated in Mianwali district of Punjab, Pakistan. It is located on the bank of Indus River. It is the site of the Kalabagh Dam. Kalabagh became small state ruled by Nawab after the collapse of Mughal Empire. Sikh conquered the Kalabagh state but later British restored the Kalabagh state after they defeated the Sikhs. The Nawab of Kalabagh ruled Kalabagh state until the independence of Pakistan.

Kalabagh Dam : The Kalabagh dam is a mega water reservoir that Government of Pakistan wishes to build across the river Indus, one of the world's greatest rivers. The proposed site for the dam is situated at Kalabagh in

Mianwali district of the north-west Punjab province, bordering NWFP. The dam project is a highly controversial and has been so since its inception. In December 2005, General Pervez Musharraf, who became the President of Pakistan after a 1999 coup, announced that he would definitely build the dam in the larger interest of Pakistan.

Kalabaland Glacier : Kalabaland Glacier of Himalaya is situated in the eastern Kumaun of the Pithoragarh district of Uttaranchal state of India. Kalabaland is situated to the north of the Milam valley and to the west of the Darma valley. This glacier is aligned at north west to south east direction and lies above the Yankcharand Sankalp glaciers. This glacier is rare in the fact that it joins Yankchar glacier to form Sankalp glacier. It is a massive mixed glacial system of Kalabaland-Burfu Kalganga glacier.The length of the glacier is 15 kms. A number of peaks completely covers Kalabaland glacier are Bamba Dhura 6,334 M, Chiring We 6,559 M, Suli Top 6,300 M, Trigal 5,983 M, Burphu Dhura 6,144 M, Suitilla 6,373 M and Kalabaland Dhura 6,105 M. Kalabaland Glacier is nestled by the horse shoe shaped Himalayan massif separating Goriganga and Lassar Yankti valley and lies to a little east of the Milam Glacier. Ralam gad river originates from glaciers of Kalabaland, Yangchar and Sankalp. Ralam gad merges with Goriganga river.The trek to the glacier is through: Munsiyari—Lilum—Pilthi—Sapodair—Ralam—Sankalpa Glacier—Kalabaland Glacier.

Kalachuris : This name is used by two minor kingdoms who had a secession of dynasties from the 10th-12th century, ruling over the Central India area (west Madhya Pradesh, Rajasthan) and were called Chedi or Haihaya (Heyheya) (northern branch) and the other Kalachuri (southern branch). They are disparately placed in time and space. Apart from the dynastic name and perhaps a belief in common ancestry, there is little in known sources to connect them.

The earliest known Kalachuri family ruled from 550–620 in central and western India; its power ended with the rise of one branch of the Chalukyas. The rise of another Kalachuri dynasty (1156–81), centered in Karnataka, coincided with the rise of the Lingayat, or Vira Shiva, Hindu sect. The best-known Kalachuri family ruled in central India with its base at the ancient city of Tripuri (Tewar); it originated in the 8th century, expanded significantly in the 11th century, and declined in the 12th–13th centuries.

Kaladi : Kaladi is a village located at 10.02 East and 76.20 East on the right of Periyar (Poorna) river, in Ernakulam district of Kerala state, south India. This is an important pilgrimage center since it was the birth place of Sri Adi Sankara, one of India's foremost philosopher saints who preached the monistic or 'advaita' philosophy.

Adi Sankara's shrine at Kalady run by the Sringeri Math is a large, partly open structure situated right on the northern bank of the river Periyar or Purna. Of the two major shrines within, one is dedicated to Sri Sankaracharya and the other to Goddess Saradamba, the main deity of Sringeri. The samadhi of Sri Sankara's mother Aryamba is also located here. A small shrine to Vinayaka, or Ganapati, is the scene of evening prayers, chanted to the rhythmic ringing of cymbals. The worship in these temples is done by Tamil or Kannada Smartha Brahmins and not by Nampoothiris. West of the Sringeri Mutt temples is a temple dedicated to Sri Krishna. The worship in this temple is done by Namboothiris.

Kalahandi : Kalahandi is a district of Orissa, India. Kalahandi District occupies the southwestern portion of Orissa, bordered to the north by the Districts of Balangir and Nawapara, to the south by the District of Rayagada, to the west by the Districts of Nawarangpur and Raipur (Chhatisgarh) and to the east by the Districts of Rayagada and Boudh. It has an area of 8,364.89 square kilometers and ranks 7th among the 30 districts of Orissa. The District Headquarters is at Bhawanipatna Town which stands almost to the eastern border.

The present District of Kalahandi was a former princely state. After Indian Independence, Kalahandi joined with the Union of India on January 1, 1948, and was subsequently merged with Orissa on November 1, 1949. The former capital of the State of Kalahandi, Junagarh, located 26 kilometers from Bhawanipatna has a well-built fort and a number of Hindu temples with sculptural evidence of the rite of sati. The District is primarily agricultural, with over half the district area covered with dense jungle forest. Industry is very limited, but bauxite and graphite deposits have been commercially exploited.

Kalamkari and Block Printed Fabrics : Kalamkari is the craft of painted and printed fabrics. It derives its name from Kalam or pen with which the patterns are traced. It is an art form that developed both for decoration and religious ornamentation. The discovery of a resist-dyed piece of cloth on a silver vase at the ancient site of Haarappa confirms that the tradition of Kalamkari is very old. Even the ancient Buddhist Chaitya Viharas were decorated with Kalamkari cloth. The great Alexander is also supposed to have acquired this Kalamkari cloth.

In Andhra Pradesh, Kalamkari is done in Machilipatnam and Srikalahasti. With their roots in temple rituals, Kalamkari cloth also followed the old tradition of religious mural paintings. Craftsmen painted the narratives of religious legends from which people learnt the stories of their Gods. Bards recited verses describing these episodes, using these paintings as illustrations.

Coming to Srikalahasti, temples were a major inspiration. The art flourished under the patronage of the temples with their demands for hangings with strong figurative and narrative components. This specialisation in figurative work continues till today. Richly displayed episodes from the Puranas and other mythological material form the themes. Little was known about printed Indian cotton before the archaeological findings at Fostat, near Cairo. The discovery unearthed a hoard of fragments of printed Indian cotton supposed to have been exported in the 18th century from the Western shores of India.

Kalanaur : Kalanaur, a historical town of Gurdaspur District, is situated towards the west of Gurdaspur at a distance of 25 Kilometres on the bank of Kiran Rivulet which originates from The Chhamb of Behrampur and flows in a Zig – Zag serpentine path and merges into the Ravi river after covering a distance of 36 miles in Amritsar District. Kalanaur was a famous place in ancient Hindu period. According to Mohammad Latif (a historian) it was founded by a Noor Tribe of Rajputs who probably migrated from South India. According to Imperial Gazetteer of India it was founded by two Muslim brothers Kala and Noor. Most probably it derived its name from the name of Kaleshwar (Name of Lord Shiva) Temple built on an ancient fort.

Kalaram Mandir : This simple, large temple was built in 1782 by Sardar Odhekar of Peshwa. The idol of lord Ram here, is of black colour, hence the name Kala Ram Mandir. The building stands in the middle of a walled enclosure with 96 pillars and entered on the east through an arched portal. The temple is made of black stones, and has a 25 m high 'Sikhara'. The stones were brought from Ramshej 200 years ago. There are great processions and festivities during Ramnavami, Dushera and Chaitra Padwa. Nearby is the *Sita Gupha cave* where Sita, wife of Rama is said to have hidden from the Demon Ravana. There is a grove of large Banyan trees near the cave.

Kalarippayattu : Kalarippayattu is a martial art practiced in Kerala, a state in South India and in parts of Tamil Nadu. It combines self-defense techniques, religion, and has elements of "martial dance" as in Capoeira.

The word "Kalarippayattu" literally means 'martial training inside the gymnasium'. The word Kalari has been derived from the Sanskrit khalurika meaning a military training ground. Kalari in common terms means school or training centre. The traditional training of Kalarippayattu is always done inside the Kalari which is specially constructed practicing area. You will see Puttara (Seven tired platform) in the South-West corner of every Kalari. Here is where the guardian deity is located. Flowers, incense and water is given to the deity every day. Before each person starts practicing they pray to the deity. Not only is the Kalari a temple of learning, it is also a temple of religious worship with a cult and ritual of its own.

In the thekkan or southern system, training usually takes place in a piece of land adjacent to the Asan or Guru's home. This type of kalari is called tharakkalari. Thara means ground or floor. The Kalarippayatt training aims at something more at the ultimate co-ordination of mind and body. The weapon is only an extension of the body, controlled by the mind and the use of these both in attack and defence attain a very high degree of perfection.

Kalasha : The Kalasha, also known as the Kalash, are an ethnic group that lives in the Hindu Kush region of Pakistan. They are an ancient Dardic people who speak the Kalasha language. Seemingly out of place in Central Asia, they are known to have light skin, eyes, and hair, similar to what one would find in Southern Europe. Many Kalash claim that they are the direct descendants of either Greek settlers, Alexander the Great's army, or even Alexander himself. The claims are questionable, as there is proof of their existence before Alexander's invasion of the Persian Empire. One theory suggests that similarities in the culture of the Kalash and Greco-Macedonian peoples stem from the pre-Indo-European expansion.

Kalat : Kalat is a historical town located in Kalat District, Balochistan, Pakistan. Kalat is the capital of Kalat District. Kalat is located roughly in the center of Balochistan, Pakistan, south and slightly west of the provincial capital Quetta. It houses the palace of the Khans of Kalat and a historic Hindu temple dedicated to Kali Devi.

Kalhora : Kalhora or Kalhoro is the name of a Sindhi tribe in Sindh, Pakistan. Kalhora tribe established Kalhora Dynasty that ruled Sindh from 1701 to 1783 AD.

Kalhora Dynasty : Kalhora Dynasty or Kalhoro Dynasty ruled Sindh, Pakistan. This dynasty was founded by Kalhora tribe. Kalhora dynasty ruled certain other parts of Hindustan (currently forming some regions of Pakistan) from 1701 to 1783 AD. Kalhoras ruled Sindh for 85 years and there were twelve Kalhora rulers during this time. By the late 1600s, the Mughal dynasty became very weak and the governor Yar Muhammad Khan Kalhora became virtual ruler of Sindh. After Nadir Shah Durrani of Iran and invaded and occupied the Mughal capital in 1739 the Kalhora became rulers of Sindh. The territory of Kalhora dynasty extended from Multan to Thatta. This period is known as the golden period of Sindhi literature. Poets like Shah Abdul Latif Bhittai, Sachal Sarmast, and Sami wrote their works in this era. Talpur army defeated Kalhora dynasty in the battle of Halani in 1783 to become rulers of Sindh.

Kali Nach : This is another dance performed during Gajan, in honour of the Goddess Kali. Here, the performer wears a mask, purified by mantras, and dances with a sword, and when worked up can make prophetic answers.

Kali River : The originates from Greater Himalayas at Kalapaani at an altitude of 3600 m, in the Pithoragarh District of Uttaranchal, India. The river is named after the Goddess Kali whose temple is situated in Kalapani near Lipu-Lekh pass at Indo Tibet border. This river forms India's continuous eastern boundary on its upper course with Nepal. River Kali has confluence with Gori Ganga at Jauljibi, a place famous for its annual trade fair. It confluences with the river Saryu at Pancheshwar. The area around Pancheshwar is called 'Kali Kumaon'. Kali descends in plains and called by the name of Sharda. Pancheswar dam, with the joint venture with Nepal for irrigation and hydro electric generation is going to be constrctuted on it. Tanakpur Hydroelectric Project is also being underway by Uttaranchal Irrigation Department, with a dam on the river near Tanakpur town of Champawat district. This river is the part of the Ganges River System. The Golden Mahaseer (Tor Putitora) is the major carp fish amply present in this river.

Kalidasa : Kalidasa was arguably India's greatest Sanskrit poet and dramatist, his title Kavikulaguru (Preceptor of All Poets) bearing testimony to his stature. Known to be an ardent worshipper of Shiva, he wrote his plays and poetry largely based around Hindu mythology and philosophy. His name means, literally, "Kali's servant". The exact dates of Kalidasa's life are disputed. These range from the 1st century BCE to the 5th Century CE. Kalidasa's play Malavikagnimitra has as its hero the second Sunga king Agnimitra. This king is known to have ruled around 170 BC. So Kalidasa had to be after him. The Aihole Prashasti of 634 AD, compares the skill of its composer to Kalidasa's. This then becomes the latest date for Kalidasa. In addition, the Indian tradition associates the poet with the court of a king Vikramaditya.

Historians generally associate Kalidasa with reigns of Gupta kings Chandragupta Vikramaditya, and his successor, Kumaragupta in the 4th century AD. Chandragupta II is known to have assumed the title of Vikramaditya and reigned over the zenith of the Gupta golden-age. It must be noted that Kalidasa does not mention any king as his patron or any dynasty other than the Sungas in his works. The fact that he named his play about Pururava and Urvashi as Vikramuurvashiiya, replacing Pururava by Vikrama in the name and calling Pururava by that name in the play, is treated as an indirect tribute to his patron. The name of his epic Kumarasambhavam is considered a pun on the name of Kumaragupta. Kumara being another name of kartikeya and the birth of this war god is tied to birth of the Gupta king.

In addition, Kalidasa's mention of Huns in Raghuvamsha is taken as veiled reference to Skandagupta's victory over them. The camapign of Raghu in the same epic is supposed to be modelled on Samudragupta's campaign. He is supposed to have composed his Meghaduta at Ramagiri, identified as Ramtek in central India near Nagpur.It is known that Prabhavatigupta, Chandragupta II's daughter was married to the Vakataka king who had his capital nearby. These clues have lead to assign Kalidasa to the Gupta age.

Kalighat Painting : Kalighat painting originated in the 19th century Bengal, in the vicinity of Kalighat temple of Kolkata, India, and from being items of souvenir taken by the visitors to the Kali temple, the paintings over a period of time developed as a distinct school of Indian painting. From the depiction of Hindu gods, goddesses, and other mythological characters, the Kalighat paintings developed to reflect a variety of themes.

Kalimpong : Kalimpong is a hill station (a hill town) nestled in the Shiwalik Hills (or Lower Himalaya) in the Indian state of West Bengal. It is located at 27.06° N

88.47° E at an average elevation of 1,247 m (4,100 feet). The town is the headquarters of the Kalimpong subdivision, a part of the district of Darjeeling. A major forward base of the Indian Army is located on the outskirts of the town.

Kalimpong is well known for its many educational institutions, which attract students from all over North East India, West Bengal, Bhutan, Nepal, and Bangladesh. In recent times, Kalimpong has become an important tourist destination owing to its temperate climate and proximity to popular tourist locations in the region. Kalimpong is also famous for its flower market, especially the wide array of orchids. It also houses several Buddhist monasteries which hold a number of rare Tibetan Buddhist scriptures.

Kalindi-Jamuna River : Kalindi-Jamuna river is one of the trans-boundary rivers which enters Bangladesh through Satkhira district. The Ichamati flows south along the eastern border of the district following the international boundary (with West Bengal of India) and is renamed as Kalindi. Flowing further south into the Sundarbans the river is again renamed as the Raymangal before debouching into the Bay of Bengal. An offshoot of the Raymangal named Hariabhanga starts at the point where the Raymangal leaves the international boundary. The Hariabhanga follows the international boundary and debouches into the Bay of Bengal. The South Talpatti Island is located at the mouth of Hariabhanga river. A distributary of the Kalindi named the Jamuna meets with the Raymangal east of the Hariabhanga and jointly debouches into the Bay of Bengal

Kalinga : Kalinga was an ancient kingdom of central-eastern India, in the province of Orissa. Kalinga was a rich and fertile land that extended from the river Subarnarekha to Godavari and from Bay of Bengal to Amarkantak range in the West. The kingdom had a formidable maritime empire with trading routes linking Sri Lanka,

Burma,Thailand, Vietnam,Borneo, Bali, Sumarta and Java. Colonists from Kalinga settled in far away places such as Sri Lanka as well as the Indonesia Archipelago. Even today Indian are referred to as Klings in Malaysia because of this. Many Sri lankan kings claimed decent from Kalinga dynasties.

Kalinga is mentioned in the Adiparva, Bhismaparva, Sabhaparva, Banaprava of Mahabharat so also is the conquest of Karna. Kalinga King Srutayu stated to have fought the Mahabharat war for the Kauravas. Kalinga is also mentioned as Calingae in Megasthenes' book on India—Indica. The Kalinga script (ref), derived from Brahmi, was used for writing. Among the offshoots, Kalinga script had the maximum resemblance with the parent script, Brahmi and later modified to Oriya script in the begining of the second millennium. This makes the Oriya Script as the most unique and least distorted script among the Indic scripts. This region was scene of the bloody war fought by the Mauryan king Asoka the Great of Magadha around 260 BCE, and whose death and destruction later served as a precursor as one of the main centers of Buddhism.

Kalinjar : Kalinjar is a fortress-city in the Bundelkhand region of central India. Kalinjar is located in Banda District of Uttar Pradesh state, near the temple-city and World Heritage Site of Khajuraho. The fortress is strategically located on an isolated rock at the end the Vindhya Range, at an elevation of 1203 feet overlooking the plains of Bundelkhand. It served several of Bundelkhand's ruling dynasties, including the Chandela dynasty of Rajputs in the 10th century, and the Solankis of Rewa. The fortress contains several temples, dating as far back as the Gupta dynasty of the 3rd-5th centuries.

Kallol : Kallol refers to one of the most influential literary movements in Bangla literature, which can be approximately placed between 1925-1935. The name Kallol or Kallol group derives from a magazine of the same name (which means Sound of waves in Bangla). Kallol was the main mouthpiece for a group of young writers starting their careers around that time. In fact, a number of other magazines that followed Kallol can also be placed as part of the general movement. These include Pragati and Kalikolom

Kalpana Chawla : Kalpana Chawla (July 1, 1961 – February 1, 2003), was an Indian-born American astronaut and space shuttle mission specialist. She was lost aboard Space Shuttle Columbia on mission STS-107 when it disintegrated during reentry into the Earth's atmosphere.

Chawla was born in Karnal, Punjab, now in Haryana, India. Her interest in flight was inspired by J. R. D. Tata, a pioneering Indian pilot. Chawla studied aeronautical engineering at Punjab Engineering College. Thereafter she moved to the United States to obtain a Master of Science degree in aerospace engineering. She earned Ph.D. in aerospace engineering in 1988 from University of Colorado. Later that same year she began working for NASA Ames Research Center.

Kalpana Chawla alias Ruchi married Jean-Pierre Harrison in 1982 and became a naturalized United States citizen in 1990. She joined the NASA astronaut corps in March 1995 and was selected for her first flight in 1996. Her first space mission began on November 19, 1997 as part of the six astronaut crew that flew the Space Shuttle Columbia flight STS-87. Chawla was the first Indian-born woman to fly in space. She was one of the seven members of the crew of STS-107 as Mission Specialist. This mission from 16/01/03 to 01/02/03 lasted 15 days, 22 hours, 21 minutes and resulted in her tragic death. The space shuttle Columbia, while returning to Earth, disintegrated in air on

1st Feb, 03 about 16 minutes before it was scheduled to touch down, killing all seven crew members.

Kalpeni : Kalpeni is an island in the Union Territory of Lakshadweep, India. It forms a single atoll along with the uninhabited island of Cheriyam, the Tilakkam and Pitti Inlet. Littered along the eastern and southern shorelines of the island is coral debris which was the result of a violent storm that hit the area in 1847. It was the first island in the Union Territory where women were allowed to go to school and get an education.

Kalpi : Kalpi is a town in the Jalaun District of Uttar Pradesh state in India, on the right bank of the Yamuna. The city of Kalpi is believed to be known as Kalpriya Nagari in the ancient times. Over the period of time the name of the city got abbreviated to Kalpi. Kalpi is said to have been founded by King Vasudeva at the end of the 4th century. In 1196 it fell to Qutb-ud-din Aybak, the viceroy of Mohammed Ghori, and during the subsequent Muslim period it played a significant part in the history of central India. During Akbar's reign, Kalpi was a governor's seat and had a mint for copper coinage. Kalpi is also considered by some as the birth place of Ved Vyas, the author of Mahabharata.

About the middle of the 18th century it passed into the hands of the Marathas. It was captured by the British in 1803, and after 1806 remained in British possession until India's independence in 1947. In May 1858 Sir Hugh Rose (Lord Strathnairn) defeated here a force of about 10,000 freedom fighters under the Rani of Jhansi.The British East India Company made it one of their principal stations for providing "commercial investment".

Kalsubai : Kalsubai is the highest mountain of the Sahyadris in India. To reach the summit there are various trekking routes and animal tracks. The main route starts from the village of Bari which is about 6 km from Bhandardara. To reach Bari, one has to travel to Igatpuri on the Mumbai Nasik route. From Igatpuri take the early morning train to Pune and alight at Bari.

Kalurghat : Kalurghat is located several miles north of the port city of Chittagong, Bangladesh, and is mostly famous for several heavy industries located there. A bridge near Kalurghat on the Karnaphuli River connects Chittagong city with the southern parts of the district. Kalurghat is also the location of the radio transmitter where Major Ziaur Rahman declared the independence of Bangladesh during the Bangladesh Liberation War in 1971. Using a makeshift radio transmitter located in Kalurghat, first M A Hannan on 26 March 1971, and later on 27 March Ziaur Rahman, an army major then, and President of Bangladesh much later, declared the Independence of Bangladesh, on behalf of the Father of the Nation Bangabandhu Sheikh Mujibur Rahman.

Kalyani : Kalyani is a raga in the Carnatic music of South India. In South Indian weddings this is a very prominently played raga. The word kalyani means 'she who causes auspicious things'.

Kalyani, today called Basavakalyana in Karnataka state, was initially capital of the Kalyani Chalukyas who ruled from 973-1195AD. Later it came under the "Hyderabad Kingdom" after 14th century. After independence from the British, this area came under "Hyderabad-Karnataka". It was ruled by a Muslim Nizam Dynasty for Centuries from approximately 14th century AD, till the formation of India and Pakistan. When the Indian Government took over all Princely States. Kalyani has its own history, culture. The Rulers of this state had their own currency, Stamps and system of governance in the pre partion era. The last living member of this dynasty is Mr. Syed Mohammad Hilal

Uddin Hussain Khan. Kalyani is also a town in the Nadia District of West Bengal.

Kamakhya Temple : The Kamakhya Temple is a Hindu temple on the Nilachal Hill on the south bank of the Brahmaputra, about five kilometres from Guwahati. The temple is considered to be one of the famous pithasthans (sacred places) of India. During the Ambubashi Festival, which occurs during the monsoon period, there is a great rush of pilgrims to Kamakhya from all over the country. The Temple is famous as the centre of Shakti worship. A road winds its way up the Temple. From the top of the Hill, a panoramic view of Guwahati and Brahmaputra can be gained.

Kamal Haasan : Kamal Haasan (b. November 7, 1954, Paramakkudi, Tamil Nadu, India) is a well known Indian movie star working mainly in the South Indian film industry.

Kamal has acted in movies made in four of the major South Indian languages—Tamil, Telugu, Kannada and Malayalam and has made inroads into the North Indian movie industry via Hindi films as well. He has been awarded the fourth highest recognition given to Indian civilians—the Padmashri in 1992. He has been conferred an honorary doctorate by Sathyabama Deemed University, Chennai in 2005.

Kamal Hossain : Kamal Hossain is a notable Bangladeshi politician, statesman and law expert. He is credited as being one of the principal authors of the Constitution of Bangladesh. Dr. Hossain served as the Minister of Law (1972-1973), Minister of Foreign Affairs (1973-1975) and Minister of Petroleum and Minerals (1974-1975) in the Government of Bangladesh during the rule of Sheikh Mujibur Rahman. The constitution of Bangladesh was written by him in 1972. But he couldn't resist the change of the constitution which was made by creating BAKSAL(Bangladesh Krishok Sramik Awamy League) by Bongobondhu Sheikh Mujibur Rahman. He had been associated with Awami League until the early 1990s, when he formed his own political party, Gano Forum (People's Forum), following disputes with Awami League leader Sheikh Hasina Wajed.

Dr. Hossain is renowned worldwide as a jurist, and has a long association with the United Nations. Between 1998-2003, he has served as the UN Special Rapporteur on Afghanistan. He is a current member of the UN Compensation Commission.

Kamala Das : Dr.Kamala Das (Madhavikutty) the internationally renowned poet, short story writer and novelist was born in 1932 at Punnayoorkulam in Kerala. She is one of the very few writers from Kerala who writes effortlessly both in English and Malayalam, yet maintaining high standards in both. One of the most influential feminist writers of our times, her language exhibits liveliness and imaginative suggestions. She started writing in Malayalam under the pen name, Madhavikutty as early as in the 50's. But she became famous in the Malayalam literary world with her work 'Ente Katha' (My Story), which is said to be her real life story. 'Ente Katha' was translated to more than 15 Foreign Languages. She is a very open and self-righteous women and portrays human emotion, love and lust in her works. Her works have an originality in their content and style.

She has received many awards for her literary contribution. Some of them are; Asian Poetry Prize for her work 'The Sirens', Kent Award for English Writing from Asian Countries for 'Summer in Calcutta', Asan World Prize, Sahitya Academy Award for 'Collected Poems' in English, Vayalar Rama Varma Sahitya Award, Kerala Sahitya Academy Award for best short story "Thanuppu".

She has also held coveted positions as Vice chair person in Kerala Sahitya academy, chairperson in Kerala forestry Board and worked as editors in Poet magazine and Illustrated Weekly of India.

Often criticized for her openness and her reluctance to live according to the societies norms, the latest controversy is her recent conversion to Islam. Her new name is Dr. Kamala Suraiyya. She has also established a political party of her own named Lok Seva Charitable Trust, to concentrate on humanitarian work as well as to provide asylum to orphaned mothers. In 1984, she was short-listed for the Nobel Prize for Literature along with Marguerite Yourcenar, Doris Lessing and Nadine Gordimer. Kamala Das is probably the first hindu woman to openly and honestly talk about sexual desires of Indian woman, which made her an iconoclast of her generation.

Kamalapuram : Kamalapuram is a village in Bellary District, in northern Karnataka, near the town of Hospet. It lies within the ruins of the old city of Vijayanagara, just outside the original 'Royal Centre'. It is mainly an agricultural village. It contains some of the ruins of the old city, and an archaeological museum. A large tank lies to the south of the village. The Archeological Museum is on the outskirts of the village. It displays many items from the ruins, and for the surrounding region. These include many images of Durga, the Lakshmi statue associated with the monolithic Narasimha of Vijayanagara. There is a scale model of the entire city centre of Vijayanagara, within a courtyard of the museum. Images and details of early and prehistoric man in the region can also be seen in it.

Kamarcut : Kamarcut is a traditional South Indian candy made out of jaggery, is made by slowly cooking jaggery with water until it achieves a honeylike consistency. Shredded coconut can be added to the mixture to create texture. It used to be available widely in South

India but has become hard to get lately in urban areas. It is still often sold in villages.

Kamarupa : Kamarupa is the ancient name of the kingdom that consisted of the Brahmaputra valley and adjoining regions. During earlier times Kamarupa was called Pragjyotisha. The kingdom is now closely associated with the Indian state of Assam. Though the historical kingdom existed between the 4th century and the middle of 7th century the notion of Kamarupa persisted and ancient and medieval chroniclers continued to call this region by this name. Muslim chronicles that were written after the end of the Kamarupa kingdom continued to call the region Kamru or Kamrud.

According to Xuanzang and Kalika Purana, the western border was Karatoya river. According to Kalika Purana and other sources, the eastern boundary was the Dikkaravasini temple near Sadiya. The kingdom was ruled by the Varman dynasty, the Mlechchha dynasty and the Pala dynasty up to the 12th century, after which the Khen dynasty moved the capital to the west and began calling their kingdom the Kamata kingdom. The Kamarupa kingdom thus ended in the 12th century with the fall of the Pala rulers.

Kamasutram : Kamasutram, generally known to the Western world as Kama Sutra, is an ancient Hindu text on human sexual behavior, widely considered to be the standard work on love in Sanskrit literature. The text was composed by Vatsyayana, as a brief summary of various earlier works belonging to a tradition known generically as Kama Shastra, the science of love. Kama is literally desire. Sutra signfies a thread, or discourse threaded on a series of aphorisms. Sutra was a standard term for a technical text, thus also the Yogasutram of Patanjali. The text is originally known as Vatsyayana Kamasutram ("Vatsyayana's Aphorisms on Love"). Tradition holds that the author was a celibate scholar. He is believed to have lived sometime between the 1st to 6th centuries AD, probably during the great cultural flowering of the Gupta period.

Kamba Ramayanam : Kamba Ramayanam is a Tamil epic that was written by Kamban during the 9th century. Running to 10,368 verses of four lines each, it describes the life of Lord Rama. Though it was based on Valmiki's Ramayana in Sanskrit, it differes from it in multiple aspects. Kamba Ramayanam is known for its brilliant use of rhyme and similes.

Kamet : Kamet is the second highest mountain in the Garhwal region of India; Nanda Devi (7,816m) is the highest. Kamet was the first mountain over 25,000 ft (7,620m) of the Himalaya to be climbed. While attempts to climb Kamet began in 1855, the first ascent was not made until 1931 by Frank Smythe, Eric Shipton, R.L. Holdsworth and Lewa Sherpa of a British-Nepalese expedition. The standard route begins from the East Kamet Glacier (camps I and II) with steep gulley climbs to the north and onto the camp III glacier. From there up the rock wall to the left of the glacier falling from camp IV, then a broken glacier fall up to camp V finishing with steep snow, possibly icy, to the summit.

Kamila Shamsie : Kamila Shamsie (b. 1973) is a Pakistani novelist, who writes in the English language. She was brought up in Karachi and attended Karachi Grammar School.

Kamleshwar : Kamleshwar (born: 6th January 1932), a prominent Hindi writer of 20th century, was born in Mainpuri district of Uttar Pradesh state, India. Kamleshwar became famous for his short stories, and some other works, which depicted the contemporary life in a vivid style of presentation. He also held important positions including Additional Director of Doordarshan, India's national television channel. Awarded Padma Bhushn 2005

Kamrup : Kamrup is an administrative district in the state of Assam in India, named after Kamarupa the name Assam was previously known in ancient times. The district, however, is now a small western part of Assam, with a distinctive native (Assamese) sub-culture and dialect (both known as Kamrupi). The distinctive dialect etc. are, however, shared with the present administrative districts of Nalbari and Barpeta, these districts being part of an un-divided Kamrup before the 1980s.

Since 2005, this pre-divided district has however again been sub-divided between the Kamrup (Metropolitan) and Kamrup (rural) districts, the former comprising of the Metropolitan city of Guwahati and the latter the rest of the district. Both of the district headquarters are located (rather side by side) in the heart of the city of Guwahati. This pair of districts occupies a total area of 4345 km^2 and has a population of 2,515,030 (as of 2001). The metropolitan district population is somewhere around a million.

Kanaka Dasa : Kanaka Dasa was one of the devotees of Krishna and an influential person in the Vaishnava bhakti movement in Karnataka. He was born in Haveri district in Karnataka state. In the 16th century, the laws of the time prohibited non-Orthodox people from entering into the sanctum sanctorum of Hindu Temples, and in Kanaka Dasa's case it was Udupi Sri Krishna Temple. According to one legend, however, a portion of the wall of the temple is said to have broke, the Krishna murti turned around, and by Krishna's grace, he was given darshan of the murti. The window is now called Kanakana Kindi. Like Tukaram, his life demonstrated that devotion to God was the sole criteria for acceptance, not ancestry.

Kanakakunnu Palace : This palace in the heart of Trivandrum city is one of the most beautiful buildings. The palace and its sprawling grounds are today the venue for many cultural meets. The Museum building is an architectural splendour. The napier museum, the natural history museum, the reptile house and the Shri Chitra Art Gallery are in the same complex amidst a well laid out garden and park.

Kanch Mandir : As the name suggests, the full temple is made up of coloured glasses (Kaanch). This Jain Temple was built by the "Cotton King" Sir Hukamchand in the early 20th century in MP. Inside this Jain temple thousands of mirrors adorn the walls, floor and ceilings, supplemented by brightly patterned ceramic tiles, Chinese lantern-type glass lamps and cut glass chandeliers. The use of glass beads and raised figures produces a pleasing 3-D effect. The paintings are done in coloured glass which depict stories from Jain scriptures.

Kancheepuram : Kancheepuram is known as one of India's Seven sacred cities. Kancheepuram was the historical capital of the Pallavas. It was under the Pallavas from 6th to 8th Century A.D. and later became the citadel of the Cholas, Vijayanagar Kings, the Muslims and the British. It has been a centre of Tamil learning and culture and religious background for centuries.

Kanchi is also a well known centre of the finest silk sarees made in the country. Kanchi has magnificent temples of unique architectural beauty bearing eloquent testimony to its glorious Dravidian heritage. Adi Sankaracharya established his episcopal seat (Kamakotipeetam) Kancheepuram is the birth place of C.N. Annadurai former Chief Minister of Tamil Nadu affectionately called as "Anna" by the people of Tamil Nadu.

Kanchendzonga : The two day festival of dance performed during the worship of snowy range of Kanchanjunga (Khang-chen-dzod-nga) is a dance peculiar to

Sikkim alone. It is celebrated in September. The third Chogyal of Sikkim, Chador Namgyal (1686-1716) introduced this dance about two and a half centuries ago as a result of a vision. Kanchanjunga is about 40 km from Gangtok and is the most unifying force in the myth and identity of the state. Khang-chen-dzod-nga means the five treasures represented by five summits of this gigantic mountain. According to tradition the five treasures are salt, precious stones, religious scripts, medicines and grains and invincible armour. The natural environment in which the Sikkimese live have made them to revere, fear and worship this mountain. They believe that their prosperity even their lives depend on the good humour of the deity, for he has the power to destroy human habitations with devastating floods and avalanches, wash away their bridges and ruin their crops by sending terrible hail storms down the valleys.

Kanchendzonga is portrayed as a fiery red—countenanced deity with a crown of five skulls, riding the mythical snow lion and holding aloft the banner of victory. Esoteric masks, flashing silks, opulent brocades and embroidered boots are the costumes of the dancers. The dancers are all male. In this warrior Dance the warlike pomp and panoply, the war deity resplendent the flaming robes, the fantastic Snow lion, comprise the essence of the dance. This mask dance is termed as Singhi Dance i.e. Lion Dance by Nepalese. They visualise the ferocious god of Kanchanjunga riding over a lion and hence call this dance as Singhi Dance.

Kanchenjunga : Kanchenjunga is the third highest mountain in the world and the second highest in Nepal and the highest in India, located in the Taplejung district straddling the frontier between Nepal and India. The rough translation of Kanchenjunga is "Five Treasures of the Snow", as it contains five peaks, four of them over 8,450 metres. Until 1852, Kanchenjunga was assumed to be the highest mountain in the world, but calculations made by the British 1849 Great Trigonometric Survey showed Mount Everest to be the highest and Kanchenjunga the third-highest.

Kanchenjunga is known for its famous views from the hill station of Darjeeling. On a clear day, it presents an image not as much of a mountain but of a white wall hanging from the sky. The people of Sikkim revere Kanchenjunga as a sacred mountain. Permission to climb the mountain from the Indian side is not allowed now. Because of its remote location in Nepal, the Kanchenjunga region is not much explored by the trekkers. It has, therefore, retained much of its pristine beauty. In Sikkim too, trekking into the Kanchenjunga region has just been permitted. The Goecha la trek is gaining popularity amongst tourists. It goes to the Goecha la Pass which is located right in front of the huge Southeast Face of Kanchenjunga. Another trek to Green Lake Basin has recently been opened for trekking. This goes to the Northeast side of Kangchenjunga along the famous Zemu glacier.

Kanchi Matha : Kanchi matha is known formally as Shri Kanchi Kamakoti Peetham. It is a religious institution based in Kanchipuram. Its head is referred to as the "Shankaracharya". During the later 20th century, it became one of the most influential institutions of Hindu religion in India. Its current head is Jayendra Saraswati. The appointed successor to the current head is Vijayendra Saraswati. The matha's official history states that it was founded by Adi Shankara of Kaladi, and that His Holiness Sri Jayendra Saraswati is its 69th head in succession. A related claim is that Adi Shankara came to Kanchipuram, and that he established the Kanchi matha in a position of supremacy (Sarvagnya Peetha) over the other mathas of the subcontinent, before his death there. This claim is disputed. Alternative accounts state that the matha was established much more recently in Kumbakonam, as a branch of the Sringeri matha, and that it later declared itself independent.

However, the list of successive Acharyas with their year of birth and death which date back to 5th century B.C, have been published by the Kanchi Kamakoti Peetham. The Kanchi Matha seems to have been moved from Kanchipuram to Kumbakonam during the 18th century when Hyder Ali invaded the region. Archeological evidence in the form of stone architecture depicting the Shankaracharya and the epigraphy by the side situated inside the precincts of the Matham indicate that the Matham is 2500 years old. Other sources, give the place of his death as Kedarnath in the Himalayas.

Kanchipuram : Kanchipuram, Kanchi, or Kancheepuram (also sometimes Conjeevaram) is the name of a temple town and the headquarters of Kanchipuram district in Tamil Nadu, India. In ancient times it is called as kachi and kachiampathi. Kanchipuram is located on the Palar River, and known for its temples and silk sarees. There are several big temples, notably Ekambaranatha Temple which is one of the five form of abodes of Lord Siva, (it is the earth abode here, other abodes include Chidambaram(Sky), Kalahasthi (air), Thiruvanika (water) and Thiruvannamalai (fire)), Kamakshi Amman Temple, Varadharaja Perumal Temple, Kumara Kottam, Kachapeshwarar Temple, Kailasanathar Temple and many more. Kanchipuram is also famous for its silk sarees, which are woven manually. These saris are considered to be of the highest quality all almost every relatively well-off South Indian woman has a Kanjivaram sari in her collection. The Kanjivaram saris woven at Kanchipuram are also prized in North India.

Kandla : Kandla is a seaport in Kutch District of Gujarat state in western India. Located on the Gulf of Kutch, it is one of major ports on west coast. Kandla was constructed in the 1950s as the chief seaport serving western India, after the partition of India from Pakistan left the port of Karachi in Pakistan.

Kangal Harinath : Kangal Harinath, which means "Penniless Harinath", refers to one of the most well-known Bauls of Bengal. Born in 1833 CE in Kushtia District, now in Bangladesh, his real name was Harinath Majumdar. Harinath is also known as 'Fakir Chand Baul'. Harinath was a disciple of Lalon Shah. He had very little formal education. However, he picked up journalism to promote the cause of poor and oppressed and started writing in Sangbad Probhakar. He established a Baul group named 'Kangal Fakir Chander Dal' (Group of the Penniless Fakir Chand) in 1880. His songs had profound influence of many thinkers of the day, including Rabindranath Tagore and Akshay Kumar Maitreya.

Kangar Valley National Park : This park was set up in the year1982 in Bastar district covering an area of 200sq.km. The nearest town is Jagdalpur at a distance of 30km which is also the railhead for visiting the park. The nearest airport is Raipur at a distance of 30km which is also the railhead for visiting the park. The nearest airport is Raipur at a distance of 330km from the park.

Kangla Palace : Palace of Kangla is an old palace at Kangla, Manipur state in India. It is situated on the western bank of the Imphal River. Only the ruins remain now. Kangla means "dry land" in old Meiteilon or Meithei. It was the traditional seat of the past Meithei rulers of Manipur. The British referred to it as the Manipur Fort.

The Kingdom of Manipur developed at Kangla. Being a political and religious centre, Kangla grew into a formidable fortress city over the centuries. It is from this capital that the Ningthouja clan gradually wielded enough political and military power to become the most dominant clan in Manipur. The royal chronicle of Manipur, Cheitharol Kumbaba, contains many references to the development of Kangla by successive reigning kings in Manipur.

The royal chronicle records that King Khagemba (1597 - 1652 A.D.) - the conqueror of the Chinese, constructed a brick wall at the western gate of 'Kangla Fort' in 1632 A.D.. It appears that the art of brick making was acquired from the Chinese prisoners who were captured during the Chinese invasion of the eastern frontier of Manipur. His son King Khunjaoba (1632 - 1666 A.D.) carried out fortification and beautification work of Kangla Fort. It is believed that the king excavated a moat (Thangapat) on the western side of the Fort. The Fort was further enlarged by King Garibaniwaz and other successive kings of Manipur.

It is famous in the history of Manipur. In the evening of March 24, 1891 British Gorkha troops attacked Juvraj Tikendrajit's residence in the Palace Compound, killing many innocent civilians including women and children who were watching a Ras Lila dance. The Manipuris struck back and the British was put on the defensive. In the ensuing chaos, five British officers including Grimwood, the then Political Agent and J.W. Quinton, the Chief Commissioner of Assam, were executed by a mob. This resulted in the Anglo-Manipuri War in 1891. The British forces finally defeated the Manipuri forces and hoisted the Union Jack in Kangla on 27 April 1892. It was occupied by the British, declaring it as the cantonment area or the 'British Reserve' till they left Manipur in 1947.

Its occupation by the Assam Rifles, an Indian paramilitary force was a major source of discontent of the local people. M. M. Jacob, the then Minister of State for

Home in 1992 had announced in a speech that the Assam Rifles would hand over the historic fort to the state government. This finally came true on November 20, 2004 when Prime Minister Manmohan Singh handed over the historic Kangla Fort to Manipur state government.

Kangra : Kangra is the most populous district of the state of Himachal Pradesh, India. Dharamshala is the administrative headquarters of the district. The district is in the western part of Himachal Pradesh, in the low foothills of the Himalayas. The Dhauladhar range adjoins the district on one side. The Beas is one of the larger rivers of this district, and contributes to the fertility of the land here. The district is bounded by the Himachal Pradesh districts of Chamba to the north, Lahul and Spiti to the northeast, Kullu to the east, Mandi to the southeast, and Hamirpur and Una to the south. The district shares a border with the states of Punjab on the southwest, and Jammu and Kashmir on the northwest.

Kangra-Lambagraon : Kangra-Lambagraon was a princely estate in British India. Lying in the present-day state of Himachal Pradesh, the estate was ruled by the ancient Katoch dynasty. "Trigarth" and "Jallandhra" were other names by which the state was known in former times. In 1947, the estate comprised of 20 villages, encompassed an area of 324 sq.km, and enjoyed a revenue of approx. Rs.40,000/-.

Kangri Language : The Kangri language is spoken in northern India, predominantly in the Kangra district of Himachal Pradesh, by the Kangri people. It is an Indo-Aryan language, classified as one of the Pahari languages, and is closely related to Dogri. Both Dogri have been considered dialects of Punjabi in the past, but speakers of those two languages "have now started seeking an independent identity."

Kangsa River : Kangsa river originates in the Garo Hills near Tura, in the eastern part of the Shillong Plateau of India and flows through Assam and Bangladesh. The river is also known as the Kangsai or the Kangsabati. After flowing south, the river enters Bangladesh 16 km north of Nalitabari upazila in Sherpur district and meets the Shomeshwari after flowing east. The joint flow of the Kangsa and the Shomeshwari is known as the Baulai river.

Kanha National Park: Kanha National Park, part of Project Tiger, is located in Madhya Pradesh, India. In the 1930s, the Kanha area was divided into two sanctuaries, Hallon and Banjar, of 250 and 300 km^2 each. Kanha National Park was created on 1 June 1955. The nearest airport is at Nagpur, around 260 km away, and the nearest railhead is Jabalpur, around 175 km away.

The lowland forest is a mixture of sal and other trees, interspersed with meadows. The higland forests are of a completely different nature. Kanha is home to about 22 species of mammals and about 300 species of birds. Commonly observed mammals include the Common Grey Langur, Wild Boar, Chital, Chousingha, Sambar and Barasingha or Swamp deer (this is the hardground swamp deer, found only in Kanha, barely 350 survive in the wild). An attempt to raise the black buck here has failed. This is tiger country (of which there are currently over a hundred). One can also find leopards, the Sloth bear and Indian wild dog. Very rarely seen are the Indian wolf, which live in the far east of the park, and the pangolin, which are nocturnal and live in the highlands. The Indian jungle fowl, which is the ancestor of domestic hens, is common. The Nilgai (blue bull), though rare, can also be found in Kanha.

Kanjut Sar : Kanjut Sar is a Himalayan mountain located in the Hispar Muztagh region of the Karakoram range. Kanjut Sar consists of two peaks: Kanjut Sar I at

7,760 metres (25,460 feet). Ranked 29th in the world. Kanjut Sar II at 6,181 metres (20,279 feet). Kanjut Sar I was first climbed in 1959 by Guido Monzino of an Italian expedition.

Kannada : Kannada is one of the major Dravidian languages of southern India. Speakers of its various dialects number roughly 40 million people. It is the state language of Karnataka, one of the four southern states in India. It is written using the Kannada script.

Kannauj : Kannauj, or Kanauj, is an ancient city lying in the Indian state of Uttar Pradesh. It is the administrative headquarters of Kannauj District. The town was in earlier times the capital of a great Hindu kingdom. Its population in 1991 was 58,932. The name Kannauj is traditionally held to be derived from the term Kanyakubja (the crooked maiden). It has given its name to a distinct dialect of the Hindi language known as Kanauji. Kannauj is known for the distilling of scents and is a market center for tobacco, perfume, and rose water.

Formerly known as Kanyakubja (called Kanogiza by Ptolemy), the town is known to have been an important center during the Gupta empire. It reached the pinnacle of its glory in the 7th century under Harsha as the capital and cultural center of the empire he built. Harsha however was greatly weakened after being defeated by the Chalukya emperor Pulakesin II; his empire fell apart soon after his death.

By the end of the 8th century, Kannauj became the focus of a three-way contest by the three dominant dynasties of the time, the Pratiharas of Malwa, the Rashtrakutas of the Deccan, and the Palas of Bengal. The Pala king Dharmapala installed a proxy king at the end of the 8th century; however, the Pratihara king Nagabhatta II conquered Kannauj in the 9th century. Kannauj became the Pratihara capital for nearly 200 years. During this period, it became known as a center for poetry. The Pratiharas ruled much of northern India in the latter half of the 8th century, but they had weakened by the early 10th century. The Rashtrakuta king Indra III captured Kannauj in 916, and by the end of that century, the Pratihara domains had been reduced to a small kingdom around the town of Kannauj.

In 1019, the town was sacked by Mahmud of Ghazni, who ushered in a chaotic period for the city. After this sacking of Kannauj, the area came to be dominated by the Chandela Rajput clan of Bundelkhand. The Gahadvala dynasty, descended from former vassals of the Pratiharas, established themselves as rulers of Kannauj at the end of the 11th century. Kannauj recovered some of its former prosperity under the Gahadvalas, but the respite was brief, for the city was sacked again in 1194 by Mohammed of Ghori, and by the early years of the 13th century it was incorporated into the Delhi Sultanate. Kannauj has never since recovered its importance.

Kannur District : Kannur District or Cannanore District is one of the 14 districts in the state of Kerala, India. The town of Kannur is the district headquarters, and gives the district its name. The old name 'Cannanore' is the anglicised form of the Malayalam name Kannur. Kannur District is bounded by Kasaragod District to the north and Kozhikode District to the south. To the east the district is bounded by the Western Ghats range, which forms the border with Karnataka state, in its districts of Kodagu and Chamarajanagar. The Arabian Sea lies to the west.

Kanpur : Kanpur is the most populous city in the north Indian state of Uttar Pradesh. Kanpur is located on the banks of the Ganga and is an important industrial center. It has an area of over 1000 km² and had a population of around 2.4 million in the 1991 census. It is home to several educational institutions, including one of the Indian Institutes of Technology.

Kanshi Ram : Kanshi Ram (born 1934) is an Indian politician of Dalit Sikh background. He founded the Bahujan Samaj Party (BSP), a political party with the stated goal of serving the traditionally lower castes of Indian society, including Sudras and Dalits. He shares the BSP's leadership with Mayawati. Their leadership brought the party to power in India's most populous state, Uttar Pradesh in 1995, at which point Mayawati became the state's chief minister.

As of April, 2005, Kanshi Ram has spent more than a year recovering from health problems and has not appeared publicly during that time. He has been convalescing at the home of Mayawati, and members of his family have claimed that she has been essentially holding him captive in order to control the BSP. On April 8, 2005, the Supreme Court of India ordered a team of doctors to examine his physical and mental condition.

Kantaji Temple : Kantaji Temple is a late medieval Hindu temple in Dinajpur, Bangladesh. Built by Maharaja Prannath, its construction started in 1722. It boast one of the greatest examples on Terracotta architecture in Bangladesh. It once had nine spires, but they were destroyed in an earthquake in the 19th century.

Kanthimathi Nellaiyappar Temple : This twin temple in Tirunelveli dedicated to Siva (Nellaiyappar) and Parvathi (Kanthimathi) is situated in the heart of the city. Built by the Pandyas in the 13C but entirely remodeled and extended in 17C—18C, the main deity is a 'Suyambu Lingam' or a Shiva Lingam which erupted from underneath the earth. The temple is worth seeing for its beautiful sculptures, musical pillars, valuable jewels, a golden lily tank and a thousand pillared mandapa. It is one of the five sacred places in Saiva religion. The famous Car festival here is celebrated during June- July. A marriage festival of Shiva and Parvathi is also celebrated during October—November months.

Kanyakumari : Kanyakumari is a town and a cape at the southernmost tip of the Indian peninsula. It is located in the state of Tamil Nadu. During British rule, it was known as Cape Comorin. The closest major city is Thiruvananthapuram, the capital of Kerala. Kanyakumari was once referred to as the Alexandria of the east. It has been a great centre for the arts, culture, civilization, and pilgrimage for years. It was also a famous centre for commerce and trade. The area abounds with many unique herbs and plants believed to have originated due to a small piece of the medical hill 'Siranjeevi' falling on this place as Lord Hanuman was carrying the hill to Sri Lanka. In addition, Kanyakumari district has many practitioners of various branches of ancient India's health systems from siddha, ayurvedha, varma kalai etc.

It is believed that Christianity arrived in this area in AD 52 through St. Thomas, one of the twelve Apostles of Christ. Similarly, Islam is believed to have entered the southern part of India through Kanyakumari during the early part of the eighth century AD through the sea route with traders and missionaries. Islam, Christianity and Jainism have also contributed to the architectural wealth and literary heritage of this place. Kanyakumari was also under the control of the Cholas, the Cheras, the Pandyas and the Nayaks who were great rulers of south India.

The architectural beauty of the temples is the work of these rulers. During the British Raj, Kanyakumari was bestowed the dry title of Cape Camorin, necessitated perhaps by the Englishmen's inability to pronounce local names. Legend has it that Kanya Devi, an avatar of

Goddess Parvati, was to wed Lord Shiva, the destroyer in the Hindu trinity. But he did not turn up at the auspicious time and the wedding never took place. The rice and cereals meant for the marriage remained uncooked. Even today, one can buy stones there that look exactly like rice and cereals. Local folks believe that they are the leftovers of the legendary marriage that could not be solemnized. As for the princess Kanya Devi, she became a virgin goddess blessing pilgrims and tourists alike.

Kapil Dev : Kapil Dev Ramlal Nikhanj, better known as Kapil was born on January 6, 1959, in Chandigarh, India. He is one of the greatest all-rounders ever seen in the game of cricket. He led the Indian cricket team to its only World Cup victory in 1983. In addition, he held the record for the most Test match wickets, between 1994 and 1999.

As a bowler Kapil was notable for a graceful action and a potent outswinger and was India's main strike bowler for more than ten years. He also developed a fine inswinging yorker during the 1980s which he used very effectively against the tailenders. As a batsman he was a natural striker of the ball who could hook and drive effectively.

A naturally aggressive player, he often helped India in difficult situations by taking the attack to the opposition, such as in a match on route to the World Cup finals of 1983, when he smashed a captain's knock of 175 against Zimbabwe helping India recover from a tenuous 5/17 - surprisingly, this was his only ODI hundred. Incidentally, this was also the first century by an Indian in an ODI.

Kaptai Lake : Kaptai Lake the largest man-made freshwater body in Bangladesh. Though created primarily for hydroelectric power generation, it contributes to produce significant quantity of freshwater fishes, navigation, flood control and agriculture, etc. The reservoir was created by damming the river Karnafuli near Kaptai town in the Chittagong hill tracts. The lake is confined within the hill district Rangamati and embraces the upazilas of Rangamati Sadar, Kaptai, Nannerchar, Langadu, Baghaichhari, Barkal, Juraichhari and Belaichhari.

The 'H'-shaped Kaptai Lake has two arms, joined by a narrow gorge near Shubalong, a part of the old Karnafuli river. Kasalong, the right arm of the lake, is fed by two streams, the Mayni and the Kasalong, in the north and laterally by the Karnafuli. The left arm, Rangamati-Kaptai is fed by two streams, the Chengi in the north and the Rinkhyong in the south.

Apart from generation of hydroelectricity, the lake has become an important resource for some other considerations. It has created a diversified and long waterway. Many places that used to take a day or even more to reach have now become an hour's trip by speedboat or launch. It has become much easier to exploit forest resources that had earlier been inaccessible. The whole lake is now a great tourist attraction. The lake's contribution to the development of agriculture and fishery is significant. Since the water level of the lake is maintained at different heights in different months of the year, the lakeshores are under an automatic irrigation system and are very fertile. People practice controlled farming in about 6,075 ha of land on leasehold basis through agreements with the local government.

Kapurthala : Kapurthala is a city in Punjab state of India. It is the administrative headquarters of Kapurthala District. It was the former capital of princely state of British India of the same name. Kapurthala, a native state of India, within the Punjab, Area, 652 sq. m.; pop. (1901), 314,341, showing an increase of 5% in the decade; estimated gross revenue, 178,000; tribute, 8700.

The Kapurthala family is descended from Jassa Singh, a contemporary of Nadir Shah and Ahmad Shah, who by his intelligence and bravery made himself the leading Sikh of his day. At one time it held possessions on both sides of the Sutlej, and also in the Bari Doab. The cis-Sutlej estates and scattered tracts in the Bari Doab were forfeited owing to the hostility of the chief in the first Sikh war; but the latter were afterwards restored in recognition of the loyalty of Raja Randhir Singh during the mutiny of 1857, when he led a contingent to Oudh which did good service. He also received a grant of land in Oudh, 700 sq. m. in extent, yielding a gross rental of 89,000. In Oudh, however, he exercises no sovereign powers, occupying only the status of a large landholder, with the title of Raja-i-Rajagan.

Raja Sir Jagatjit Singh, K.C.S.I., was born in 1872, succeeded his father in 1877, and attained his majority in 1890. During the Tirah expedition of 1897-98 the Kapurthala imperial service infantry took a prominent part. The territory is crossed by the railway from Jaladhar to Amritsar. The state has a large export trade in wheat, sugar, tobacco and cotton. The hand-painted cloths and metal-work of Phagwara are well known. It also has the much renowned Sainik School, housed in what was formerly the palace of the erstwhile maharajah of Kapurthala state, HRH Maharajah Jagatjit Singh. The palace building has a spectacular architecture based on the Palace of Versailles and Fontainbleau spread over a total area of 200 acres.

Other places of interest include the famous Shalimar Gardens, District Courts buildings, Moorish Mosque, Panch Mandir ("Five Temples"), State Gurudwara, a wetland resort, Guru Nanak sports stadium, Jagjit Club, and the NJSA Government college.This is the college from where His Highness Sir Atul Aswal, the royal prince of Garhwal

Dynasty, who reside in G.D. Park now, has done his graduation.

Kar Hunnive : This is observed on the Full moon day of Jyestha (June) by worshipping the bullocks and the agricultural implements in Karnataka. A special feast is prepared in the afternoon. In the evening a function called Karihariyodu is performed, in which the chief event is bullocks race. Many pairs of bullocks participate in the running race and the pair which come first is acclaimed by the public. If the bullocks which comes first are red or brown colour, it is supposed that red variety of jowar will grow in abundance during the ensuing season and if they are white in colour, white jowar is supposed to grow in plenty.

Kara Film Festival : The Kara Film Festival is the only internationlly recognized film festival of Pakistan, annually held in the city of light — Karachi. It is organized under the aegis of the Kara Film Society, a grouping of committed young filmmakers of Karachi. The Kara Film Society is a not-for-profit, non-political and non-governmental body, headed by Hasan Zaidi. The society organizes the annual KaraFilm Festival, screenings, talks and workshops. Kara Film Festival was first held, in 2001, since then it has been annualy held in December in Karachi. This year, Kara Film Festival is going to be held on December 1st - 10th, 2005, Karachi. The great success of Kara Film Festival within a short span of time has caught the attention of world film makers and renowned film critics and now it is ranked amongst some of the most prestigious film festivals of the region.

Karachi : Karachi is the largest city in Pakistan and the capital of the province of Sindh. A native of Karachi is referred to as a Karachiite. Karachi is the financial and commercial hub of Pakistan and an important port in the region. The city is located on the coast of the Arabian Sea, northwest of the delta of the Indus River. It accounts for the lion's share of Pakistan's GDP and generates about 65% percent of the national revenue. Karachi claims highest per capita income in South Asia. It is the nucleus of regional business and technological activities and has one of the highest literacy rate in the country. It is also the home of distinguished academic and research institutions. With a population that is unofficially estimated at approximately 12 million, Karachi is the most populous city of the country and one of the largest cities in the world.

Karachi District : Karachi district is the most populous of the Districts of Pakistan. It was formed by the merger of the five districts of Karachi Central, Karachi East, Karachi South, Karachi West and Malir. It is largely conterminous with Pakistan's largest city, Karachi. Karachi began as a small fisherman village and emerged to become the largest city of Pakistan with a population of 9.2 Million, boasting the largest inland citizen migration in the sub-continent.On 14th August 2001 under to Devolution Plan City District Government Karachi came into being with 18 Town Administration and 178 Union Councils.

Karachi Stock Exchange : Karachi Stock Exchange has been declared as the "Best Performing Stock Market of The World For the year 2002". As on December 31, 2004, 661 companies were listed with the market capitalization of Rs. 1,723.45 billion having listed capital of Rs. 405.65 billion. The KSE 100 Index closed at 6218.40 on December 31, 2004. KSE has been well into the 3rd year of being one of the Best Performing Markets of the world as declared by the international magazine "Business Week". Similarly the US newspaper, USA Today, termed Karachi Stock Exchange as one of the best performing bourses in the world.

Karaikal : Karaikal, also Karikal or Karaikkal, is one of the four Districts of the Union Territory of Pondicherry.

Karaikal is located in a small coastal enclave of territory which was formerly part of French India, and, together with the former French coastal enclaves of Pondichery, Yanam, and Mahé, forms the Union Territory of Pondichery. Karaikal is bounded on the North and South by Nagapattinam district of Tamil Nadu state, on the west by Tiruvarur district (also belonging to Tamil Nadu), and on the East by the Bay of Bengal. Located 132 km south of the city of Pondicherry, Karaikal is known for its rich religious heritage, and is the destination for those who seek and solicit leisure, serenity and piety.

Karak : It is a tale ballet singing form sung by a community called 'Jogies'. They narrate a popular folk tale in their dance style, performed by three members with accompaniement of typical folk instrument called 'Rabab'.

Karakam Dance : Karakam is a folk art developed along with the cult of Mariamman in Tamil Nadu. It is of two varieties- the religious and the professional. The religious type is called Sakti Karakam. A small pot is filled with water and sealed with a coconut. Flower wreaths decorate it and a lime fruit is placed at the top of the Karakam. The temple priest or his nominee carries it with great ceremony and sentimental attachment since this is one of their hereditary privileges. The professional type is known as Attak Karakam and is performed anywhere by anyone with necessary practice and skill. It is one of the Tamil Nadu's regular showpieces at the republic day floats in New Delhi every year.

Karakoram : Located in the mountainous regions of Gilgit, Ladakh & Baltistan, Gilgit and Baltistan are in Pakistan, the Karakoram is one of the great Himalayan mountain ranges, with many of the highest and most daunting peaks of the world. It is located on the border of Pakistan and India with China, about 500 km (300 mi) in length, and is the most heavily glaciated part of the world outside of the polar regions. Karakoram means "black gravel" in Turkish, as many of the surrounding glaciers are covered in rubble.

Due to its altitude and ruggedness, the Karakoram is much less inhabited than parts of the Himalayas further east. European explorers first visited early in the 19th century, followed by British surveyors starting in 1856. The Muztagh Pass was crossed in 1887 by the expedition of Colonel Francis Younghusband and the valleys above the Hunza River were explored by George Cockerill in 1892. Explorations in the 1910s and 1920s established most of the geography of the region.

The Karakoram and the Himalaya are important to Earth scientists for several reasons. They are one of the world's most geologically active areas, at the boundary between two colliding continents. Therefore, they are important in the study of plate tectonics. Mountain glaciers may serve as an indicator of climate change, advancing and receding with long-term changes in temperature and precipitation. These extensive ranges may have even caused climate change when they were formed over 40 million years ago. The large amounts of rock exposed to the atmosphere are weathered (broken down) by carbon dioxide. This process removes the greenhouse gas from the atmosphere, and could have caused the global climate to cool, triggering an ongoing series of ice ages.

Karakoram Highway : The Karakoram Highway (KKH) is the highest international road in the world. It connects China to Pakistan across the Karakoram mountain ranges, through the Khunjerab Pass at a recently confirmed altitude of 4,693 metres (15,397 feet). The highway runs about 1,200 km from Kashgar, China to Havelian in the Abbottabad District of Pakistan. An extension of the highway meets the Grand Trunk Road at Hasan Abdal, west of Islamabad, Pakistan. Large part of highway runs through Azad Kashmir.

Karakoram Pass : The Karakoram Pass (5,575 m or 18,291 ft) 35°27′N 77°54′E was the highest pass on the ancient caravan route between Leh, Ladakh and Yarkand in the Tarim Basin. The high altitude was responsible for the deaths of innumerable pack animals, and the route across the Pass was notorious the strewn trail of bones along the way.

It is in a saddle between two mountains and about 45 metres wide. There is no vegetation or icecap and is generally free of snow due to the winds. However, the winds are often very high accompanied by low temperatures and there are frequent blizzards. In spite of all this, the Karakoram Pass was considered a relatively easy pass due to its relatively gradual ascent on both sides, and lack of ice.

Karakoram Ranges : Far away from here are seen the Karakoram ranges also known as Mustagh in Kashmir. Some of its peaks rising over 25,000 ft and among them the World-famous K2 (over 28,000 ft.), the second highest in the world, stands out boldly in its mountain glory. To the east of the valley stands the noble, snow-clad peak of Haramukh (16,903 ft.) overlooking it.

Karam : The another extensively celebrated festival is Ind-Karam which is held on the 11th day of the phases of moon in Bhadra month in Jharghand. It is the festival of youthfulness and for the youth. The youth of villages get together in the forest. Where they dance, sing and collect fruits and flowers for the worship of the deity known as Karma Devta. At the evening, when the worship is over, dancing and signing go all through the night. The entire plateau resounds with dance of damsel, song of spirit and joy of juvenalia. It is indeed a rare example of such a vital and vibrant youth festival.

At the same time, the unmarried girls celebrate the Jawa festival, which has its own kind of dance and songs. This is held mainly with an expectation of fertility and better household. The unmarried girls decorate a small basket with germinating seeds. It is believed that the worship for good germination of the grains would increase the fertility as well. The girls also offer a green melon to the deity as a symbol of 'son'. This reveals the primitive expectation of human being, i.e grain and children.

Karatoya River : Karatoya river is an intriguing river, formerly the main channel of the Tista, and perhaps a distributary of the Brahmaputra. In the Siyar-al-Mutakhkhirin it is recorded that this river was three times the size of the ganges when Bakhtiyar Khalji invaded the Northern Region (1115 AD). Tectonic disturbances had broken it up into four distinct parts. The northern part, called the Dinajpur-Karatoya, is the main source of the Atrai. It rises in a marsh in Baikanthapur in Jalpaiguri (India), but also receives water from underground streams. In Khansama upazila its name changes to Atrai. The Dinajpur-Karatoya was connected with the Rangpur-Karatoya north of Khansama, but very little water now passes down that channel. The upper part of Rangpur-Karatoya originates in the Jalpaiguri district of India and is known as the Deonai-Jamuneshwari up to Gobindaganj upazila.

Karauli : Karauli (also formerly spelled Karoli or Kerowlee) is a town lying in the Indian state of Rajasthan. The town is the administrative center of Karauli District, and was formerly the capital of the erstwhile princely state of Karauli. The town dates from 1348, and is situated in a position naturally defended by ravines on the north and east, while it is further protected by a great wall. The

Maharaja's palace is a handsome block of buildings, some of them dating to the late 1700's.

Legend has it that the princely state of Karauli was founded about 995 by Raja Bijai Pal; ot is claimed that he was 88th in descent from the hindu god Krishna. Little is however known about the early history of the family; the state was long a fief in Jaipur state until the HEIC chose, in the early 19th century, to recognise Karauli as being an independent principality. In 1818, Karauli was made part of the Rajputana Agency.

The state had an area of 3,178 km^2 (1242 square miles). In 1901, the population of the state was 156,786, and that of the town was 23,482. Millets, the staple food of the people, was the main agricultural produce. As of the early 20th century, there were no major industries; a little weaving, dyeing, wood-turning and stonecutting constituted the notable cottage industries. Most goods, as also salt, sugar, cotton, buffaloes and bullocks, were imported; rice and goats comprised the main exports. After India's independence in 1947, the state under Maharaja Ganesh Pal Deo acceded to the dominion of India on 7 April 1949; Karauli later merged with the union of India and became part of the state of Rajasthan.

Karbis : The Karbis, mentioned as the Mikirs in the Constitution Order of the Government of India, constitute an important ethnic group in the hill areas of Assam. They do not call themselves Mikir rather Karbi, and sometimes Arleng, which literally means a man. Presently they inhabit the Karbi Anglong district and some Karbi inhabited pockets are found in the North Cachar Hills, Kamrup, Morigaon, Nagaon and Sonitpur districts also.

Kargam : Kargam is the most common form of folk dance in Tamil Nadu.

Kargam is essentially part of a ritual and is performed by men balancing pots filled with uncooked rice, surrounded by a tall conical bamboo frame covered with flowers. The musical accompaniment comprises a drum and a long pipe.

Kargil : The contemporary district of Kargil was one of the districts of Ladakh Wazarat/Province before Partition of Ladakh in 1947. The other two districts of Ladakh Wazarat were Skardo Baltistan and Leh Central Ladakh. Today, Kargil is one of the districts of Ladakh region in the Indian state of Jammu and Kashmir. Kargil lies on the line of control facing Pakistan Occupied Kashmir's region of Baltistan. Zanskar Zangskar is part of Kargil district along with Suru, Wakha and Dras valleys. Some parts of Kargil district like Gultari, Shingo-Shigar, Olding, Brolmo, Tse-tse thang, Rganogs and Marol villages are in Pakistani occupation since 1947.

Kargil Town : Kargil town serves as the headquarters of Kargil District in Jammu and Kashmir of India. It is located 60km and 204km from Drass and Srinagar to the west respectively, 234km from Leh to the east, 240km from Padum to the southeast and 1047km to Delhi in the south. Kargil is located 10,000 feet above sea level, along the banks of Suru river. People in Kargil are of mixed Dard and Tibetan descent. The inhabitants of Kargil were adherents of Tibetan Buddhism until the 14th-15th centuries when Muslim missionaries began to proselytise to the local people. Today, 90% of Kargil's population are Shia Muslim, 5% Sunni and 5% Tibetan Buddhist. The architecture of older mosques in Kargil combines Tibetan and Iranian styles, while newer mosques architectural styles tend to follow those of modern Iranian and Arabic styles.

Kargil War : The Kargil War, also known as the Kargil conflict (I), was an armed conflict between India and Pakistan that took place between April and June 1999 in

Kashmir. The cause of the war was the infiltration of Pakistani soldiers and Kashmiri militants into positions on the Indian side of the Line of Control, which serves as the de facto border between the two nations. Pakistan blamed the fighting entirely on independent Kashmiri insurgents; however, documents left behind by casualties and later statements by Pakistan's Prime Minister and Army Chief showed involvement of Pakistani paramilitary forces. The Indian Army, supported by the air force, attacked the Pakistani positions and, with international diplomatic support, eventually forced a Pakistani withdrawal across the Line of Control.

The war is one of the most recent examples of high altitude warfare, in mountainous terrain, and posed significant logistics problems for the combating sides. This was the first ground war between the two nuclear powers. (India and Pakistan both test-detonated fission devices in May 1998, though the first Indian nuclear test was conducted in 1974.) The conflict led to heightened tensions between the two nations and increased defense spending on the part of India. In Pakistan, the aftermath caused instability to the government and the economy, and on October 13, 1999, a coup d'etat by the military placed army chief Pervez Musharraf in power.

Karimnagar : Karimnagar is a town in Andhra Pradesh state of India. It is the administrative headquarters of Karimnagar District. The town has a population of 253,819 (agglomeration 345,782) (2006 census}. Karimnagar derives its name from Syed Karimullah Shah Saheb Quiladar, and was a centre for Vedic learning. It was one of the capitals during the rule of the Nizams, and there are several famous people like P.V. Narasimha Rao, Former Indian Prime Minister, who hail from here. Karimnagar District is home to many tribes such as Gonds, Koyas, and Chenchus all who live in their own settlements and speak their own dialects. The town is known for its silver filigree work, a very delicate form of metal craft.

Karma : The karma is a famous autumn festival which starts from the eleventh day of the bright fortnight of the month of Bhadrab and continues for some days in the month of Ashwina. The festival is celebrated in most of Orissa's villages in Sambalpur and Phulabani districts.

Karma Dance : Among the Gonds, Baigas and Oraons of the north-west fringes of Madhya Pradesh, the Karma dance is very common. This form is associated with the fertility cult and essentially related to the Karma festival that falls in the month of August. The Karma dance symbolizes the bringing of green branches of the forest in the spring. Sometimes a tree is actually set up in the village and people dance round it. The dance is filled with breath of trees. The men leap forward to a rapid roll of drums. Bending low to the ground the women dance, their feet moving in perfect rhythm to and fro, until the group of singers advances towards them.

There are other variants of the Karma. The songs associated with these variants differ with each pattern. The Thadi, the Lahaki, the Khalha, the Jhumar and the Jharpat are the variations of Baiga Adivasis dance. The Karma seems to have been the oldest dance form of the Adivasis of Madhya Pradesh. It is the only dance which is common to the many ethnic groups of India.

Karnafuli River : Karnafuli river is the largest and most important river in Chittagong and the Chittagong Hill Tracts, originating in the Lushai hills in Mizoram State of India. It travels through 180 km of mountainous wilderness making a narrow loop at Rangamati and then follows a zigzag course before it forms two other prominent loops, the Dhuliachhari and the Kaptai.

The Rangamati and the Dhuliachhari loops are now under the reservoir of the Kaptai earth-filled dam. The hydroelectric dam is situated just before the entrance of the river into the Kaptai loop. After coming out from the Kaptai loop the river follows another stretch of tortuous course through the Sitapahar hill range and flows across the plain of Chittagong after emerging from the hills near Chandraghona. Therefore, the river drains into the Bay of Bengal cutting across several hill ranges, viz the Barkal, Gobamura, Chilardak, Sitapahar and Patiya of the Chittagong Hill Tracts and Chittagong. It has possibly maintained its older course keeping pace with the uplift of the hill ranges and can be classified as an antecedent river. The Karnafuli is narrow and straight from Prankiang to Waggachhari along Kaptai-Chandraghona road. The straightness of the river is probably due to a fault, which controlled the channel from Prankiang to Wagga. The main tributaries of the Karnafuli are the Kasalong, Chengi, Halda and Dhurung on the right and the Subalong, Kaptai, Rinkeong and Thega on the left.

Karnal : Karnal is a city in Karnal District, in Haryana, India. The district has an area of 1,967 sq km and its population is 8,85,000. The district headquarter is situated in Karnal city. Karnal was founded by the Kauravas around the time of the Mahabharat for King Karna. It is 123 km from Delhi on the National Highway NH1, also called the GT Road, and 126 km from Chandigarh. Karnal is well known world over for Shoes, Basmati Rice and agriculture research Institutions.

Karnal District lies on the western bank of river Yamuna forming eastern boundary of the district. It is called as the city of Daanvir Karan has ever been a walled town as far as it is possible to trace and may even have had a citadel one time. In 1739, the Persian King Nadir Shah defeated the Mughal ruler Muhammad Shah in the Battle of Karnal. Karnal was annexed by the Raja of Jind in AD 1763 and was taken from him by George Thomas in 1797. The British established a cantonment in 1811 but abandoned it after 30 years due to the outbreak of malaria.

Karnam Malleswari : Indian weightlifter from Andhra Pradesh. She became the First Indian woman ever to win an Olympic medal. She won bronze in 69kg category at Sydney Olympics 2000. She has also won gold in Istanbul World Championship (1994) and Asian Championships (54-kg category) at Pusan, Korea (1995).

In World Weightlifting Championship at Guangzhou (China) on November 19, 1995 Malleswari set a new world record by winning three golds in 54-kg category. She was awarded 'Rajiv Gandhi Khel Ratna Award' in 1994-95.

Karnaphuli : Karnaphuli is a river in the south-eastern part of Bangladesh. Originating from the Lushai hills in Mizoram, India, it flows through Chittagong Hill Tracts and Chittagong into the Bay of Bengal. A large hydroelectric power plant using Karnaphuli river was built at Kaptai during the 1960s. The mouth of the river hosts Chittagong sea port, the main port of Bangladesh.

Legend has it that a princess from neighbouring Arakan (now in Myanmar) fell in love with a tribal prince of Chittagong. The lovers were once enjoying a moonlit boatride on the river. While admiring the reflection of the moon dancing on the rippled water surface, the princess leaned slightly and a flower tucked in the hair over her ear by the prince suddenly fell into the river. The princess was grief-stricken at losing the flower, which she held very dear as a present from her charming prince. She immediately jumped into the river to retrieve the flower but could not. Instead she was carried away by the fast-flowing current and vanished in the river. The prince dove into the river to rescue the princess but his attempt was in vain. Out of sorrow he drowned himself in the river to unite with the princess after death. This tragedy gave the river its name Karnafuli from the word 'karnaphul' meaning 'flower adorning the ear'. The river is known to the Marma tribe as the Kynsa Khyong.

The Karnaphuli Hydro-power station, the only hydro-electric power plant in Bangladesh, was constructed in Kaptai in 1962. An earth-filled dam on the Karnaphuli River created the Kaptai Lake, which acts as the water reservoir for the hydropower station. The power plant produces a total of 230 megawatts of electricity.

Karnataka : Karnataka or Karnataka is one of the four southern states of India. Before 1973, the state was known as Mysore state, as it was formed out of the former Kingdom of Mysore in 1950, and enlarged in 1956 to include the Kannada-speaking regions of neighboring states. Karnataka's capital Bangalore is the only city in the state with a population of more than 1 million. Other major cities include Mysore, Mangalore, Hubli-Dharwad, Bellary and Belgaum. Kannada is the official language of Karnataka. As of 2001, it is one of 10 Indian states with a population greater than 50 million.

KaroKari : KaroKari or Honour Killing is the practice in Sindh, which looks towards killing of (mostly) women by family members in order to preserve family "honour".A news-making case occurred on December 28, 2005, when one Nazir Ahmed slit the throats of his three young daughters and stepsister.

Karol Bagh : Karol Bagh is an old market in West-Central Delhi. Once centred around the main street, called Ajmal Khan Road, the market has now expanded into the lanes that lead off it, swallowing once-residential areas which now house a large concentration of mid-range hotels. Some of the best-known shops on Ajmal Khan Road include Roopak's, a spice store and a plethora of shops specializing mainly in clothes (including branches of famous trousseau shops Ram Chandra Kishan Chandra and Zohra, which were featured in Mira Nair's film Monsoon Wedding). Other landmark shops include Cheap Silk Stores, South India Cloth House, and Jainsons Westend.

Famous eating places are mostly old-fashioned sweetshops, including Punjab Sweets and Roshan da Kulfi (supposedly one of the oldest and best kulfi places in the city. These are also well-known for their traditional Punjabi vegetarian food options and snacks, such as aloo tikki and excellent Chole Bhature. The area between Gurudwara Road and Ajmal Khan Road, at the Pusa Road end, specialises in motorcycle and automobile parts. A little further down, where Ajmal Khan Road meets Pusa Road, is a station of the soon-to-be-opened third line of the under-construction Delhi Metro, which will link it to Connaught Place and most of West Delhi.

Kartalab Khan's Mosque : Kartalab Khan's Mosque situated in the Begum Bazar area in old Dhaka, was built by Diwan murshid quli khan alias Kartalab Khan in 1701-04. It is also known as the 'Begum Bazar Mosque'. The baoli of this mosque, which appears to be a monument by itself, deserves special mention. It is the only one of its kind in Bengal. Its origin may be traced to the Deccan, where Kartalab Khan had long stayed before coming to Bengal

Kartarpur Gurudwara : Kartarpur located 16km from Jalandhar is famous for its Gurudwara built by the Fifth Sikh Guru, Guru Arjun Devji in 1656 A.D. A fair is held every year on his birth anniversary. Large number of devotees attend the fair. There is a Smarak here for Swami Virjanad who was the teacher of Swami Dayanand Saraswathi; the founder of Arya Samaj. Kartarpur is also famous for its furniture industry.

Karthi : Karthi is the only mixed dance of men and women in Punjab, which used to be more popular in the hills, than in the plains. While the Bhangra and the Jhumar are not preceded by any ritual to a deity, in the Karthi, offerings are first made to a deity, at a harvest time. This is followed by women leading the processions and singing songs. The men follow, and then a circle is formed with men and women alternating and linking hands. The accompanying songs are sentimental, and tell of battles fought and victories won, of the union and quarrels of lovers. The tempo of the Karthi is a slower than the tempo of the other two dances. There is much clapping of hands both singly and in pairs. While no wind instruments are used in the Bhangra and the Jhumar, a folk Shenai and other wind instruments are in evidence in the Karthi.

Karthigai Deepam : Karthigai Deepam or the festival Lights is celebrated in Tamil Nadu from the days of Tolkappiam. Every house is illuminated with a large number of flat earthen lamps and there is great rejoicing, children using crackers and lighting lamps. Vaishnavites in some areas of Tamil Nadu use a type of light prepared by themselves to illuminate their homes. It is called Pori Vaanam and is made of a stick called Kavattaik-kambu with cloth, cloth rope, saw-dust, konkani resin and Maruthankai being the fruit of Maruda trees. This combination produces a sparkling light. Elephant shaped lights (made by the potters) are sent by parents to their daughters on this occasion.

This day comes in November-December on the Karthigai constellation day is specially important to Thiruvannamalai. Birth in Tiruvarur, death at Varanasi, worship at Chidambaram give salvation to human beings. At Thiruvannamalai, Shiva is supposed to have appeared as a pillar of fire, one of the five elements, on the

Karthigai day. The local hills is said to been established by God, so that the holyday may be observed in perpetuity, by the annual appearance of a blaze of light at the top, witnessed by the presiding deity, Arunachaleswarar.

Karthigai synchronises with the full moon and people greet the deity with shouts of Annamalaiyarku Arọhara. In a big copper urn, large quantities of high quality camphour ghee and wicks are placed and as the flame is lighted on the hill at 5.00 pm, ignorance fades to merge with God in glory.

Karunanidhan Bandyopadhyay : Karunanidhan Bandyopadhyay (1877-1955) a Bengali poet and patriot, was born on 19 November 1877 in Shantipur of the Nadia district. His father, Nrisingha Bandyopadhyay, was a school teacher. Karunanidhan passed the Entrance examination in 1896 from Shantipur Municipal School and FA from Calcutta Metropolitan Institution in 1899. He studied for the BA at General Assembly's School, Kolkata, but failed to pass the examination. He then began teaching. He taught at a number of schools: the Shantipur Municipal School, Gaibandha High School, Calcutta Sri Krishna Pathshala, Hughli Government Branch School and Uttarpara Government High School.

Karunanidhan was influenced by rabindranath tagore. The themes of his poems include romantic love, the pleasures of conjugal life, love for nature and spiritualism. In recognition of his literary contributions, he was awarded the Jagattarini Medal by the university of calcutta in 1951. He died on 5 February 1955.

Karur : Karur is a city and District in Tamil Nadu state of south India. One of the ancient cities in Tamil Nadu, it was ruled by the Cheras, Cholas, the Nayaks, and the British successively. There is proof that Karur may have been the centre for old jewellery-making and gem setting (with the gold imported mainly from Rome), as seen from various excavations. According to the Hindu mythology, Brahma began the work of creation here, which is referred to as the "place of the sacred cow."

Karur District, with headquarters at Karur, is the most centrally located district of Tamil Nadu. Its about 371 km south west of Chennai (Madras), the capital of Tamil Nadu. Karur has a very long history and has been sung by various sangam poets. In history, it has been the battleground of various Tamil Kings like Chera, Chola, Pandya and Pallavas because of strategic location. The district has a very rich and varied cultural heritage. The district is made fertile by the perenial flows of the Kaveri River on the northern side and also the Amaravati, Nanganjiyar and Noyyal rivers. Its economy is mainly agrarian. Presently, the district is famous world-wide for its handloom products.

Karuva Dance : Karuva dance is popular in East Godavari district. Eight men dressed as Gopika's and eight dressed as Krishna's stand in a circle alternately. In the middle of the circle stand two more dancers dressed as Radha and Krishna. They dance to different rhymes. The movements in this dance are the most important. The gatis generally employed are Chaturasara, Trisara and Misra. The classical dance forms of Andhra Pradesh are mainly Kuchipudi and Bhamakalapam. They belong to the ancient school of Bharatnatyam. The temple dances and the court dances too have their own styles in Andhra.

Karwa Chauth : 'Karwa Chauth' is celebrated by married women in some parts of India by fasting for the life of their husbands. It is celebrated on the fourth night after the full moon in the month of kartik in the Hindu calendar. Karwa means clay pot and chauth means fourth night after the full moon. It has a great social and cultural significance and mostly practised in northern part India. The wife starts her fast in the night just after the appearance of the moon in the sky and then sight of husband. Women wait eagerly for the appearance of moon and look at the moon in the sky and then look at her husband's face who then gives with his hands first bite of food and first drops of water of the day to her wife and then she takes her meal.

Karwar : Karwar is a small seaside town situated on the west coast of the Indian Sub-continent. It is the capital of Uttara Kannada district in Karnataka, one of the southern states of India. The town lies about 15 kilometres south of the Karnataka-Goa Border. Since it is sandwiched between the sea on one side and Western Ghats on the other, Karwar is rich in flora and fauna, The Monsoons last long and it rains heavily, the climate is similar to Goa, but is ignored in terms of tourism. Konkani is the local language of the inhabitats and the official language is Kannada.

Recently a bay near the town was chosen as the site for a new naval base for the Indian Navy called INS Kadamba, as part of Project Seabird. Karwar is also the site of a nuclear reactor Kaiga. Karwar has a number of beautiful beaches and it's idyllic beauty inspired the great Indian poet Rabindranath Tagore, to pen his first play.

Kasaragod : Kasaragod (also spelled Kasargod or Kasargode) is the northern-most district in the state of Kerala, south India. It is one among the 14 districts in the state of Kerala and was formed on 24 May 1984.

The place was famous in ancient times as Harkwillia, a port city in the west coast of India. Many Arab travellers, who came to Kerala between ninth and 14th centuries, visited Kasaragod as it was then an important trade centre. They called this area Harkwillia. Duarte

Barbosa, a Portuguese traveller who visited Kumbla near Kasaragod in 1514, had recorded that rice was exported to Mali Island whence coir was imported. Dr. Francis Buccanan, who was the family doctor of Lord Wellesley, visited Kasaragod in 1800. In his travelogue, he has included information on the political and communal set-up in places like Athipramba, Kavvai, Nileswaram, Bekal, Chandragiri and Manjeshwaram.

Kasauli : Kasauli is a small town in Himachal Pradesh, India. The cantonment was established in 1842 by the British colonial rulers as a hill station. Located 77 km from Shimla and 70 km from Chandigarh, it still retains the old world charms and is a throwback to the past. Kasauli largely remains untouched by civilization. During off-season (November-February) it is still possible to walk kilometers without running into other people (unlike its neighbouring cities).

The Pasteur Institute, founded in 1900 by Sir David Semple, is the oldest in India, producing anti-rabies vaccines and also treating sufferers. Legend has it that Kasauli came into being when Lord Hanuman, on his way to getting the Sanjeevani herb, stepped here for jumping on to the Sanjeevani hill. At Kasauli there is a Hanuman Mandir atop the 300 m high hillock, called Monkey Point, where Hanuman is supposed to have rested his feet. This temple lies within the confines of an air force base and is subject to security restrictions.

Kashmir Earthquake (2005) : The Kashmir earthquake (also known as the Northern Pakistan earthquake or South Asia earthquake) of 2005 was a major earthquake whose epicenter was the Pakistan-administered disputed region of Kashmir. The earthquake occurred on October 8, 2005. It registered a minimum magnitude of 7.6 on the moment magnitude scale making it a major earthquake similar in intensity to the 1935 Quetta earthquake, the 2001 Gujarat

Earthquake, and the 1906 San Francisco earthquake. As of 8 November, the Pakistani government's official death toll was 87,350. Some estimate that the death toll could reach over 100,000.

Most of the affected areas are in mountainous regions with access impeded by landslides that blocked the roads, leaving an estimated 3.3 million homeless in Pakistan. The UN reported that more than 4 million people were directly affected, prior to the commencement of winter snowfall in the Himalayan region. It is estimated that damages incurred are well over US$ 5 billion (Rs. 30 billion) Five crossing points were opened on the Line of Control (LoC) between India and Pakistan to facilitate the flow of humanitarian and medical aid to the affected region.

Kashmir Valley : Kashmir is a region where the northern part of South Asia and the southern part of Central Asia meet. The term Kashmir historically described the valley just to the south of the westernmost end of the Himalayan mountain range. Currently, 'Kashmir' refers to a much larger area which includes the regions of Kashmir, Jammu and Ladakh. The main "Valley of Kashmir" is a low-lying fertile region surrounded by magnificent mountains and fed by many rivers. It is renowned for its natural beauty and quaint lifestyle.

Srinagar, the ancient capital, lies alongside Dal Lake and is famous for its canals and houseboats. Srinagar (alt. 1,600 m. or 5,200 ft.) acted as a favoured summer capital for many foreign conquerors who found the heat of the Northern Indian plains in the summer season to be oppressive. Just outside the city are the beautiful Shalimar, Nishat, and Chashmashahi gardens created by Mughal emperors.

The region is currently divided between three countries: Pakistan controls the northwest portion (Northern Areas and Azad Kashmir), India controls the central and southern portion (Jammu and Kashmir and Ladakh), the Siachen Glacier is controlled by both India and Pakistan, and the People's Republic of China controls the northeastern portion (Aksai Chin and the Trans-Karakoram Tract). Though these regions are in practice administered by their respective claimants, India has never formally recognized the accession of the areas claimed by Pakistan and China. India claims that these areas, including the area ceded to China by Pakistan in 1963 (the Trans-Karakoram Tract) are a part of its territory, while Pakistan claims the region excluding Aksai Chin and Trans-Karakoram Tract. Both countries view the entire Kashmir region as disputed territory, and do not consider each other's claim to be valid. An option favoured by many Kashmiris is independence, but both India and Pakistan oppose this for various reasons. Kashmir is considered one of the world's most dangerous territorial disputes due to the nuclear weapons capabilitites of India and Pakistan. The two countries have fought two of their three full-scale wars over the Kashmir issue: the first Kashmir war in 1947 and the second Kashmir war in 1965. More recently, in 1999, there was a limited border conflict (also referred to by some as the third Kashmir war) in the Kargil area of India-controlled Kashmir.

Kashmiri : Kashmiri is a Dardic language spoken primarily in Kashmir, an Asian region now split between India, Pakistan and China. It has about 4,611,000 speakers. It belongs to the Indo-Aryan branch of the Indo-European family of languages. It is an SVO language. Kashmiri has remained a spoken language up to the present times, though some mansuscripts were written in the past in the Sharada script, and then in Perso-Arabic script. Currently, Kashmiri is written in Perso-Arabic script with some modifications. The earliest literary composition in Kashmiri that has survived is the poetry of Lalleshvari, a 14th century mystic poetess.

Kasturba Gandhi : Kastürba Gandhi (April 11, 1869 – 22 February 1944), affectionately called Ba, was the wife of Mohandas Gandhi, whom she married at the age of 13.

Born to wealthy businessman Gokuladas Makharji of Porbandar, Kasturba married Mohandas Gandhi in May 1882. At the time, she was illiterate, and so Gandhi taught her to read and write — a potentially radical move, given the position of women in India at that time. When Gandhi left to study in London in 1888, she remained in India to raise their newborn son Harilal. She had three more sons—Manilal (1892), Ramdas (1897), and Devdas (1900).

In 1906, Mohandas Gandhi decided to practice brahmacharya, and the couple became celibate. Although she stood by her husband, she did not always easily accept his ideas. Gandhi had to work hard to persuade her to see (and agree to) his side of the viewpoint. Kasturba was deeply religious. Like her husband, she renounced all caste distinctions and lived in ashrams.

Kasturba often joined her husband in political protests. She traveled to South Africa in 1897 to be with her husband. From 1904 to 1914, she was active in the Phoenix Settlement near Durban. During the 1913 protest against working conditions for Indians in South Africa, Kasturba was arrested and sentenced to three months in a hard labour prison. Later, in India, she sometimes took her husband's place when he was under arrest.

In 1915, when Gandhi returned to India to support indigo planters, Kasturba accompanied him. She taught hygiene, discipline, reading and writing to women and children. Kasturba suffered from chronic bronchitis. Stress from the Quit India Movement's arrests and ashram life caused her to fall ill. After contracting pneumonia, she died from a severe heart attack on February 22, 1944.

Kasu Brahmananda Reddy National Park : Kasu Brahmananda Reddy National Park located at Jubilee hill, Hyderabad covers an area of 156.30 hectares. The park established in 1994 to safeguard the biodiversity and richness of the area, is named after late Kasu Brahmananda Reddy, the former Chief Minister of Andhra Pradesh. The vegetation here is southern tropical deciduous and is the last remaining representative of the indigenous flora of Hyderabad region. The park has nearly 600 species of trees, shrubs, climbers, herbs, grasses, besides several pteridophytes, bryophytes and xerophytes.

Kasur : Kasur, located 55 km southeast of Lahore, is one of the oldest cities in Pakistan. Kasur is adjacent to the Indo-Pak Border. It is a major tourist attraction because of the famous guard changing ceremony (at the Ganda Singh Border which is a couple of minutes drive away). It is also famous for it very spicy fish which is prepeared by only a couple of the local restaurants. Apart from that, it is also the birthplace of Noor Jehan, the famous Pakistani singer and actress who gained popularity in the 1950's.

Politically, the Kasur District is an important district of the Punjab. Some big wigs of politics are contesting election from this district. The total population of the district is 2375875. Total register voters are 1173524. A large number of non-muslim voters also reside in the District. The city of Kasur is a town of considerable antiquity. It is situated upon the north bank of the old bed of the Beas upon the Ferozpur Road 53 Kilometer south-east of Lahore. It is built upon the high bank which marks the termination of the Majha, and looks down upon the lowlands of the Sutlej and Beas.

Kathak : Kathak which is a major classical dance forms of North India literally means a story-teller or Kathakar. In ancient India, there were Kathakars or bards who used to recite religious and mythological tales to the accompaniment music, mime and dance. These rahapsodists and minstrels were associated with temples and shrines. Their particular dance-forms, which had its origin in simple story-telling, later came to be known as Kathak. Kathak is danced by both men and women.

A Kathak dancer is not required strictly to adhere to fixed steps and stages in a fixed order. He or she can change the sequence of stages to suit his or her aptitude and style of dancing. There is a sort of contest during the performance in which the drummer plays and weaves a complex design which in turn is danced by the dancer, specially in the item which is technically known as jagaj dikhana. It is a kind of friendly challenge and competition between the two full of innovations and improvisations.

Kathakali : Kathakali, is an efflorescent art form of Kerala. It has been described as a true representation of the artistic traditions of India and one of the most magnificent theatres of the imagination.

Kathakali is a highly stylised dance-drama which serves to present story themes derived from the Ramayana, the Mahabharata and other Hindu epics, myths and legends. The dance aspect consists of pure dance (nritya) as well as mime (abhinaya).

Kathakali was traditionally the preserve of men, but now women also perform the dance. The themes have also changed with times and the latest innovation is Shakespeare's King Lear. What is most striking about Kathakali, is the emphasis given to aharya abhinaya, the use of costumes, ornaments and facial make-up. According to the qualities that they represent, the characters fall into five main types and the makeup illumines these types.

Kathakali makes strenuous demands on its exponents because it is the only dance form in which the entire body, both skeleton and muscles, down to even the smallest facial muscle are used to portray emotion. The actor in kathakali never speaks expect with his hands. The text of the drama is sung for him and is the baseline for his interpretation. It is in histrionics or interpretive dancing that the Kathakali artist excels, the spectator's experience enhanced by the thrilling drum beats

Kathgodam : Kathgodam is the place in the Nainital district of Uttaranchal state of India.It is the part of twin township of Haldwani -Kathgodam. Kathgodam is the last railway station for entering in the Himalayan state.From this place uphill journey to Himalayan Mountains starts.This place is near to Himalayan tourist destinations like Nainital, Bhimtal and Sattal,etc. Kathgodam is situated on the banks of Gaula river. Mountain roads to Almora, Nainital and Bhimtal.

Kathiawar : Kathiawar is a peninsula in western India. It is part of Gujarat state, bounded on the north by the great wetland of the Rann of Kutch, on the northwest by the Gulf of Kutch, on the west and south by the Arabian Sea, and on the southeast and east by the Gulf of Cambay. A person from Kathiawar is called a "Kathiawadi". The major cities of Kathiawar are Rajkot in the center of the peninsula, Jamnagar on the Gulf of Kutch, Bhavnagar on the Gulf of Cambay, Porbandar on the west coast, historic city of Junagadh on the South. Diu, an island town formerly part of Portuguese India and now part of the Indian union territory of Daman and Diu, lies off the south coast of Kathiawar. The city of Somnath and its famous temple are also located on the south coast.

Kathiawar-Gir Dry Deciduous Forests : The Kathiawar-Gir dry deciduous forests are a tropical dry broadleaf forest ecoregion of western India. The Kathiawar-Gir forests have a disjunct distribution. The main part of the ecoregion comprises the Aravalli Range and the eastern half of Rajasthan state, extending into eastern Gujarat and the Malwa region of Madhya Pradesh. A small enclave of the ecoregion covers the peak of Girnar on the Kathiawar peninsula of western Gujarat. The drier Northwestern thorn scrub forests ecoregion lies to the west, covering the remainder of the Kathiawar Peninsula and the strip of western Rajasthan between the Aravalli Range and the Thar Desert. To the northwest the Kathiawar-Gir dry deciduous forests transition to the Upper Gangetic Plains moist deciduous forests. To the southeast lies the Narmada Valley dry deciduous forests ecoregion, which covers the Vindhya Range and Narmada River valley. The ecoregion also borders on the North Western Ghats moist deciduous forests in southeastern Gujarat.

The ecoregion has tropical monsoon climate, with most of the rainfall during the southwest monsoon (June-September), and arid for the remaining months of the year. Rainfall averages 550 to 700 mm/year. Temperatures often exceed 40 °C. Higher elevations of the Aravallis stay cooler, and the windward slopes (generally southeast-facing) receive higher rainfall.

Kathua : A gateway to the northernmost Indian state of Jammu and Kashmir, Kathua lies just 88 kilometers south of the state's winter capital of Jammu. Kathua is the name of both a city and one of the fourteen administrative districts that comprise Jammu and Kashmir. The Kathua district is surrounded by Jammu to the northwest, the Doda and Udhampur districts to the north, the state of Himachal Pradesh to the east, Punjab to the south, and Pakistan to the west. Its terrain is diverse, consisting of rich agricultural areas along the Pakistani border, plains sweeping eastward to the foothills of the Himalaya, and a mountainous Pahari region in the east. The traditional language of Kathua is Dogri, although Punjabi is also widely spoken in the district. The Pahari language is prevalent in the mountainous area of the east. The principal media of education are English, Hindi, and Urdu, which is also an official language of Jammu and Kashmir.

Kaundinya Wildlife Sanctuary : Kaundinya Wildlife Sanctuary in Palamaneru is located 50 Km from Chittoor and 120 Km from Bangalore by road. It covers an area of 358-sq-kms. The area is covered by southern tropical thorn type of forests.

Kavadi : Lord Muruga or Subrahmanya, the son of Lord Shiva, has annihilated all the evil forces of demons. He is said to be reside in six embattled field-camps called Padaiveedus. Palani and Thirupparakundram in Madurai district are two such holy places. They are hillocks described in mythology as carried by a giant called Idumban slung on the two ends of a pole placed on his shoulder. This Idumban became one of the principal devotees of Lord Subrahmanya. He has a shrine half-way up the Palani hill and receives the first honours from all devotees proceeding to worship Subrahmanya. Actually the worship of Lord Subrahmanya without paying homage to Idumban is considered ineffective. The carrying of Kavadi by pilgrims is symbolic of Idumban carrying the hillocks, the abodes of the Lord slung on a pole.

Kavadiyattam : It is a ritual dance offering in Subramanya temples. The group of devotees wearing bright yellow or saffron costumes with ash smeared all over the body, dance in a frenzy carrying *kavadis* (colourful bow shaped wooden structures) on their shoulders.

Kavaratti : Kavaratti is an island in the Union Territory of Lakshadweep off the coast of the state of Kerala. The territorial capital Kavaratti is located here. It is one of the smallest union territory capitals in India. 52 mosques located throughout the island, inculding the Usra Mosque.

Kaveri River : The Kaveri River is one of the great rivers of India and is considered sacred by the Hindus. The headwaters are in the Western Ghats range of Karnataka state, and flows through Karnataka and Tamil Nadu and empties into the Bay of Bengal. The river has supported irrigated agriculture for centuries, and the Kaveri has been the lifeblood of the ancient kingdoms and modern cities of South India. The source of the river is Talakaveri located in the Western Ghats about 5000 feet above sea level.

Talakaveri is a famous pilgrimage and tourist spot set amidst Bramahagiri Hills near Madikeri in Kodagu district of Karnataka. Thousands of piligrims flock to the temple at the source of the river especially on the specified day known as Tula sankramana when the river water has been witnessed to gush out like a fountain at a predetermined time. It flows generally south and east for around 765 km, emptying into the Bay of Bengal through two principal mouths. Its basin is estimated to be 27,700 square miles, and it has many tributaries including Shimsa, Hemavati, Arkavathi, Kapila, Honnuhole, Lakshmana Tirtha, Kabini, Bhavani, Lokapavani, Noyyal and Amaravati.

Kavirajamarga : Kavirajamarga (850AD) is the first extant literary work in the Kannada language. It is ascribed to early 9th century Rashtrakuta king Nripatunga Amoghavarsha and famous Kannada poet Sri Vijaya Ponna of those times.

Kawal Wildlife Sanctuary : This Sanctuary was established in 1965. The sanctuary spreads over 893sq.km with dry deciduous teak forest, bamboo and miscellaneous species of flora. Cheetal, Sambar, Nilgai, Muntjac (barking deer), Indian Bison (Gaur), are found in this sanctuary.

Kayang : Kayang is a folk dance of the Kinnaur district where men and women dance in semi-circles around the musicians. It is based on a legend from the epic Mahabharata.

Kaykobad : Kaykobad is the pen name of the poet Kazem Ali Quereshi. Kaikobad (1857-1951) was an epic Bengali poet and writer. He was born in the village of Agla under nawabganj thana in the district of Dhaka in what is now Bangladesh, in 1857. He was the son of Shahamatullah Al Qureshi, a lawyer at the Dhaka District Judge Court.

Kaikobad studied at Pogose School and St Gregory's School in Dhaka. He then went to Dhaka Madrasah where he studied up to the Entrance Examination. However, he did not sit for the examinations, returning instead to his native village to take up the job of postmaster, where he worked until his retirement. In 1932, he presided over the main session of the Bangiya Muslim Sahitya Sammelan in Kolkata.

Kaikobad revealed his poetic genius early. His Birahabilap was published in 1870, when he was about thirteen. Kaikobad was influenced by the epics written by hemchandra banerjee and nabinchandra sen and, in 1904, published Mahashmashan (The Great Crematorium), based on the Third Panipat War. The epic, which shows the destructive nature of war in both victory and defeat, is considered his masterpiece.

Kazi Nazrul Islam : Kazi Nazrul Islam (b. May 1899, d. August 29, 1976) was a Bengali poet. He is the national poet of Bangladesh, and is revered in West Bengal, India as well. He is also known as Bidrohi Kobi, the rebel poet.

Nazrul's place in the Bengali literary canon was secured when he published Bidrohi (Rebel) in 1922. Set in a heroic meter, this long poem invokes images from Hindu, Muslim and Greek mythology.

Nazrul's literature can hardly be separated from his politics. After Nazrul achieved fame as a poet, he started editing a weekly political and literary magazine called Dhumketu (The comet). It launched with a now famous adulation from Rabindranath Ay chole ay re dhumketu, andhare badh agnisetu (O comet, come, create the firebridge in the darkness). Dhumeketu openly opposed British rule in India, and soon enough, it was shut down and its workers, Nazrul foremost, were imprisoned. Over the years, Nazrul was imprisoned several times.

Nazrul was unequivocal in his demand for India's freedom from British colonial rule. Nazrul was among the first of British India's intellectuals to demand the complete independence of India, as opposed to Swaraj as promoted by Gandhi at that time or dominion status. Nazrul vehemently opposed swaraj, literally meaning "self rule", and supported armed rebellion against the British, in contrast with the non-violent methods adopted by Gandhi. At one point, Nazrul joined Langol (The plough), a major socialist newspaper. Nazrul, a Muslim, was also strongly against the Pakistan movement which demanded a separate homeland for Indian muslims.

Kazi Shahadat Hossain : Kazi Shahadat Hossain (born August 7, 1986 in Dhaka) is a Bangladeshi cricketer. Having been discovered in Narayanganj, he was called up for the Bangladesh A team. He has a strong, fast run-up and an angular delivery. His debut Test against England was something of a sober experience, as he had a rate of runs per over conceded of 8.33, however, if he continues to develop as he has been, he could find himself thrust in the centre of the action in the future.

Kaziranga National Park : Kaziranga National Park is situated on the south bank of the Brahmaputra river in Assam, India. It is famous as a refuge for the Indian or one-horned rhinoceros (Rhinoceros unicornis). Stretching over an area of 430 km^2, Kaziranga is one of the last refuges of the Indian rhino. The national park is a vast stretch of coarse, tall elephant grass, marshland and dense tropical moist broadleaf forests. The Park celebrates its centenary in 2005.

Kaziranga reserve was created to preserve Indian rhinocerous numbers, it was established as a proposed forest reserve on June 1, 1905, and Kaziranga was declared a reserve forest in 1908 by the British and was officially closed for shooting in 1926. In 1938 the Park was opened to visitors. In 1950 the area was declared a wildlife sanctuary, in 1954, the rhino was given legal protection through the Assam (Rhinoceros) Bill that laid down heavy penalties for killing it. In 1974 Kaziranga was designated a national park, the first national park in Assam. Bounded by the misty blue hills of Barail and Karbi Anglong to the south, the national park was declared a UNESCO World Heritage Site in 1985. Today it holds the world's largest population of Indian rhinos, numbering more than one thousand.

Kaziranga is home also to elephants, sloth bears, tigers, leopards, jungle cats, hog badgers, capped langurs, hoolock gibbons, wild boars, jackals, porcupines, pythons, water buffaloes, Indian bison, swamp deer, sambar deers and hog deer. Besides these, the park has a respectable avian population, which increases considerably in the winter, when migrating birds visit the park.

K Balachander : K. Balachander is a director, writer, and producer from Tamil Nadu. He was born in 1930 in Nannilam, Thanjavur, India. Throughout his career, he has encouraged growth in the Tamil film industry in South India, and introduced many successful actors, such as Kamal Hassan and Rajni Kanth. He is a recipient of the Padma Shri award.

Writer, director and producer of more than 90 films in Tamil, Telugu, Kannada and Hindi. K. Balachander is an artist with a message. Starting as an amateur dramatist and rising to become the legendary producer-director today, K. Balachander has crossed several milestones. He got his break in films as a scriptwriter for Deivathai (1964), he made his directorial debut in 1965 for the film Neerkumizhi, which was based on one of his plays; after that, he never looked back.

A rare and successful exception to the makers of potboilers, he specialises in providing thought-provoking films in commercial mainstream cinema. So K. Balachander is an inspiration to most upcoming filmmakers today. by Rajinikanth, Kamal Haasan and Prakash Raj. Abaddam is released with a tagline of 'Vayasuki abaddam andam'.

Kebab : Kebab (kebap in Turkish, kabab in Iran, India and Pakistan, also spelled kebob, kabob) means "grilled (or broiled) meat" in Persian and Turkish. Kebab is usually made of lamb and beef, although chicken and fish can be used for some styles. Pork is never used by Muslims because of religious belief but is sometimes used by non-Muslim sellers. There are many varieties of kebab and the term means different things in different countries. The generic term kebab usually refers to döner kebab in Europe and to shish kebab in the United States, though its meaning can vary. Perhaps the earliest recipe is in the tenth-century Kitab al-Tabeekh by Ibn Sayyar al-Warraq of Baghdad. His recipe for Kebab Khalis uses thin slices of lean meat, salted and grilled in an ungreased frying pan.

Kech : Kech or Turbat district is in the south west of Balochistan province of Pakistan. Kech was notified as a district, with its name as Turbat, on July 1, 1977, when Makran district was given the status of a division and was divided into three districts. Previously it was one of the 3 tehsils of Makran district. In 1995, the name of the district was changed from Turbat to Kech, the old name for the area, when even Awaran was part of it. For administrative purposes, Kech district is divided into 4 sub-divisions, i.e., Turbat, Buleda, Dasht, and Tump.

Kechadmaru : Kechadmaru is celebrated by the tribals called Mathuras who inhabit Utmur Taluq in Adilbad district which is in Andhra Pradesh. This festival is meant, for unmarried girls. This is celebrated on the new moon day in the month of Shravana. All the unmarried girls of the village gather at the Naik's house on that day and sings songs in the name of the guru to the accompaniment of drums and eat Gogri (mixture of wheat or Bengal Gram and Jaggery).

All the girls dance in the morning and evening for nine days. On the tenth day they get clay, wheat or Bengal Gram and wet them with water. The clay is placed on the Patasa leaves. This ritual is known as Dhovi. This wheat or Bengal gram is sown in this clay. The` girls continue singing till the next full moon day in Rakhi Purnima. They tie the rakhi to the Mathura men present there. The men folk offer presents to the girls. The group singing continues for three days.

On the third day, the girls observe a fast and each one of the unmarried girls prepares feminine idol in her house and worship it. After the worship, the fast is broken. This is called Teez. In the morning of the following day, the brothers of the girls, kick away the clay idols of their respective sisters. Then the girls take the idols to front-yard of the Naik's house and keep them there. All the Mathura men folk, young and old, gather at the Naik's house and dance around these idols. The Naik offers them tea and paan. The girls collect the idols, remove the seedlings from the clay and later the clay is immersed in the nearby stream. The girls take' Purampuri' with them and eat it here. The seedlings are distributed among the male members after they return to their houses. The men offer some presents and with that the festival concludes.

Kedareshvara Temple : It is the most important Shiva temple of the Uttar Pradesh. The stone linga here is said to have emerged spontaneously. The myth narrate that a pure hearted devotee of Shiva prayed for a chance to visit the famous Kedareshvara Shiva temple in the Himalayas. Shiva, who is the god of destruction is always kind to his bhaktas (devotees). Shiva was touched by his bhakta's piety and instead of bringing him to the mountain, Shiva brought his image to the bhakta. This image (linga) emerged out of a plate of rice and lentils. It can be still seen by the believers on the rough surface of the natural stone linga.

Kedarnath : Kedaranath, situated in the Garhwal Himalayas at a height of 10,500 ft. above sea level, is in the Uttar Kashi district of the northern state of Uttaranchal. Kedarnath with one of the 12 jyothir lingas of Shiva, is amongst the premier pilgrimages in India.

The uniqueness and greatness of this temple is mentioned in the Vedas, Ithihaas and the Epics. It is at the base of Mandakini river, in a valley two and half km, surrounded by high snow covered mountains. Besides its religious significance, it is also visited by those who love to conquer the rough terrain of Garhwal.

According to legend, the Pandavas sought Lord Shiva's blessings for redemption from the sin of killing of Kauravas. But the Lord eluded them by taking the form of a bull in Kedarnath and when followed further by the Pandavas, he went down into the earth, leaving behind the hump there. This conical protrusion about five feet by four feet or 'jyothirlingam' is worshipped as the idol in the Kedarnath temple. Other parts emerged at four other places: arms at Tungnath, face at Rudranath, belly at Madmaheswar and the locks of hair with head at Kalpeshwar. All the five shrines are worshiped as 'Panch Kedar'.

The original temple (now extinct) with 12 Jyothirlingas, was built by the Pandavas at the present site and Adi Sankaracharaya restored the present Kedarnath temple. The Samadhi of Adi Sankaracharya lies behind this temple. The statue of Nandi, the divine bull of Shiva, stands at the entrance of the temple. Inside the temple, there are marvellous sculptures of Kedaragouri, Krishna, Pandavas, Draupadi, Karthikeyan etc. The shrine is covered by snow for 6 months in a year (closed from Oct-Nov up to Apr-May). The statue is carried to Ukhimath, and is reinstated in Kedarnath in the month of May.

The Bhairavnath temple, situated to the south of the main temple of Kedarnath, is dedicated to Lord Bhairav, the deity who guards the main temple in winter when it is closed.

Keibul Lamjao National Park : It covers an area of 25 sq km. It is the only floating sanctuary existing in Manipur. A small population of thamin (Sangai), the brow-antlered deer (one of the most endangered species of deer in the world), hog deer, panther, fishing cat, wild boar and water birds are the most interesting wild animals and birds seen here. Tourism is not only of great economic significance but also a means for achieving national integration, international understanding and peaceful co-existence among the people.

Nestled in valley among hills far above the sea level, Manipur is the land of Polo's birth. The martial tradition of Manipur is reflected in their indigenous games even today. Surcharged with nature's pristine glory, Manipur lies on a melting pot of culture as one of the world's most beautiful spots. Rajshree Bhagyachandra created the Ras

Lila, the classical dance of Manipur in his enchanting dream by the grace of Lord Krishna. Manipur's mythological concept of creation is revealed in her famous folk dances.

Kejimikujik Lake : Kejimikujik lake (sometimes Kejimkujik or even Kedgeemakoogee) is the namesake lake and the largest lake in Kejimkujik National Park. The work 'Kejimkujik' is agreed by all to be a word derived from the Mi'kmaq language, but depending on the source will be said to mean "attempting to escape" or "swollen waters". The park's official stance is that Kejimkujik is a Mi'kmaq word meaning "tired muscles". The lake is featured in The Tent Dwellers by Albert Bigelow Paine, a book chronicling his fishing trip through the central Nova Scotia wilds in the early 1900s.

Kejimkujik National Park : Kejimkujik National Park consists of two parts: the main section of the park, located in the uplands of south-central Nova Scotia, and the seaside adjunct, located nearby on the Atlantic coast. The park covers an area of 381 km^2. The main section of the park is a forested upland plain that contains many lakes and rivers. These interior waterways were important canoe routes between the Bay of Fundy and the Atlantic for the ancestors of the Mi'kmaq. The park also contains the petroglyphs that these people left behind. The seaside adjunct includes white sandy beaches and coastal wetland areas. The park includes habitat for the endangered Piping Plover and other coastal birds. It is located off Nova Scotia Highway 103 near the towns of Port Mouton, Nova Scotia and Port Joli, Nova Scotia.

The park is named after Kejimkujik Lake, the largest lake inside the park. The lake's Mi'kmaq name has been translated as "attempting to escape" or "swollen waters", possibly related to fishing weirs placed on the lake. The park's official stance is that Kejimkujik is a Mi'kmaq word meaning "tired muscles".

Kendrapara District : Kendrapara District is an administrative district of Orissa state in eastern India. The town of Kendrapara is the district headquarters. Kendrapara District is situated in the eastern portion of the state, and is bounded on the north by Bhadrak District, on the east by the Bay of Bengal, on the south by Jagatsinghpur District, on the west by Cuttack District, and on the northwest by Jajpur District. Kendrapara District lies in the river delta formed by the Brahmani and Baitarani rivers. The Bhitarkanika Mangroves, Bhitarkanika National Park, and Gahirmatha Beach lie in the district.

Keokradong : Keokradong is a mountain peak located in South-Eastern Bangladesh. Keokradong (or Keokradang) (883 metres) is widely reported to be the highest point in Bangladesh at 1230 metres. However, recent SRTM and other data show that it is not the highest point, and that its height is around 347 metres less than previously reported.

Keoladeo National Park : The Keoladeo National Park in Rajasthan, India is a famous avifauna sanctuary that sees thousands of rare and highly endangered birds such as the Siberian Cranes nest here during the winter season. Over 230 species of birds are known to have made the National Park their home. It is also a major tourist centre with scores of ornithologists arriving here in the hibernal season. It was declared a protected sanctuary in 1971. It is also a declared World Heritage Site.

The sanctuary was created 250 years ago and is named after a Keoladeo (Shiva) temple within its boundaries. Initially, it was a natural depression; and was flooded after the Ajan Bund was constructed by Maharaja Suraj Mal, the then ruler of the princely state of Bharatpur, between 1726 to 1763. The bund was created at the confluence of two rivers, the Gambhir and Banganga. The park was a happy hunting ground for the maharajas of Bharatpur, a tradition dating back to 1850, and duck shoots were organised yearly inhonor of the British viceroys. In one shoot alone in 1938, over 4,200 birds such as mallards and teals were killed by Lord Linlithgow, the then Governor-General of India. After India's independence, the rulers of the princely states were allowed shooting rights until 1972. In 1982, grazing was banned in the park, leading to violent clashed between the local Meena and Gujjar communities and the government.

The sanctuary hosts a small wintering population of the rare Siberian Cranes. Other species include the ruddy shelducks, gulls, northern shovelers, northern pintails, coots, garganey, tufted ducks and common pochard. In late 2004 however, the Rajasthan government led by Vasundhara Raje succumbed to pressure from farmers to prevent water from being diverted to the sanctuary. The water supply to the park dropped from 540,000,000 to 18,000,000 cubic feet (15,000,000 to 510,000 m^3). The result was an ecological disaster with the marshlands turning dry and inhospitable. Most of the birds flew off to alternate avenues as far as Garhmukteshwar, Uttar Pradesh on the river Ganga for breeding. This resulted many of the birds being hunted for their meat. The act was criticised by leading environmentalists, leading to a Public Interest Litigation being filed in court.

Kerala : Kerala is a state on the southwestern tropical Malabar Coast of India. Kerala borders Tamil Nadu and Karnataka to the east and northeast; to the west and south lie the Indian Ocean islands of Lakshadweep and the Maldives, respectively. Kerala also envelops Mahé, a coastal exclave of the Union Territory of Pondicherry. With a population of around 3.18 crore and 819 persons per km^2, Kerala is among India's most densely populated regions. With a 73-year life expectancy and a 91% literacy rate, Kerala is also one of India's healthiest and best-educated states.

Prehistoric Kerala's rainforests and wetlands, then thick with malaria-bearing mosquitoes and man-eating tigers, were largely avoided by Neolithic humans; indeed, no evidence of habitation prior to around 1,000 BCE exists. Only then did tribes of megalith-building proto-Tamil speakers from northwestern India settle in Kerala. Subsequent contact with the Mauryan Empire spurred development of new Keralite polities — including the Cheran kingdom and feudal Namboothiri Brahminical city-states — and an indigenous Keralite culture, including kalarippayattu, kathakali, and Onam. More than a millennium of overseas contact and trade culminated in four centuries of struggle between and among multiple colonial powers and native Keralite states. This period ended when Kerala was granted statehood on November 1, 1956. Radical social reforms begun in 1911 by the kingdoms of Kochi and Travancore — and spurred by such leaders as Narayana Guru — were continued by post-Independence Communist and leftist governments, making Kerala among the Third World's longest-lived, healthiest, and most literate regions. Kerala now has a stable democratic socialist political system and unusually equitable gender relations.

Kerala Backwaters : The Kerala Backwaters are a chain of brackish lagoons and lakes lying parallel to the Arabian Sea coast (known as the Malabar Coast) of Kerala state in southern India. The network includes five large lakes (including Ashtamudi Kayal and Vembanad Kayal) linked by 1500 km of canals, both manmade and natural, fed by 38 rivers, and extending virtually the entire length of Kerala state. The backwaters were formed by the action of waves and shore currents creating low barrier islands across the mouths of the many rivers flowing down from the Western Ghats range.

Kerala Congress : The Kerala Congress is a political party in Kerala, India. It is quite fragmented and some of the fragments are even represented in the Lok Sabha.

Kerala Kalamandalam : Kerala Kalamandalam is a major center for learning Indian Performing Arts especially those that developed in the South Indian state of Kerala. It is situated in the village of Cheruthuruthy in Trissur district near the banks of Bharathapuzha.

The Kalamandalam was founded in 1930 by late poet Vallathol Narayana Menon and Manakkulam Mukunda Raja. Kalamadalam imparts training in Kathakali, Mohiniyattam, Koodiyattam, Thulall and Panchavadyam. Kalamadalam follows the Gurukula system of education, the ancient Indian education system.

Keshab Chandra Sen : Keshab Chandra Sen (1838 to 1884) was a Bengali scholar, orator and religious leader. He was trying to envision and establish a syncretic/ synthetic religion with amalgamation of the best principles in Christianity and Hinduism. However, his Brahmo Samaj was against idol or image worship. Their faith was in saguna nirakara aspect of God—God without form but with benevolent attributes—if one may say so. Quite a few bright and young college students came under the influence of this seemingly new, progressive, and liberal reformist religious movement.

He was the third chief of Brahmo Samaj and his Service Book for Samaj meetings, the Slokasangraha, was a collection of texts from Hindu, Buddhist, Jewish, Christian, Islamic and Chinese scriptures. It was a movement brought to birth by the conflict of East with West in the realm of intellect, and still is an attempt of educated Hindus to find relief from the impossibilities of the faith of their childhood.

Pandit Shiva Nath Sastri gives an insider's view of History of the Brahma Samaj. Incidentally, despite the differences in ideals, he and Sri Ramakrishna became friends. Keshab and, following him, other Brahmos publicized Ramakrishna before the larger public of Bengal through their speeches and writings. The discovery of Ramakrishna was one of the greatest gifts of the Brahmos to the Bengali intelligentsia of the nineteenth century.

Keshava Baliram Hedgewar : Dr. Keshava Baliram Hedgewar (April 1, 1889 - June 21, 1940) was an Indian nationalist. He was the founder of Rashtriya Swayamsevak Sangh(RSS). Hedgewar founded the RSS at Nagpur in 1925. RSS began as an organisation promoting the Hindu Rashtra. This is a widespread misconception about RSS. The problem is that concept of indian or hindu "rashtravad" is not same as the western concept of nationalism. The hindu concept of "rashtravad" is not a political concept but essentially a spiritual concept. And so the hindu concept of nationalism is a cultural and spiritual concept which is not given by Dr. Hedgewar.

This concept is emphasized many a times by various spiritual giants and reformers like Vivekanand, Aurbindo, B. G. Tilak, Swami Ramateertha etc. Hedgewar just tried to reiterate the same indian or hindu concepts of nationalism in front of the society.

KeshGarh Sahib : KeshGarh Sahib (the birth place of the Khalsa) is located in Anandpur, it was created by Guru Gobind Singh in 1699. KeshGarh Sahib is where the first Khalsa where initiated by Guru Gobind Singh Ji on Baisakhi Day March 30, 1699 (this date is considered sacred). It is one of the five most sacred places in Sikhism.

Kettuvallam : Kettuvallam is a kind of house boat in Kerala, India. Kettuvallam literally means "bundle" or "package" boat (Kettu means tied with ropes, and vallam means boat—Malayalam language). A house boat is about 60 to 70 feet in length and has a width of around 15 feet in the middle. The boat is made of wooden planks joined and stiched together using coconut fiber ropes. Usually the wood used will be 'Anjili', The roof covering is made of bamboo poles and palm leaves. Outside of the boat is painted using cashew nut oil, which acts as a protective coating.

Nowdays, they are mainly used as houseboats for Kerala's ecotourism industry. Connected by artificial canals, the backwaters form an economical means of transit, and a large local trade is carried on by inland navigation. Fishing and fishcuring is an important industry. Kettuvallam in the backwaters are one of the best tourist attractions in Kerala.

Khagrachari : Khagrachari is a district in south-eastern Bangladesh. It is a part of the Chittagong Division and the Chittagong Hill Tracts.

Khairagarh : Khairagarh is a town in central India, situated in Rajnandgaon District of Chhattisgarh state. Khairagarh is a generally tranquil place, which complements the musical and academic fervor of the university. Khairagarh was a feudatory state of the former Central Provinces of British India. The chief, who is descended From the old Nagvaansh royal family, received the title of Raja, The King, as an hereditary distinction in 1898. The state included a fertile plain, yielding rice and cotton. Its prosperity was promoted by the Bengal-Nagpur railway, which has a station at Dongargarh, the largest town, connected by road with Khairagarh town, the residence of the Raja.

Khairpur : The Khairpur district is a district in the Sindh province of Pakistan. Khairpur is the principal city of the district. Khairpur District is located in the Northern

Sindh and bounded on the north by Shikarpur and Sukkur on the east by India. on the south by Sanghar and Nawabshah and on the west by Larkana and drives its name from the town the total are of the district is 15910 square kilomeres. At the time of independence.Khairpur was one of the Soveriegn states that acceded the subjects of defence, communications and foreign affairs to Pakistan between 1947 to 1949. Khairpur was Ruled by Mirs (ameers) of the Talpur dynasty from 1783 to 1955 until it merged with the state of Pakistan which abolished the Monarchy.

Khaja : Khaja is a sweet delicacy of Bihar state, India. Refined wheat flour, sugar and edible oils are the chief ingredients of khaja. It is believed that, even 2000 years before, Khajas were prepared in the fertile land on the southern side of the Gangetic Plains of Bihar. These areas which are home to khaja, once comprised the central part of Maurya and Gupta empires. Presently, Khajas are prepared and sold in the city of Patna, Gaya and several other places across the state of Bihar, yet Khajas of Silao and Rajgir areas have a distinct superiority over khajas of all other places. Silao and Rajgir are the places where one can get puffy khaja, which melts in the mouth.

From Bihar Khajas have travelled to some other parts of India, including Andhra Pradesh. Khaja of Kakinada, a coastal town of Andhra Pradesh, is famous. First,a paste is made out of wheat flour,mawa and oil.Then it is deep fried until crisp.Then a sugar syrup is made which is known as "Pak".The crisp croissants are then soaked in the sugar syrup until they absorb the sugar syrup.The speciality of Kakinada Khaja is that it is dry from outside and full of sugar syrup from inside and is juicy. It melts as soon as one puts it in one's mouth.

Khajuraho : Khajuraho is a city in the Indian state of Madhya Pradesh, located in Chhatarpur District, about 385 miles (620 kilometres) southeast of Delhi, the capital city of India. One of the most popular tourist destinations in India, Khajuraho has the largest group of medieval Hindu temples, famous for their erotic sculpture. The name Khajuraho is derived from the Hindi word khajur meaning date palm.

The city was once the religious capital of the Chandela Rajputs, a Hindu dynasty that ruled this part of India from the 10th to the 12th centuries. The Khajuraho temples were built over a span of a hundred years, from 950 to 1050. The whole area was enclosed by a wall with eight gates, each flanked by two golden palm trees. There were originally over 80 Hindu temples, of which only 22 now stand in a reasonable state of preservation, scattered over an area of about 8 square miles (21 km^2).

The temples of Khajuraho are an example of religion laced with erotica. They are fine examples of Indian architectural styles that have gained popularity due to their salacious depiction of the traditional way of life during medieval times. They were rediscovered only during the 20th century and the jungles had taken a toll on some of the monuments. The Khajuraho group of monuments has been listed as a UNESCO World Heritage Site.

Khaksar Tehrik : The Khaksar Tehrik, based in Lahore, Pakistan, was established by Allama Mashriqi in 1930, keeping in mind the plight and poor condition of the masses in India. The Tehrik was created to free India from foreign rule, to uplift the masses, and to revive the lost glory of the Muslims, who had previously ruled India for almost one thousand years. Although Mashriqi firmly believed that the right to rule India belonged to the Muslims, at the same time, he wanted to create an environment of fairness, justice, and equal rights for non-Muslims as well. For this reason, non-Muslims were allowed to join the Tehrik and the Tehrik was kept free of prejudice against any people, regardless of caste, color, creed, or religion.

Khal Lam : *Khal Lam* is another popular dance of Mizos in which a group of boys wearing specially made shawls dance to the beat of drums and gongs. The dancers wear one type of striped loin cloth (puan) and a uniform striped shawl (puandum). While one beats a gong, the dancers in a row more gradually forward, with small forward-backward steps, keeping with the time. On occasions of Chapchar Kut festival the boys and girls would dance chai the whole night. The boys would sit with their backs to the wall. Each boy would have a girl sitting in front of him, in between his knees, with her back towards him. Individual dancers would perform in the clearing in the middle, all the others joining in the music.

The young folk would perform another type of dance in the open courtyard. They would make a circle with a girl in between two boys with their arms over the shoulders of the girls. In the midst of the circle, one would beat a drum or gong and all in the circle would move forward and backward and would also progress slowly along the circle. The person in the middle would chant a song and the refrain would be taken up by all.

Khaled Mosharraf : Khaled Mosharraf Bir Uttom, was a Bangladeshi army officer and war hero. He was one of the sector commanders of Mukti Bahini during the Bangladesh Liberation War of 1971.

He also led the ill-fated 3 day coup in November 3, 1975, which put him in power for only 3 days. He was executed by yet another coup on November 7, 1975.

Khaleda Zia : Khaleda Zia (born August 15, 1945) is the Prime Minister of Bangladesh. She was Prime Minister from 1991 to 1996, the first woman to do so, and then again from 2001 to the present. She is the widow of assassinated president Ziaur Rahman, and leads his old party, the Bangladesh Nationalist Party. Khaleda Zia was born to Iskandar Majumder and Taiyaba Majumder at Dinajpur District in 1945 in what is now north-western Bangladesh. She studied in Dinajpur Government Girls High School and later in Surendranath College. In 1960, she married Ziaur Rahman. Her husband later became the President of the Republic and formed the Bangladesh Nationalist Party (BNP).

Until the assassination of Khaleda Zia's husband, President Ziaur Rahman in an abortive military coup in Chittagong on 30 May 1981, Khaleda Zia had taken little interest in either politics or public life. Even when her husband was propelled to power after the political changes in 1975, she remained a shy and withdrawn housewife spending most of her time raising her two sons. After the 1981 assassination of President Ziaur Rahman, Vice-President Justice Abdus Sattar took over as the acting President and also as Chairman of the BNP. Army Chief of Staff General Hossain Mohammad Ershad overthrew Justice Sattar in 1982. In March 1983, Justice Sattar appointed Khaleda Zia vice-chairman of BNP. On February 1984, she became the chairperson as Justice Sattar retired from politics. On 10 August 1984 the party elected her the chairperson.

Meanwhile, BNP formed a seven-party alliance in September 1983 to step up movement against the autocratic regime of General Hossain Mohammad Ershad. Khaleda was detained seven times during almost nine years of autocratic rule under President Ershad before Ershad's resignation on 6 December 1990. The BNP restored the parliamentary system through the 12th amendment to the Constitution in 1991. A neutral caretaker government oversaw elections on 27 February 1991. Khaleda Zia was elected as Bangladesh's first woman Prime Minister in elections that were broadly considered to be free, fair and truly democratic.

When in power, the government of Khaleda made some headway in the education sector, introducing compulsory free primary education, free education for girls up till the 10th grade, stipend for girl students and food for education programme. It also increased the age-limit for entry into government services from 27 years to 30 years and made highest budgetary allocation in the education sector. She became Prime Minister for the second consecutive term after the BNP had a landslide victory in 15 February 1996 general election to the sixth Jatiya Sangsad. The election was, however, boycotted by all other major parties. The short-lived parliament introduced the Caretaker Government through 13th amendment to the Constitution, and then was dissolved to pave the way for the parliamentary elections. In the 12 June 1996 polls, BNP lost to Sheikh Hasina's Awami League but emerged as the largest opposition party in the country's parliamentary history with 116 seats.

Aiming to return to power, the BNP formed a four-party opposition alliance on 6 January 1999 with the Jatiya Party, the Jamaat-e-Islami and the Islami Oikya Jot and launched several agitation programmes against the ruling Awami League. The alliance then participated in the 1 October 2001 general elections and won the election with a two-third majority and Khaleda Zia was once again sworn in as the Prime Minister of Bangladesh.

Khalid Maqbool : Lieutenant Gen. (Retired) Khalid Maqbool, born in 1948 is the current Governor of Punjab, the most populous province of Pakistan. He was commissioned in the Pakistan Army in May, 1966. He has vast experience of instructional assignments including Chief Instructor at premier institutions of Pakistan i.e. National

Defense College and Command and Staff College, Quetta, where he dealt with matters related to strategy and defense policy at the national level.

In addition, he served as the Defence and Military Attache to the U.S. for two and half years. He was Chairman, National Accountability Bureau for over one year before he was sworn in as Governor of the Punjab Province on October 29, 2001. For meritorious services, he is recipient of the high award of Hilal-e-Imtiaz (Military) and Hilal-e-Imtiaz.

Khalilabad : Khalilabad is a town in Uttar Pradesh state of northern India. It is the district headquarters for Sant Kabir Nagar District. The town is small but has a history which can be traced back to Mughal emperors. Mughal Emperor Aurangzeb deputed his captain 'Khalilurehman' to suppress any revolts by hindu rajputs from near by villeges, notable among these were two brothers named Jai Singh and Vijay Singh. Vijay Singh was killed in a battle by Aurangjeb's forces and Jai Singh was forced to convert to Islam. Jai Singh was later known as Jasim Khan. His kin and relatives still live in a nearby villege called 'Pach Pokhri'.

Khalilabad was a major trade centre for spices and handloom products. Traders from across India used to visit the weekly markets for trading spices and handloom products. Now the spices trade is totally gone, but the handloom market still thrives. Khalilabad is named after the Mughal ruler of the place, Qazi Khalilurehman. There is a small fortress in the town, a part of which is being used as Police Headquarters. Facing this fort is a small temple of Goddess of Time (Samay Mai). This goddess is in form of an elephant statue. It is said that Qazi Khalilurehman was facing problems in construction of the fortress, walls used to collapse all of sudden, and someone suggested to him that if you can bring the Goddess of

Time and get a temple made in front of your fortress, your problems will vanish. Qazi did so and succeeded in making of the fortress.

Khalistan : Khalistan (lit. "pure-land") is the name given to the proposed nation-state encompassing the present Indian state of Punjab and all Punjabi-speaking areas contiguous to its borders being proposed by separatist organisations. A movement for Khalistan precipitated when the Indian Army attacked the Harmandir Sahib complex, along with 37 other gurduaras simultaneously, in June 1984. The attack had been planned several months beforehand and coincided with an important anniversary in the Sikh calendar when thousands of pilgrims were present. The attack caused widespread anger amongst the Sikh community, even amongst Sikhs opposed to the idea of Khalistan. However, the movement lost its support amongst the people in the 1990s and Tatla concludes, "The realpolitik of resources bargaining and distribution has returned, the Indian state has 'managed' another ethnic conflict and the aggrieved group has retuned to normal politics by sharing power for the state government".

The army operation was followed by killings of Sikh males between the ages of 15 and 35 in Punjab's villages. These violent events, together with pogroms against Sikhs in India's major cities in November 1984, and daily terror families subsequently experienced in Punjab's villages, gave rise to resistance. A Sarbat Khalsa (general congregation of the Sikh people) was convened at the Akal Takht, the Sikh seat of temporal authority in Amritsar, on 26 January 1986. The gathering passed a resolution (gurmatta) favouring the independence of Punjab (Khalistan). Khalistan is envisaged by its proponents as a secular state.

Khalsa : Khalsa which means 'Pure' is the name given by Guru Gobind Singh to all Sikhs who have been baptised or initiated by taking Amrit in ceremony called Amrit Sanchar. The first time that this ceremony took place was on Baisakhi, which fell on 30 March 1699 at Anandpur Sahib in India. The Sikhs celebrated the 300th anniversary of the day in 1999 with thousands of religious gatherings all over the world.

Historically, one of the male children (usually the first) of many Khatri Hindu families in the Punjab was intiated as a Khalsa Sikh. The Khalsa must carry the five symbols, Panj Kakar, or the Five Ks:

— Kesh – uncut hair to represent the natural appearance of saintlihood.

— Kanga – a small comb.

— Kacha – shorts/underwear to denote chastity.

— Kara – steel bangle/bracelet as a sign of restraint and bondage, and a symbol of dedication to the Guru.

— Kirpan – a sword for defence. The Kirpan is a symbol of dignity, power and courage. Kirpan is from Kirpa (act of kindness, Sanskrit) + Aan (self respect, Persian).

A Sikh is to lead his life according to the Guru's teaching and repudiate non-Sikh rites and ceremonies. This includes leaving any caste. All Sikhs were taught to treat all in the community as equals; no distinction was made of the different tiers of 'craftsmen' and professions.

Khamba Lim : It is performed by two groups of men and women who stand in two rows. A similar dance is known as the Akhu.

Khamba Thoibi Dance : It is a duet of male and female partners, a dance of dedication to the sylvan deity, Thangjing of Moirang.

Khambhat : Khambhat, formerly known as Cambay, is a town in Gujarat state, India. It was formerly an important trading center, although its harbor has gradually silted up, and the maritime trade has moved elsewhere. Khambhat lies on an alluvial plain at the north end of the Gulf of Khambhat, which is noted for the extreme rise and fall of its tides, which can vary as much as thirty feet in the vicinity of Khambhat.

Khambhat was the capital of a princely state of British India within the Gujarat division of Bombay. It has an area of 350 square miles (906 km²). As a separate state it dates only from about 1730, the time of the dismemberment of the Mughal empire. Its Nawabs were descended from Momin Khan II, the last of the Mughal governors of Gujarat, who in 1742 murdered his brother-in-law, Nizam Khan, governor of Khambhat, and established himself there.

Khammam : Khammam is a town in the Khammam District of India's Andhra Pradesh state. The name of the town Khammam derives from the name of the hill of stambhadri(name of an old temple called Narasimha Swamy Temple on a small hill top in Khammam town believed to have existed since Treta Yuga) later it became kambadri, kamba, khammam mettu, at last when it became the district headquarters, it is known to be khammam. Khammam district has a lot of historical importance in Andhra Pradesh.

Khammam town which was the seat of Taluk Administration was part of the larger Warangal District, till 1st October, 1953. Five taluks of the Warangal district viz., Khammam, Madhira, Yellandu, Burgampadu and Paloncha (Now Kothagudem) were carved out and a new district KHAMMAM with Khammam as District Headquarters. In 1959 Bhadrachalam Revenue Division consisting Bhadrachalam and Nuguru Venkatapuram Taluks of East Godawari district, which were on the other side of the river Godawari were merged into Khammam on grounds of geographical contiguity and administrative viability. There is a festival held in khammam remembering the old name "Stambhadri".

Khampti : The Khampti is a tribal group found in the Lohit district of Arunachal Pradesh in India as well as in northwestern Myanmar. Smaller numbers can be found in parts of Assam as well as the East Siang district of Arunachal Pradesh. The Khampti, whose name is also spelt as Khamti, is a sub-group of the Shan people. As of 1990 their total population was estimated to be around 70,000, but it was recalculated that it actually stood at 13,100 in 2000, of which 4,235 lives in Myanmar.

The Khampti whom inhabit in the region around the Tengapani basin were descandants of 18th century migrants who came during the 18th centuary were from the Bor-Khampti region, the mountainous valley of the Irrawady. The Khampti possess East Asian features. The Khampti are followers of Theravada Buddhism, but they do not abstain from meat. They used a variant of the Tai script, known as Lik-Tai, for the use of their language.

Khampti Dances : Khampti Dances are dances of Arunachal. The Kamptis, who are Buddhists, have many dance-dramas through which they unfold some stories or depict mythical events bearing ethical lessons. These dramas are generally staged during the religious festivals of Potwah, Sankian or Khamsang, constituting the entertainment part of the festivals.

The dance is called Ka and the dance-drama is called Kapung (Ka-dance; Pung-story) and actually means a story depicted through the dance. The rehearsal of a drama starts about one month before a festival. This may be done in the monastery or in any house of their choice. The well-to-do-villagers invite the drama-party when the drama is staged in the front courtyard or in some suitable open space near their house. Women do not take part in the drama. The female role, if any, is played by a man in woman's costume.

After the performances, the party is given a remuneration of seven, fourteen, twenty-eight or forty-two rupees-always an amount divisible by seven. They purchase with this money the costumes and masks used in the dramas. The surpluses, if any, is shared by the members of the drama party.

Khan Abdul Ghaffar Khan : Khan Abdul Ghaffar Khan (b. at Hashtnagar in Utmanzai, Peshawar, North-West Frontier Province, India, 1890; d. in Peshawar, NWFP, Pakistan, 20 January 1988) was a Pashtun (Afghan) political and spiritual leader known for his non-violent opposition to British rule during the final years of the Empire on the Indian sub-continent. He was a lifelong pacifist and a devout Muslim. He was known as Badshah Khan (sometimes written as Bacha Khan), the 'Khan of Khans', and 'Frontier Gandhi'.

Ghaffar Khan was educated in a small school run by Christian missionaries. His childhood was in sharp contrast to his contemporaries. Education as a means of social advancement remained an ideal throughout his life. Ghaffar Khan's goal was a united, independent, secular India; to achieve this end, he founded the Khudai Khidmatgar [Servants of God] (also known as the 'Red Shirts') during the 1920s. The organization recruited over 100,000 members and became legendary in opposing the British-controlled police and army.

Ghaffar Khan forged a close, spiritual, and always uninhibited friendship with Mahatma Gandhi, the pioneer of non-violent mass civil disobedience in India. The two had a deep admiration towards each other and worked together for the rest of their lives. He strongly opposed the partition of India. While the Red Shirts were willing to work with Indian politicians, some Pashtuns desired independence from both India and the newly created state of Pakistan following the departure of the British. However, there was no option that included independence or merger with Afghanistan and when given a choice between Pakistan and India, most voters chose Pakistan by a margin of 9 to 1 in 1947. A loya jirga in the Tribal Areas garnered a similar result as most preferred to become part of Pakistan. Khan was exiled to Jalalabad, Afghanistan, but subsequently returned to Pakistan. In 1962 Abdul Ghaffar Khan was awarded "Amnesty Internationals Prisoner of the Year ". Ghaffar Khan died in Peshawar under house arrest in 1988 and was buried in Jalalabad according to his wishes.

Khan Abdul Jabbar Khan : Khan Abdul Jabbar Khan (1882—May 1958) popularly known as Dr Khan Sahib was a pioneer in the Indian Independence Movement and a Pakistani politician. He was born in the village of Utmanzai, near Charsadda in the North-West Frontier Province. His father, Bahram Khan was a well known Khan in the Hashtnagar area. In 1935, Dr. Khan Sahib was elected as the NWFP's sole representative to the Central Legislative Assembly in New Delhi. With the grant of limited self-government and announcement of provincial elections in 1937, Dr. Khan Sahib led his party to a comprehensive victory. The Frontier National Congress, an affiliate of the Indian National Congress emerged as the single largest party in the Provincial Assembly.

Khan Abdul Qayyum Khan : Khan Abdul Qayyum Khan (nicknamed the "Lion of the Frontier" by his supporters) was a major figure in Pakistan politics, in particular in the North West Frontier Province where he served as deputy speaker, Chief Minister and Minister in the Central Government as well as Federal Interior Minister.

Qayyum Khan a barrister by profession was of Kashmiri origin his father Khan Abdul Hakim was Tehsildar in the North West Frontier Province. An honest man, but a harsh ruler he is known in his later life for his development work in the province especially for the construction of Peshawar University and his deep dislike as well as brutal suppression of the Khudai Khidmatgar movement. His role in ordering the Babra Sharif massacre is one which he faces much criticism for, that in combination with the brutal crackdown against his former colleagues in the Congress party earned him their lasting hatred.

Arrested by the Ayub Khan regime, he was disqualified from politics and imprisoned for 2 years before finally being released. Contesting the 1970 elections from three seats as leader of the Pakistan Muslim League-Qayyum faction he won all National Assembly seats and entered into alliance with the PPP after the separation of east Pakistan. Appointed Federal interior Minister by Zulfiqar Bhutto he served in that post till the 1977 elections when his party suffered a near total rout. After Zia-ul-Haqs assumption of power, Qayyum Khan tried to unify all the disparate Muslim League factions. His efforts were inconclusive and he passed away on 22, October 1981.

Khan Abdul Wali Khan : Khan Abdul Wali Khan (b. January 11, 1917, d. January 26, 2006) was a controversial person in Pakistan politics.

He was called hero, saint, traitor or villain at varying stages during his life. However with his recent death there has been increased appreciation from a wide cross section of society, including former bitter rivals, of his contribution to the politic of Pakistan.

Khan, Ataur Rahman : Khan, Ataur Rahman (1907-1991) was the prime minister of Bangladesh from 30 March 1984 to 9 July 1986. He was born in 1907 at village Balia under Dhamrai thana of Dhaka district. He began his career in politics as an activist of the Krishak Praja Samiti. He was secretary of the Dhaka district unit of the Party in 1934-35 AD. He joined the Muslim League in 1944, and was a member of the Dhaka district committee and vice president of the Manikganj Sub-divisional unit committee of the Party. Ataur Rahman had played a substantial role in floating the Awami Muslim League (1949), and had been the vice president of the party since its inception till 1964. As a member of the Sarbadaliya Rastrabhasa Karma-parisad he played a vital role in piloting the Language Movement, and was later elected convenor of the reconstituted working committee in March 1952.

Ataur Rahman Khan was the joint secretary of the United Front formed for launching the 1954 general elections. He was elected a member of the East Bengal Legislative Assembly as a nominee of the Front. He was a member of the provincial cabinet of Sher-e-Bangla Ak Fazlul Huq in charge of the Ministry of Civil Supplies. He was elected a member of the Pakistan Constituent Assembly in 1955. He was simultaneously the leader of the opposition parliamentary party in the provincial assembly (1955-56) and the deputy leader of the opposition parliamentary party in the constituent assembly.

Ataur Rahman Khan became the Chief Minister of East Pakistan in 1956 and continued to hold this position till the promulgation of martial law in the country in 1958. As one of the leaders of National Democratic Front (NDF) formed under the leadership of Huseyn Shaheed Suhrawardy in 1962 he played a vital role in the movement for the restoration of democracy in the country. He was elected president of the Dhaka High Court Bar Association in 1969 and a member of the bar council in 1970.

Ataur Rahman Khan floated a new political party styled as Jatiya League in 1969, and was elected its president. During the War of Liberation in 1971 he was arrested by the Pakistan occupation army, and was however released in September after confinement for five months. Ataur Rahman was elected a member of the Jatiya Sangsad in 1973. He joined the Bangladesh Krishak-Sramik Awami League (BAKSAL) in 1975, and was made a member of its central committee. After the fall of BAKSAL Ataur Rahman revived his party Jatiya League in 1976. He was elected a member of the Jatiya Sangsad in 1979. Under his leadership the Jatiya League as a member of the seven party alliance took active part in the movement against the military rule of General Husain Muhammad Ershad. Later he joined the cabinet of General Ershad, and was made the Prime Minister in 1984 which office he held till 1 9 July1986.

Khanda : The Khanda is one of the most important symbols of Sikhism. Its importance is emphasised by the fact that many Sikh flags, including the Nishan Sahib have the Khanda on them. It is a collection of four weapons commonly used by Sikhs at the time of Guru Gobind Singh. The weapons are:

— A double-edged sword called a Khanda sits in the middle.

— A Chakkar is a circular weapon that surrounds the Khanda

— Two daggers, or Kirpans are crossed at the bottom and sit on either side of the Khanda and Chakkar. They are called Miri and Piri.

The weapons have symbolic meanings. The Khanda symbolises knowledge of God, the Chakkar symbolises the oneness of God, Piri symbolises spiritual sovereignty and Miri symbolises political sovereignty. The Khanda is an important emblem in Sikhism and can be compared to the Cross to Christians, or the Star of David to Jews. The current flag of Iran bears an emblem which is visually similar to a Khanda, but is not referential to Sikhism.

Khandagiri and Udayagiri Caves : Twin hills honeycombed with Jain caves that reveal the sculptural art of the 2nd century BC makes an interesting study of the life and times of Jain ascetics. The coarse -grained sandstone which forms Khandagiri and Udayagiri rises nearly 40m above the surrounding lateritic and infertile plain. Khandagiri has 19 caves and Udaigiri has 44 caves.

Khandesh : Khandesh is a region of central India, which forms the northwestern portion of Maharashtra state. Under British rule there was also a Kandesh District. The name Khandesh originates from palkhi word Kandesh. Some people believe its origins from Mughal Empire. The terms "Khandesh" and "Deccan" thus connote historical and political affiliations, as well as geographical zones. Khandesh lies on the northwestern corner of the Deccan plateau, in the valley of the Tapti River, and is bound to the north by the Satpura Range, to the east by the Berar (Vidarbha) region, to the south by the Desh region of Maharashtra, and to the west by the northernmost ranges of the Western Ghats, and beyond them the coastal plain of Gujarat.

Khanewal : Khanewal is district in the province of Punjab, Pakistan. It most widely known for being the host city to the second largest Trian Stattion in Pakistan. The larges Train Station in in Lahore, which is capital of Punjab. It is also the home town of two the Pakistan's national cricket team's players : Shabbir Ahmed and Iftikhar Anjum.

Khang-chen-dzod-nga Dance : The two day festival of dance performed during the worship of snowy range of Kanchanjunga (Khang-chen-dzod-nga) is a dance peculiar to Sikkim alone. It is celebrated in September. The third Chogyal of Sikkim, Chador Namgyal (1686-1716) introduced this dance about two and a half centuries ago as a result of a vision. Kanchendzonga is portrayed as a fiery red—countenanced deity with a crown of five skulls, riding the mythical snow lion and holding aloft the banner of victory. Esoteric masks, flashing silks, opulent brocades and embroidered boots are the costumes of the dancers. The dancers are all male. In this warrior Dance the warlike pomp and panoply, the war deity resplendent the flaming robes, the fantastic Snow lion, comprise the essence of the dance. This mask dance is termed as Singhi Dance i.e. Lion Dance by Nepalese. They visualise the ferocious god of Kanchanjunga riding over a lion and hence call this dance as Singhi Dance.

Kharagpur : Kharagpur is a town in India. It is located in the Midnapore West district of the state of West Bengal. Features that distinguish it from the multitude of other small towns spanning India are its railway platform, purportedly the longest railway platform(1.072 km or 3,517 feet) in the world. It is the most important station of the South Eastern Railway, originating from Howrah Station, the tracks trifurcate here for Tatanagar (going west towards Nagpur, SE Railway was formerly known as BNR or Bengal Nagpur Railway), Midnapore (going north) and Balasore (heading southwards along the coast of the Bay of Bengal).

The other notable site in Kharagpur is the prestigious Indian Institute of Technology, which has a campus in Kharagpur, started at Hijli. Kharagpur was chosen as the location of the first campus of the prestigious Indian Institutes of Technology (IITs). The IITs are the premier technical education institutes in India and are internationally recognised for their academic and technical excellence. Unlike other IITs, this IIT has been long known for its ability to offer unusual courses not found in other IITs. This IIT has also has a reputation for student bonding, unique hostel life and extensive extra-curricular activities. Kharagpur also has one of the biggest Railway workshops in India which includes all the workshops for A-Z of Railways.

Kharan : Kharan is a district in the north west of Balochistan province of Pakistan. Kharan was notified as a district in 1951 and the Deputy Commissioner's office started functioning on March 15th 1952. It is one of the oldest districts of Balochistan. The Deputy Commissioner directly supervises all activities in the district. He also supervises the functions of all Departments through the district-level heads of these Departments. To facilitate the administrative services, the district is divided into four tehsils i.e. Kharan, Basima and Kashkhel, eleven Patwar circles and 394 Mauzas. Over 99% of the people of the area are Muslims.

Khardung La : Khardung La (La means Pass in Tibetan, the local language) located in the Ladakh region, Jammu and Kashmir, India, is a high motorable mountain pass rising to a height of 5,359 m (17,582 feet). The pass on the Ladakh range lies North of Leh and is the gateway to the Shyok and Nubra Valleys.The Siachen Glacier lies partway up the latter valley. Built in 1976, it was opened to motor vehicles in 1988 and has since seen many automobile, motorbike and mountain biking expeditions.

Maintained by the Indian Army's 14 Corps, the pass is strategically important to India as it is used to carry essential supplies to the Siachen. Khardung La is historically important as it lies on the major caravan route from Leh to Kashgar in Chinese Central Asia. About 10,000 horses and camels used to take the route annually, and a small population of Bactrian camels can still be seen in the area north of the pass, mute witnesses to history. During World War Two there was a futile attempt to transfer war materiel to China through this route.

Kharias : The vast majority of the Kharias are found in the Ranchi and Singhbhum districts. The hill Kharias practice a crude type of shifting cultivation and hunt with bows and arrows, sticks and with spears. The Birhors are mostly found in the districts of Hazaribagh and usually live in huts made of twigs and leaves but during the rains in semi-permanent settlements. They sustain themselves by gathering wild forest produce, including honey and beewax, by hunting deer and other animals and by catching birds and monkeys.

Khasi : (1) Khasi is an Austro-Asiatic language spoken primarily in Meghalaya state in India. Khasi is part of the Mon-Khmer group of languages, and is distantly related to the Munda branch of the Austroasiatic family, which is found in east-central India. Although most of the 865,000 Khasi speakers are found in Meghalaya state, the language is also spoken by a number of people in the hill districts of Assam bordering with Meghalaya and by a sizable population of people living in Bangladesh, close to the Indian border. Khasi is rich in folklore and folktale, and behind most of the names of hills, mountains, rivers, waterfalls, birds, flowers, and animals there is a story.

(2) The Khasi are a tribe in Meghalaya, India who call themselves Hynniew trep (which means "the seven huts" in their local language). They comprise almost fifty percent of the population of Meghalaya. Most Khasis are Presbyterian or Roman Catholic. Some are also found in the hilly areas of Sylhet, Bangladesh. The Khasi tribes are usually dependant upon Zoom cultivation in which the vegetation is left to grow totally under the care of the nature. One of the main product the Khasis produce by zoom cultivation in bangladesh is betel leaf. Khasi society

is matrilineal, i.e. descent is through the mother. Traditionally, only women can inherit property or own land. As in many matrilineal societies, the maternal uncle is an extremely important figure in a child's life. The main deity in the Khasi pantheon is the god simply referred to as U Blei ("the God"). Sometimes, this deity is seen as an androgynous being, and referred to as U Blei-Ka Blei ("the God-Goddess").

Khasi Hills : The Khasi Hills are part of the Garo-Khasi range in Meghalaya, India. It is inhabited mainly by tribal dwellers. Cherrapunji, the world's wettest place, is located here. It is part of the patkai range. The range is part of the Meghalaya subtropical forests ecoregion.

Khatam-Band : Khatam-band is a speciality in Kashmir woodwork and comprises ceilings of rooms, made from thin panels of pine wood, cut into geometrical designs. Builders of houseboats have kept this old craft alive.In Kashmir the shrine of Khwaja Naqshband, near the Jama Masjid of Srinagar, presents the best example of this craft. The Kashmiri carpentry and wicker-work industries are notable. The boats (float-bottomed mostly) that the carpenter makes are of many sizes, and include the famous house-boats, the favourite residence of summer visitors. In wicker-work, Lunch and flower baskets, chairs and tables and various other articles of common use are turned out in elegant designs. Kangri, the Kashmiri chafing vessel, its earthen bowl encased in wickerwork, is also made as an artefact ornamented with wicker rings and coloured mica for the mantelpiece.

Khatris : The Khatris are an elite community of the Kshatriya caste that originated in the Potwar Plateau region of Punjab, a region historically connected a region historically connected with the composition of the Vedas and classics like the Mahabharata and Ashtadhyayi. The

Kshatriya are members of the Hindu military order. As administrators and rulers, Kshatriya are assigned with protecting the Hindu Dharma, and serving humanity. In course of time, however, as a result of economic and political exigencies, the Khatri also expanded into mercantile occupations.

When Pakistan and India gained independence, most of the Khatris in what became Pakistan migrated to India. Today Khatris live in all regions of India, but are concentrated in Punjab, Haryana, Delhi and Uttar Pradesh. While most Khatris are Hindu, some are also Sikh and a small minority are Jain. Khatris of all these faiths collectively form one community. In modern times, the Khatri play a dominant role in the Indian economy, serving as businessmen, civil and government administrators, landlords, and military officials. They are by far the most educated group in Punjab.

Khawaja Nazimuddin : Khawaja Nazimuddin (Bengali:(July 19, 1894 - 1964) was the second Governor-General of Pakistan, and later the second Prime Minister of Pakistan as well. He was born in Dhaka, Bengal (now in Bangladesh) into the family of the Nawabs of Dhaka. He received his education from Aligarh Muslim University, and later Trinity Hall, Cambridge until the mid-1930s.

After returning to the South Asia, he became involved in politics in his native Bengal. Nazimuddin was initially the Education Minister, but climbed the ranks to become the Chief Minister of the province prior to independence. Nazimuddin also became the head of the Muslim League in Eastern India.

Upon the formation of Pakistan, he became an important part of the early government. After the early death of Muhammad Ali Jinnah, Nazimuddin succeeded him as the Governor-General of Pakistan. At this point in time, the position was largely ceremonial, and executive power rested with the Prime Minister. The first Prime Minister of Pakistan, Liạquat Ali Khan was assassinated in 1951, and Nazimuddin stepped in to replace him.

During Nazimuddin's time as Prime Minister, Pakistan saw a growing rift within the Muslim League, especially between Punjabi and Bengali groups, as those were the two largest ethnic groups of Pakistan, but were separated by India. On 21 February 1952, a demonstration in the Language movement demanding equal and official status to Bangla language turned bloody, with many fatalities caused by police firings. During his reign, a framework was begun for a constitution that would allow Pakistan to become a republic, and end its Dominion status. Progress was made, but Nazimuddin's time as Prime Minister would be cut short in 1953.

In 1953, a religious movement began to agitate for the removal of the Ahmadi religious minority from power positions, and demanded a declaration of this minority as non-Muslims. Nazimuddin resisted such pressures; but riots broke out in The Punjab against both the government and followers of this religious minority. Nazimuddin responded by changing the governor of that province to Feroz Khan Noon, but the decision came late.

Ghulam Muhammad, the Governor-General, asked the Prime Minister to step down. Khawaja Nazimuddin refused, but Ghulam Muhammad got his way by invoking a reserve power that allowed him to dismiss the Prime Minister. The Chief Justice, Muhammad Munir, of the "Federal Court of Pakistan" (now named as the Supreme Court of Pakistan), did not rule on the legality of the dismissal, but instead forced new elections. The new prime-minister was another Bengali born statesman, Muhammad Ali Bogra. The dismissal of Nazimuddin, the Prime Minister, by the Governor-General, Muhammad, signaled a troubling trend in Pakistani political history. The Nazimabad and North Nazimabad suburbs of Karachi have been named in honor of Khawaja Nazimuddin.

Khecheopalri Lake : Khecheopalri lake in West Sikkim district of the Indian state of Sikkim is considered to be a holy lake both by the Buddhist and the Hindu population. The lake is enveloped in a dense forest cover of temperate vegetation and bamboo. The placid waters of the lake are visited by many pilgrims and tourists. The closest town is Pelling. A peculiar aspect of the lake is the absence of leaves floating on the waters. This is explained by the duck population who are known to remove the leaves as soon as they fall on the surface, giving it a clear and smooth surface.

Kheda : Kheda is a town in the Gujarat state of India. Kheda, also known as Kaira, is 35 km from Ahmedabad. The National Highway no. 8 connecting Ahmedabad and Mumbai passes through Kheda. It forms the administrative center of Kheda District. The town of Kheda passed to the Babi family early in the eighteenth century, with whom it remained until 1763, when it was taken by the Marathas. The Marathas ceded the district to the British in 1803, and it became part of the Bombay Presidency of British India. It was a large military station till 1830, when the cantonment was removed to Deesa.

Khemkaran : Khemkaran is a section of India bordering Pakistan. It was the site of a major tank battle in 1965 reulting it also being known as the graveyard of tanks. The 1965 India-Pakistan War was witness to the largest tank battle in military history since World War II. This battle lead to the creation of Patton Nagar (or Patton City) at the site of the battle viz., Khemkaran. This is due to the fact that a lot of Patton tanks fielded by the Pakistani forces were either captured or slain at the scene.

Khewra Salt Mines : The Khewra Salt Mines are situated 160 km from Islamabad and 260 km from Lahore in Tehsil Pind Dadan Khan District Jhelum. THey are easily accessible via Lahore – Islamabad Motorway through Lilla Interchange. It is a tourist attraction, with up to 40,000 visitors per year.

Khichuri : Khichuri is a very popular vegetarian dish in eastern India especially Bengal. The main ingredients are rice and lentil (moong and moosoor dal). Addition of vegetables such as cauliflower, potato, and green peas is very common. In Bengali tradition it is customary to cook Khichuri during rainy days. Common accompaniment with Khichuri are beguni—deep fried eggplants and other vegetables in a besan (chick pea flower) batter. Other popular accompaniment is ghee (clarified butter) and achar (oil based pickle). It is traditional in Bengal to cook Khichuri as a lunch at the Saraswati Puja during the month of February—the invocation of the goddess of learning. It is also customary to cook Khichuri for lunch in other popular pujas such as Durga Puja. While Khichuri is cooked as a rather rich and delectable delicacy in Bengal, it is cooked very differently in North India—a very plain dish that is normally associated with bland taste and diet for people when sick.

Khilafat Movement : The Khilafat Movement (1919-1924) was a movement amongst the Muslims of British India (the largest single Muslim community in one geo-political entity at the time) to ensure that the British, victors of World War I, kept a promise made at the Versailles. The promise was that the Caliphate, then claimed by the Ottoman emperor, would not be abolished.

Ottoman emperor Abdul Hamid II (1876-1909) had launched his Pan-Islamic program in a bid to protect the Ottoman empire from Western attack and dismemberment, and to crush the Westernizing democratic opposition in

Turkey. He sent an emissary, Jamaluddin Afghani, to India in the late nineteenth century. Some Indian Muslim leaders endorsed his efforts. One Muslim journalist, Maulana Mohammad Ali, spent four years in prison (1911-1915) for preaching resistance to the British and support for the Ottoman caliph.

In September 1919, Maulana Muhammad Ali and his brother Shaukat Ali, together with Maulana Abdul Kalam Azad, Dr. Mukhtar Ahmed Ansari, and Hasrat Mohani, started a new organization, the Khilafat Movement. Their avowed aim was to use whatever leverage they had with the British, as residents of a British colony, to protect the Caliphate. They organized Khilafat Conferences in several northern Indian cities. In 1920 they published the Khilafat Manifesto.

The Ali brothers then made a strategic alliance. They convinced Mohandas Karamchand Gandhi to join a Hindu-Muslim alliance for self-rule (Indian Independence, or Swaraj). Gandhi's followers would support the Khilafat Movement if the Muslims would support Gandhi's efforts for swaraj. Gandhi became a member of the Central Khilafat Committee and at the Nagpur session (1920) of the Indian National Congress Gandhi proposed a non-cooperation campaign, of non-violent satyagraha, in support of swaraj and khilafat.

Khilchipur : Khilchipur is a town in Rajgarh District of Madhya Pradesh state in central India. It is the administrative headquarters of Khilchipur was formerly the capital of a princely state of the same name, under the Bhopal Agency of British India's Central India Agency. It had an area of 273 square miles, and a population of 31,143 in 1901. Its estimated revenue in 1911 was 7000 rupees, and it paid a yearly tribute to Sindhia of Gwalior of 700 rupees. Its rulers were Khichi Rajputs of the Chauhan clan. The rulers acceded to the Government of India after India's independence in 1947, and the Khilchipur became part of the new state of Madhya Bharat. Madhya Bharat was merged into Madhya Pradesh on November 1, 1956.

Khilji Dynasty : Khilji or Khalji was a ruling dynasty of Turkic origin that conquered and ruled northern India (1290-1320). They were the second Muslim dynasty to rule the Delhi Sultanate. Ikhtiar Uddin Muhammad bin Bakhtiar Khilji, one of the generals of Qutb-ud-din Aybak, conquered Bihar and Bengal in the late 12th century, and the Khiljis were feudatories of the Slave Dynasty of Delhi Sultans. Jalal ud din Firuz Khilji took control of the Delhi Sultanate in 1290, and three Khilji sultans ruled the empire from 1290 to 1320. Mahmud Khilji established himself as ruler of Malwa in 1436, and his successors ruled Malwa until 1531, when Malwa was conquered by the Sultans of Gujarat.

Khindsi : Famous mainly for its large and picturesque lake in Maharashtra. Boating facilities are also offered. Khindsi is very close to Ramtek, in fact you can combine the two places in a single trip.

Khirbhwani : Khirbhwani is 22.5 Kms. from Srinagar. Every year a very big fair is held there in June. This is also a place of pilgrimage for Hindus.

Khondaker Moshtaq Ahmad : Khondaker Moshtaq Ahmad (1918-1996) is a Bangladeshi political figure. He served as the President of Bangladesh from 15 August until 6 November 1975. He was the successor of Sheikh Mujibur Rahman. Ahmad was one of Sheikh Mujib's closest associates since his earliest days as a student leader. Ahmad was senior to Mujib in age and association in politics. When the younger charishmatic leader eclipsed Ahmad, he remained a follower of Mujib.

During the Bangladesh Liberation War in 1971, Ahmad was the foreign minister of the government in exile.

Ahmad allegedly maintained a back channel trying to reconcile with Pakistan. His efforts were thwarted by Tajuddin Ahmed, who later removed him from his position. After liberation, Ahmad is reported to have maintained close relationships with various anti-Mujib, anti-Bengali-nationalist and anti-secular groups. He conspired with Major Rashid and Major Faruk Rahman to assassinate Mujib. When their mutual interests culminated in the assassination of Mujib by a group of renegade army officers led by Rashid and Rahman, Ahmad ascended to the Presidency. However, he always remained a puppet of all these forces, never having the competence or courage to consolidate his power. He was ousted in yet another coup in November, 1975 and handed over his power to the then chief justice. Later, Ahmad made some futile efforts to gain political influence, but finally faded into political inconsequence. He died in 1996.

Khonghampat Orchidarium : The Orchid yard of the Forest department, on National Highway No. 39, abolt 7 km from Imphal, is another place of interest. More than 110 varieties of Orchids, including several rare species, are grown here. Peak season is April-May.

Khoria : This dance is performed by women at weddings and is marked by happy cajoling and joyful teasing. It resembles the Ghoomar dance of Rajasthan.

Khoria Dance : This dance is a variety of Jhumar dance. It is performed by woman only. It is popular in the central areas of Haryana. It is connected with the daily life of the people and with the most important events like harvest. Singing a folk song, the girls enter dancing place and make a ring. The simple movements acquire form and colour with the swirling off their full-gold-work skirts and coloured chundries and the gleam and jingle of heavy rustic jewellery. The graceful steps give place to faster tempo until two or three pairs of the girls break from the ring into the centre with crossed arms joined together swirling on the axis of their feet. The girls in the ring clap to the beat of the drum. In final stage the dance is around the circumference.

Khuaichhiah : Honey collection from the forest was an important source of food for the Mizos. The chief was entitled to a share of the honey collected by his subjects. This due was called Khuaichhiah. This included honey and wax.

Khuda Baksh Oriental Library : Khuda Baksh Oriental Library in Bihar is one of the national libraries of India, Khuda Baksh Oriental library has a rare collection of Arabic and Persian manuscripts, books from the University of Cordoba, Spain and Rajput and Mughal paintings.

Khudai Khidmatgar Movement : Khudai Khidmatgar (Persian) literally translates as the servants of God. It represented a non violent freedom struggle against the British Empire by the Pashtuns of the North West Frontier Province. The movement was led by Khan Abdul Ghaffar Khan known locally as Bacha Khan or Badshah Khan. Formed out of the society for reformation of Afghans (Anjuman-e-Islah-e-Afghan), it initially targetted social reformation and launched campaigns against prostitution. Bacha Khan as it's founder seemed to be influenced by the realisation that whenever British troops were faced with an armed uprising they eventually always overcame the rebellion. The same could not be said when using non violence against the troops.

The movement started prior to the Qissa Khwani bazaar massacre, when a demonstration of hundreds of non violent supporters were fired upon by British soldiers in Peshawar. It's low point and eventual disappaition was after Pakistan's inependance in 1947 when the Muslim

League Chief Minister Abdul Qayyum Khan banned the movement and launched a brutal crackdown on it's members which culminated in the massacre at Babra Sharif massacre. At it's peak the KK movement consisted of almost 100,000 members.

Khudai Khidmatgar: Khudai Khidmatgar literally translates as the servants of God. It represented a non violent freedom struggle against the British Empire by the Pashtuns of the North West Frontier Province. The movement was led by Khan Abdul Ghaffar Khan known locally as Bacha Khan or Badshah Khan. Formed out of the society for reformation of Afghans (Anjuman-e-Islah-e-Afghan), it initially targetted social reformation and launched campaigns against prostitution. Bacha Khan as it's founder seemed to be influenced by the realisation that whenever British troops were faced with an armed uprising they eventually always overcame the rebellion. The same could not be said when using non violence against the troops.

The movement started prior to the Qissa Khwani bazaar massacre, when a demonstration of hundreds of non violent supporters were fired upon by British soldiers in Peshawar. It's low point and eventual disappaition was after Pakistan's inependance in 1947 when the Muslim League Chief Minister Abdul Qayyum Khan banned the movement and launched a brutal crackdown on it's members which culminated in the massacre at Babra Sharif massacre. At it's peak the KK movement consisted of almost 100,000 members.

Khullong Ishei : It is a folk song of Manipur, commonly sung by the Meities in villages when they go to work in the fields or go for fishing. There is no set system of words and sentences. The theme is love. The singer adjusts his words and stanzas of verses of his own to the tune.

Khulna Division : Khulna Division is an administrative region in south-west Bangladesh. Its headquarter is Khulna district. The region borders the Rajshahi Division to the north, the Dhaka Division and Barisal Division to the east, the Bay of Bengal to the south and State of West Bengal (in India) to the west. Part of the Ganges River is in the north of the region. Other rivers include the Maghumait River, the Bhairab River and the Kabadak River. The region also has several islands in the Bay of Bengal.

Khulna University : Khulna University is a state run university situated near Gollamari, Khulna in south-western Bangladesh. Khulna University was established in 1987 in order to cater to the growing educational needs of the country. The academic program of the University commenced in August 1991 with four disciplines: Computer Science and Engineering, Architecture, Business Administration, and Urban and Rural Planning. In the following year, Forestry and Wood Technology and Fisheries and Marine Resources Technology disciplines started their academic activities. Now there are sixteen disciplines under five schools. It is the only university in Bangladesh where student politics is not allowed.

Khumi : Khumi is a small tribe of Chittagong hill tracts. The Khumis are also called Khami, which means the best race. Kha in the Khumi dialect means man and mi means the best. The Arakanese call Khumis Khemi, which implies a race of very low social hierarchy. Khe in the Arakanese language means dog and mi denotes race. Khumis have Mongoloid features. They migrated from Arakan towards the end of the 17th century. In Bangladesh they live in Ruma, Rowangchhari and Thanchi upazilas of Bandarban district.

Khunjerab National Park : Khunjerab National Park one of the highest altitude parks in the world, provides the habitat for a number of endangered and threatened species like the Snow leopard, Marco Polo sheep, and Himalayan ibex. It is also one of the most important alpine biodiversity regions within Pakistan. Implementation of the management plan to protect the alpine flora in Khunjerab National Park will on focus on community-based conservation with a strong element of environmental awareness raising. The aim is to control grazing, and increase the population of the Snow leopards, Marco Polo sheep, and Blue sheep. To ensure sustainable management, training and building the capacity of government staff is also an important part of the strategy.

Khunjerab Pass : The Khunjerab Pass is a high mountain pass on the northern border of Pakistan with China. It peaks at 4,693 metres (15,397 ft) and is the highest point on the Karakoram Highway. This section of the road was completed in 1982 and is possibly the highest metalled border crossing in the world. The pass is often snow covered and during the rainy season (December-April) the pass is closed to all vehicles except large trucks because of mudslides.

Khunyang Chhish : Khunyang Chhish is a mountain in the Karakoram region of Pakistan. Alternate variations of the name include Kunyang Chhish and Khiangyang Kish. The mountain is the highest peak south of the Khunyang Glacier while Distaghil Sar dominates the glacier on it's northern end. The first climbing attempt on Khunyang Chhish was made in 1962 but the climb was aborted after an avalanche killed two climbers. The next attempt was in 1965 but another climber died after the collapse of a narrow ridge at 7,200 m (23,600 ft).

Khurda : Khurda is a town in the Indian state of Orissa. It is also the district headquarters of Khurda district located at 20.11° N 85.40° E. It was the capital of Orissa from 1568 to 1803. Khurda is known for its brass utensils, cottage industries, railway coach manufacturing, and cable manufacture. It is also known for its fort, often described as the "last independent fort". The town lies on the banks of the rives Daya and Kuakhai. Khurda Road, the railway station that serves the town is also the divisional headquarters of the East Coast Railway of the Indian Railways.

Khurshid Ahmad : A world renowned research scholar, an educationist, an economist, a versatile writer and a preacher of Islam, Prof Khurshid Ahmad was born in Delhi on March 23, 1932. He holds Bachelor's degree in Law and Jurisprudence, Master's degrees in Economics and Islamic Studies, and also an Honorary Doctorate in Education.

His in-depth comparative study of the oriental as well as occidental philosophies in religion, academics, economics, constitutional matters and commitment for Islam has led him to be entrusted with key positions in the national as well as international organizations on these socio-economic and other multi-dimensional disciplines.

Khushab District : Khushab district, situated between Sargodha and Mianwali, is one of the districts of Pakistan. It has two tehsils, khushab and noorpure. It is an old city near the river Jehlum. Its headquarter is at Jauharabad. Population of Khushab is 8,88,194 people. There is a beautiful valley called Soon Sakaser Valley. Globally renowned tribe Awans live there.Tiwana are also famous landlords of khushab. They are headed by Mr. Qadir Yar Khan Tiwana he is practicing lawyer in lahore. He is also famous for his horses and he love to play Golf and is famous for his whole in one at jimkhana club course.

Khuzdar : Khuzdar is a small town located in Khuzdar District in Balochistan, Pakistan. Khuzdar is the capital of Khuzdar district. It is a district and divisional headquarter town in Balochistan. Khuzdar was notified as a separate district on 1st March 1974. Previously, it was included in Kalat District. Khuzdar used to be the main city of Jhalawan state. The district is subdivided into three tehsils: Khuzdar, Naal and Wadi. It is at the apex of a narrow valley at an elevation of 1,237 m (4.000 feet). Over 99% of the people of the area are Muslims. The population of Khuzdar district is estimated to be over 525,000 in 2005. The major tribes in the district are Bizenjo, Jattak, Hasni, Zehri, Mengal, Ahmadzai, and Zarakzai.

Khuzdar District : Khuzdar district is located in the center of Balochistan province of Pakistan. Khuzdar is the capital of Khuzdar district. It is a district and divisional headquarter town in Balochistan. Khuzdar was notified as a separate district on 1st March 1974. Previously, it was included in Kalat District. Khuzdar used to be the main city of Jhalawan state. The district is subdivided into three tehsils : Khuzdar, Naal and Wadi. It is at the apex of a narrow valley at an elevation of 1,237 m (4.000 feet). Over 99% of the people of the area are Muslims.

Khwaja Abdul Ghani : Khwaja Abdul Ghani (1813-1896) the nawab of Dhaka, was also a philanthropist and social worker. Born on 30 July 1813 at Begumbazar, Dhaka. Khwaja Abdul Ghani was the son of Khwaja Alimullah (d 1854) and Zinat Begum. His mother tongue was Urdu, but he spoke Bangla too. In his childhood, Ghani learnt Arabic and Persian at home. One of the first batch students of Dhaka Collegiate School, Ghani was also proficient in English. Abdul Ghani's intellect and sagacity was duly noticed by his father who appointed him Mutawalli of all family properties by executing a waqfnama in 1846. Abdul Ghani brought prosperity to his father's property as well as to their zamindari and eventually became the richest zamindar in East Bengal.

During the Sepoy Revolt of 1857, Khwaja Abdul Ghani rendered his support to the British Raj supposedly to ensure the safety of the city people against the onslaught of the British Army. After the revolt was over, he tried to assuage the British Army to give amnesty or at least minimise the punishment of the sepoys allegedly joining the revolt. He also donated a huge amount of money to the Debt Fund for people's welfare launched by the government at that time.

In 1861 the British Government made him an Honorary Magistrate. The perfection in arbitration judgement that he had developed prompted people to come to him for arbitration instead of going to the Courts. He was made a member of the Bengal Legislative Assembly in 1866 and a member of the Governor General's Legislative Council in 1867. In 1869 he settled a violent Shia- Sunni riot through arbitration. Abdul Ghani died on Monday 24 August 1896 at the Ahsan Manzil and lies buried at the family graveyard at Begumbazar in Dhaka.

Khwaja Alimullah : Khwaja Alimullah was the founder of the Nawab Family of Dhaka. Born in Begum Bazar, he was the son of Khwaja ahsanullah (d 1795 AD). Alimullah lost his father in childhood and was brought up under the care of his uncle, Khwaja Hafizullah who was childless. Hafizullah made his fortune in trade and commerce. Leather and salt were the major items of his business. He had some Greek trading partners. Alimullah took major responsibilities in the business of Hafizullah. After the permanent settlement, Hafizullah purchased some zamindari estates and indigo factories in Barisal. Alimullah became his sole heir and himself bought extensive landed estates in Barisal, Khulna, Dhaka, Mymensingh and Tripura. He acquired extensive landed property in and around Dhaka city. He had a moneylending business and was one of the major shareholders and directors of Dhaka Bank.

In 1830, Alimullah purchased the French Trading House at Kumartuli and renovated it into his own residence. This mini palace subsequently became the nucleus of the famous ahsan manzil of Dhaka. Khwaja Alimullah died on 16 Bhadra, 1261 corresponding to 1854 AD in Dhaka and was buried in the family graveyard at Begum Bazar.

Khwaja Mir Dard : Khwaja Mir Dard (1721–1785) is one of the three major poets of the Delhi School—the other two being Mir Taqi Mir and Mirza Sauda—who could be called the pillars of the classical Urdu ghazal. Dard was first and foremost a mystic, a prominent member of the Naqshbandi Mujaddidi order, and the head of the Muhammadi path in Delhi. He regarded the phenomenal world as a veil of the eternal Reality, and this life as a term of exile from our real home. Dard inherited his mystical temperament from his father, Khwaja Muhammad Nasir Andalib, who was a mystic saint and a poet, and the founder of the Muhammadi path.

Dard received his education in an informal way at home, and in the company of the learned, acquiring in due course a command of Arabic and Persian, as also of Sufi lore. He also developed a deep love of music, possibly, through his association with singers and qawaals who frequented his father's house. He renounced earthly pleasures at the young age of 28, and led a life of piety and humility.

The secret of Dard's appeal as a poet lies not in his mysticism, but in his ability to transmute this mysticism into poetry, and to present transcendental love in terms of human and earthly love. Although he has written ghazals which are unambiguously mystical in their intent, his best couplets can be read at both the secular and spiritual levels, and are, for this reason, acceptable to all and sundry. In addition, Dard had also written ghazals which deal with a patently sensuous and earthly love, and deserve to be classed with the best poetry of this kind. Dard generally excels in short ghazals of about seven to nine verses, written in comparatively short measures. His style is simple, natural and musical; his content, thoughtful and thought-provoking. His poetry includes a collection of Urdu ghazals and a divan in Persian.

Khyal : Khyal is the modern genre of classical singing in North India; its name comes from an Arabic word meaning "imagination". It appeared more recently than dhrupad. Like all Indian classical music, khyal is modal, with a single melodic line and no harmonic parts. The modes are called raga, and each raga is a complicated framework of melodic rules.

Khyal bases itself on a repertoire of short songs (two to sixteen lines). The singer uses these as raw material for improvisation, accompanied by a set of two hand drums, the tabla, and usually a harmonium or bowed string instrument such as the sarangi, violin or dilruba playing off the singer's melody line. A typical khyal performance uses two songs, one slow (vilambit) and one fast (drut). The slow song, the bada khyal or great khyal, comprises most of the performance; the fast song (chote khyal, small khyal) is a used as a finale. The songs may or may not be preceded by improvised alap without drum accompaniment; alap is given much less room in khyal than in other forms of classical music in north India.

As the songs are short, and performances long, the lyrics lose much of their importance. Improvisation is added to the songs in a number of ways: for example improvising new melodies to the words, using the syllables of the songs to improvise material (bolbant, boltaans), singing the names of the scale degrees — sa, re, ga, ma, pa, da and ni (sargam) — or simply interspersing phrases sung on the vowel A, akar taans. Now and then, the singer returns to the song, especially its first line, as a point of reference.

Khyber Pass : The Khyber Pass (also called the Khaiber Pass or Khaybar Pass) is the most important pass connecting Pakistan with Afghanistan. Throughout history it has been an important trade route between central Asia and the Subcontinent and a strategic military location. The actual pass summit is 5 kilometers inside Pakistan at Landi Kotal.

Kikli : Kikli is a popular dance among younger girls in Punjab. They form pairs and then the two girls of each pair stand opposite each other holding each other's hands crosswise. Then they lift their heels and swing round and round on their toes. The movements gets faster and faster, the upper part of the body bends backward and the arms remain fully stretched. As the spinning gathers momentum, it creates an ecstasy and the girls go on and on till they reach the point of exhaustion. Even though they move very fast, they are very careful to maintain rhythm and keep singing various kinds of songs about the mother, the father, the brother, the mother-in-law and about various incidents connected with daily life.

Luddi and Jhumar are also famous dances especially for auspicious occasions. Luddi is generally danced to celebrate a victory. Dancers lift both arms, hop on one foot and move in a circle, swinging their bodies and shaking their shoulders. Though no songs are sung with Luddi, it is a dance bursting with enthusiasm.

King Edward Medical University : King Edward Medical University is the highly regarded medical institution of Pakistan. It was established in 1850. It is the second medical institution established in Sub-continent after Bengal Medical College that was established in Calcutta in 1835. Initially its name was Lahore Medical College. Later in 1864 its name was changed to Lahore Medical School. Initially the attached hospital, like the school, was very small named as the Lahore Dispensary, situated close to the college. Since 1870 examinations and diplomas were granted by Punjab University which was established in 1870. On December 21, 1911 college was named as King Edward Medical College. In 1935, on its 75th birthday college was again recognized for M.B.,B.S. degree by General Medical Council of Great Britain in 1936.

Kingdom of Cochin : The Kingdom of Cochin or Kochi (also known as Perumpadapu Swaroopam, Madarajyam, Gosree Rajyam, or Kuru Swaroopam; Malayalam) was a former state in the area of present Kochi (Cochin), Thrissur, Palakkad and Malappuram in what is now the Indian state of Kerala. Later, it was merged with Travancore to create Travancore-Cochin, which was in turn merged with the Malabar district of Madras State on November 1, 1956 to form the new state of Kerala.

Kingdom of Mysore : The Kingdom of Mysore was a kingdom of southern India, which was founded about AD 1400 by the Wodeyar dynasty, who ruled the state until the independence of India in 1947, when the kingdom was merged with the Union of India. The kingdom originated as a small state based in the city of Mysore, and was established by two brothers, Vijaya and Krisha Wodeyar. It remained a kingdom tributary to the Vijayanagara empire until the collapse of the latter in the second half of the 16th century. In common with every other feudatory of that Empire, Mysore, under the Wodeyar dynasty, then assumed the trappings of independence. It was in the reign of Raja Wodeyar and his successor, the celebrated Kantheerava, in the mid-1600's, that the kingdom really asserted its independence, and expanded to include most of the southern part of modern-day Karnataka, as also parts of neighbouring states.

After Chamaraja Wodeyar VI, the failure of the direct male line not only necessitated the adoption of an heir, but also precipitated a minority. The Arasus (feudal barons) of Kalale came to hold sway over the affairs of the Kingdom of Mysore, and the position of "Dalavoy" or supreme commander of the Royal army, became effectively hereditary to that family. The situation was compounded by extensive intermarriage between the royal family of Mysore and that of the Arasus of Kalale. The influence of the family is regarded as having been benign, given the continuance of the legitimate dynasty, as also the similarity and alliance between the two families. This influence continued even into the 20th century; HH Maharani Kempa Nanjammani Vani Vilasa Sannidhana Avaru, regent of Mysore (1894-1902) and mother of HH Maharaja Krishnaraja Wodeyar IV, hailed from this family.

During this period, Hyder Ali, who joined the army as a foot soldier, came to prominence. By many accounts, he enjoyed the confidence of Maharaja Krishnaraja Wodeyar II, and hence essayed a meteoric rise in the affairs of the Kingdom. During the minority of Maharaja Nanjaraja Wodeyar, Hyder Ali rose to become the de facto ruler of the state, retaining the Wodeyars as nominal rulers. His son Tipu Sultan dispensed with this charade and assumed full royal powers. Tipu Sultan prosecuted a brilliant military career; his rule contributed a golden chapter to the history of India.

Both Hyder and Tipu brought in many technological innovations, modernizing the Mysorean army and expanding Mysore's foreign trade. They also aligned themselves by and large with the French, whose French East India Company was politically very active in southern India at the time. By the end of the eighteenth century, the Mysore Kingdom found itself in a series of four wars with the British East India Company, which was then expanding its control in India. In 1799 Tipu Sultan was finally defeated by the British in the fourth Mysore War, led by Arthur Wellesley, 1st Duke of Wellington, the future 1st Duke of Wellington. The British, who purported to wage that war in support of the legitimate dynasty, reinstated the Wodeyars on the throne in the person of the 5-year-old Krishnaraja Wodeyar III. After the final defeat of Tipu Sultan, the British annexed a large part of Mysore state, the remainder becoming a princely state in British India. The 5 year old Krishnaraja Wodeyar III ascended the throne under the regency of his adoptive grandmother, HH Maharani Lakshmi Ammani Avaru, relict of HH Maharaja Krishnaraja Wodeyar III. Diwan Purnaiya was appointed diwan or first minister.

The capital was moved to Bangalore in 1830. Charging the Wodeyars with financial mismanagement, the British took direct control of Mysore in 1831 and retained it for half a century. This act manifests the greed for land that characterised the British East India Company in the run up to the indian rebellion of 1857, and is of a piece with its annexation, in the same period, of other princely states like Thanjavur, Satara, Sind, Avadh and Jhansi. The Maharaja chose to argue his case in British courts, and a favourable verdict resulted in the Rendition of 1881, which restored the Wodeyar dynasty to the throne. Mysore again took its place as one of the three highest-ranking princely states in India. For the next seventy years, Mysore enjoyed the reputation of being a model state.

India became independent on 15 August 1947, and a new republican order was established. All the princely states were merged with the Union of India, and provinces were later reorganised on the basis of language. Inevitably, the kingdom of Mysore lost its distinct identity. HH Maharaja Jayachamaraja Wodeyar, signed the Instrument of Accession on 9 August, 1947 and the state acceded to the

Dominion of India. With the merger of Mysore with the Union of Inḍia, the reign of the Wodeyars came to an end. The kingdom initially became a separate state within the union of India and in 1956 Kannada-speaking areas belonging until then to the neighbouring provinces of Madras, Bombay and Hyderabad were merged with Mysore to create a create a Kannada-speaking state that retained the former name. The name of the state was changed to Karnataka in 1973.

Kinnaur Kailash : The Kinnaur Kailash is a mountain in the Kinnaur district of the Indian state Himachal Pradesh. The Kinnaur Kailash has a height of 6050 meters and is considered as sacred by both Hindu and Buddhist Kinnauris. This mountain is sometimes confused with the Mount Kailash in Tibet.

Kinnerasani Dam : The Scenery of Kinnerasani Dam is very beautiful with greenery and natural landscape in Andhra Pradesh. Glasses Rest House constructed by Singareni Collieries at Kinnerasani has given a boost to attract the tourists.

Kinnerasani Wildlife Sanctuary : This Wildlife Sanctuary lying on the Right Bank of the Godavari River forms a part of the Dandakaranya forests in Khammam district. It is situated 12-km from Paloncha, Khammam District in Andhra Pradesh.

Kinoo : The Kinoo is a variety of citrus fruit grown in Pakistan, which resembles Mandarin oranges. Indonesia is the largest export market for the fruit. Kinoo has a lot of seeds per wedge, compared to any other citrus fruit. The normal seeds of kinoo are diploid and tetraploid. But now scientists have made triploids, which means they have come up with seedless varieties. They are still testing however, whether the fruit is healthy for consumption. Kinoo has the longest growing period, and is a late maturing variety with short crushing and processing period. This causes problems to citrus industry. Due to soft skin, the fruit is damaged during harvesting and transportation, thus causing heavy post harvest losses.

Kiran TV : Kiran TV is the second Malayalam language channel from Sun Network, which is based in Chennai, Tamil Nadu, India. It's a 24 hour Music channel, with more than 12 hours of LIVE Film Songs dedication and Instant Live SMS Facility. The channel also airs one movie everyday and plays a wide range of songs regularly. This is the first full time music channel of Kerala.

Kirpan : The kirpan is the ceremonial shortsword carried by Sikhs, as a reminder to fight for justice and against oppression. It is one of the Five Ks, of Khalsa Sikhs. The word kirpan has the literal meaning of weapon of defence, as opposed to the talwar, the weapon of offence. Typically made from iron, kirpans range in size although a recommended size is said to be 8+ inches. It is required that all Baptised Sikhs wear the kirpan at all times. To Sikhs, it is a highly important religious symbol; it is rarely used as a weapon. Nevertheless, the requirement that baptised Sikhs wear the kirpan has caused problems for believers in many areas, especially where the custom clashes with local ordinances against carrying weapons. In cases where safety regulations conflict with wearing the kirpan, such as boarding an airplane or entering a prison, Sikhs are usually advised to comply with authorities.

It was first established as a principle that one must fight for peace. A Sikh should never use the Kirpan in anger or for a malicious attack. However, a Sikh may use it in self-defence or to protect a person in need. Some Sikhs choose to learn the art of Gatka. This is a martial art devised by the Sikh Gurus' that uses circular movements to effectively swing a sword.

Kirtankhola River : Kirtankhola river is starting from Sayeshtabad in Barisal district, the river Kirtankhola ends into the Gajalia near Gabkhan khal (canal). This old river is now known as the Barisal river. The total length of the river is about 160 km. In ancient times, the Ganges used to flow in three courses in Bengal namely the Nalini, the Haldini and the Pabni. The Pabni, meeting with the ancient Padma joint flow of which termed as the Sugandha, flowed through madaripur south of Faridpur, again renaming as the Andar Khan or the Arial Khan. The Arial Khan branched out in several courses in Madaripur and flowed through Barisal. Flowing forward and receiving various names, the Arial Khan fell into the Bay of Bengal as the Haringhata.

Kirthar Mountains : Kirthar Mountains range is loacted in Balochistan and Sindh provinces of Pakistan. It extends southward for about 190 miles (300 km) from the Mula River in east-central Balochistan to Cape Muari (Monze) west of Karachi on the Arabian Sea. The Kirthar National Park is one of the largest wildlife reserve in Pakistan. The range forms the boundary between the Lower Indus Plain (east) and southern Balochistan (west). It consists of a series of parallel, rock hill ridges rising from 4,000 feet (1,200 m) in the south to nearly 8,000 feet (2,500 m) in the north. It is drained in the north by the Kolachi River and in the south by the Hub River and Lyari River, which flow to the Arabian Sea. The inhabitants of the region, chiefly Balochi, Sindhi, and Brahui tribes, subsist by flock grazing.

Kirthar National Park : Kirthar National Park is located in Kirthar Mountains range. It is second biggest National Parks of Pakistan, while Hingol National Park being the biggest. It is also the first National Park from Pakistan to be included in the 1975 United Nation's list of National Parks around the world. Kirthar is an area of outstanding beauty and cultural heritage which provides important habitat for a variety of mammals, birds and reptiles characteristic of the arid subtropics Approximately one third of the park lies in the north of Karachi district and two thirds in the south-west of Dadu district. The park is part of a 4,471.61 km^2 protected areas complex, being contiguous with Mahal Kohistan Wildlife Sanctuary (705.77 km^2) to the south and Hab Dam Wildlife Sanctuary (272.19 km^2) to the south-west. Surjan, Sumbak, Eri and Hothiano Game Reserve (406.32 km^2) lies just to the east of the park. There are two tourist centers in the Park managed by Sind Wildlife Management Board, namely Khar and Karchat. The centres offer cottage and dormitory accommodation and guides are available. There are some 671km of unmetalled roads within the park, most of which are negotiable only by four-wheel drive vehicle.

Kirti Chakra : Kirti Chakra is an Indian military decoration awarded for valor, courageous action or self-sacrifice away from the battlefield. It may be awarded to civilians as well as military personnel, including posthumous awards. It is the peacetime equivalent of the Maha Vir Chakra. It is second in order of precedence of peacetime gallantry awards; it comes after Ashoka Chakra and before Shaurya Chakra. Before 1967, the award was known as the Ashoka Chakra, Class II.

Kirti Mandir : Porbandar which is a seaside town in Saurashtra was the birth place of the Father of Nation. It has also a mythological association. Lord Krishna's classmate, Sudana hailed from this place. The town was formerly known as Sudanapuri. The house where Mahatma Gandhi was born has been turned into a national monument Kirti Mandir. The memorial contains within it a library of books on Gandhism, a spinning hall, a children's nursery and a prayer hall where prayers of all faith are held regularly.

Kishore Kumar : Kishore Kumar was one of the most popular play back singer in Hindi films. He was not only a singer but also an actor, producer and director. He was more popular among the young people because of his gay style of singing.

He was born at Khandwa, Madhya pradesh on August 4, 1929. Later he came to Mumbai and began his career as a musician. Kishore's real name was Abhas Kumar Ganguly. He sang thousands of songs. Some of his songs became memorable. His song 'Marne Ki duyaen kyon mangu' gave him instant popularity. He gave his voice to top actors of that time like Dev Anand, Rajesh Khanna and Amithabh Bachchan. Kishore acted in about 81 films, both Hindi and Bengali. His famous films were Bhai Bhai (1956), Asha (1957), Musafir (1957), Jhungroo (1961) Door Gagan kki chaon mein (1964) and Padosan (1968). Some of his memorable songs are 'Ek Ladki Bhigi Bhagi si', 'Yeh dil na hota Bechara', 'yeh sham mastani', 'Mere sapno ki rani', 'Tere mere milan ki raina' and 'Jindagi ka safar'. He died on October 13, 1987. It was a great loss to the music world and his fans.

Kishtawar National Park : The park was started in 1981, covering an area of 310sq. km in Kishtawar district. The nearest town is Kishtawar at a distance of 60km. The airport and railhead for the park are at Jammu at a distance of about 245km. The fauna of the park include musk deer, Kashmir stag, Languor markhar, ibex, Himalayan tahr, black bear, leopard cat, leopard and snow leopard. The birds commonly found are monal pleasant, golden eagle, koklas, golden oriole, flycatcher.

Kite Festival : It is amusing and well - known festival organized on 14th January every year in India. The kitists from all over the world demonstrate unimaginable kite forms and skills at this festival.

K J Yesudas : Padmashree Dr. Kattassery Joseph Yesudas, the great South Indian singer, was born on 10th January 1940 in Fort Cochin, Kerala. Born to parents Augustine Joseph Bhagavathar and mother Elizabeth Joseph, Yesudas was initiated into Carnatic music at a very young age by his father who was a classical musician himself. Although financially restrained, his father recognizing the boy's musical talent decided to provide him musical education at any cost. His decision proved to be right...a great musician was born, with mastery over both classical and light music who has over 30000 song recordings to his credit in a career spanning four decades.

Yesudas got his first recognition at the tender age of seven, when he won a gold medal for music at a local competition in Fort Cochin. He went on to have training from the Music Academy, Tripunithura and Swati Tirunal Music Academy, Trivandrum and obtained diplomas in 'Sangeetha-bhushanam' and 'Ganabhushanam'. Initially he struggled a lot for a break and suffered many hardships when he roamed around Chennai looking for an opening, living mainly on tap water and faced rejections from music directors and All India Radio Trivandrum. But young Yesudas patiently endured and persisted to achieve his life's goal. He became closely associated with 'Kalabhavan', an art institute which encouraged upcoming artists, began to give public concerts and started becoming popular and at last in 1961, he got a break as a playback singer in the Malayalam film ' Kalpadukal' directed by K.S Antony. The rest is history.

Dr. Yesudas soon was making a mark for himself, tearing down language barriers and singing in all South Indian languages and later almost all Indian languages. In 1976, Salil Chaudhary gave him a chance in Hindi films with 'Anand Mahal'. Although his number ' Aa Aa Re Mitwa' in the film was noticed, it was the film 'Chitchor' that really launched him in Hindi films. 'Gori Tera Gaon Bada Pyaara' and 'Jab Deep Jale Aana' were two of his memorable numbers of which the former earned him the National award for best singer in 1979. He has won the coveted National award seven times- in 1977 for the song "Manushyan Mathangale Sristichu" in the film 'Achanum Bappayum' (Malayalam), "Padmatheerthame" in the film 'Gayathri' (Malayalam,1973), 'Chitchor' (Hindi,1979), 'Mekha Sandesham' (Telugu, 1985), 'Unnikale Oru Katha Parayaam' (Malayalam, 1987), in 1992 for 'Bharatham' (Malayalam) and in 1993 for 'Sopanam' (Malayalam).

He has also won numerous state awards to the extend of monopolizing the Kerala state award at one time and other awards & honours in recognition of his talent. He received the 'Padmashri' from the President of India in 1977 and in 1991 an honorary doctorate degree from the Annamalai University, Chennai in recognition for his contributions to music and art. Government of Kerala honoured him with the title 'Asthana Gayakan'. He also became a Senate member in the International Parliament for Safety and Peace, an organization incorporated in the U.S. More recently he received the Padma Bhushan from the President of India in January 2002.

Yesudas who is a down to earth, humble person believes in Shri Narayana Guru's principle of 'One caste, One religion and One God for all'. In spite of his popularity in film Music he enjoys Carnatic classical more. In 1980 he launched a recording studio Tharangini in Thiruvanathapuram. He has many album releases to his credit including devotional, light and classical music. Married to Prabha his devoted fan of many years, the couple has three boys Vinod, Vijay and Vishal. His second son Vijay follows his fathers footsteps in Music. This Musical maestro, shifts base frequently from Madras to Fort Lauderdale, Florida, USA where he has a studio and back and continues to enchant his fans with his wonderful voice.

K Kamaraj : K Kamaraj (July 15, 1903–1975) was an Indian politician widely known as a kingmaker in Indian politics. He was instrumental in bringing to power two Prime Ministers, Lal Bahadur Shastri in 1964 and Indira Gandhi in 1966. He was involved in the Indian independence movement and was a close ally of Jawaharlal Nehru, the first Prime Minister of India. He was born to Kumarasamy and Sivakami Ammal at Virudhunagar in Tamil Nadu. His was from a poor family belonging to the Nadar caste (a mercantile caste) and retained a spartan life style and bachelorhood throughout his lifetime. Despite dropping out of school in the seventh grade he rose to political prominence joining the struggle for Indian independence at the age of sixteen.

Kamaraj became Chief Minister of Madras Presidency in 1954 and ruled the state for thirteen years. He was also president of the Indian National Congress for five years. As Chief Minister, he initiated massive reforms in the educational and the social sectors of the state. He introduced the Mid-day meal scheme in Tamil Nadu, which was later popularised by M. G. Ramachandran and this scheme is being considered by the Government of India to be introduced in all public schools in the country. It was his government, which built most of the existing dams in Tamil Nadu.

Kamaraj is known for his honesty, integrity and simplicity. He denied any special treatments extended to him or his mother just because he was the chief minister. He lived in a rented house and had a possession of only 120 rupees and 6 dhothis when he died—a hard gesture from a Chief Minister of Indian history. He was awarded the Bharat Ratna, the highest civilian award posthumously in 1976.

K Karunakaran : K. Karunakaran (born July 5, 1918) is a veteran Congress party leader, freedom fighter, trade unionist, and former Chief Minister of Kerala, India. Like many during his time, he entered into politics during India's freedom struggle. He started off as an activist in the Kochi Rajya Praja Mandalam and later entered electoral politics as member of the Thrissur Municipal Council from 1945 - 1947. He was a founding member of the INTUC. He was elected 7 times to the Kerala Legislative Assembly between 1965 and 1995 and served as Chief Minister four times.

Due to the differences in opinions with the Congress Leadership, Karunakaran left the Congress Party and formed a new party called Democratic Indira Congress (Karunakaran). His children are also active in the state politics.

K Karunanidhi : Kalaignar Muthuvel Karunanidhi (born June 3, 1924) is one of the founder members and the present leader of the DMK party in Tamil Nadu, India. He is the president of the DMK party since 1969. He has been the Chief Minister of Tamil Nadu four times (1969-71, 1971-74, 1989-91, and 1996-2001).

Karunanidhi started his career as a script-writer working in the Tamil film industry, but his wit and oratorical skills rapidly made him a popular politician. He was famous for writing historicals and mythological stories which propagated the socialist and rationalist ideals of Dravidian movement to which he belonged to. His long political career has spanned over 60 years. He has championed the cause of Tamil language in the past and has rallied against the "imposition" of Hindi in Tamil Nadu. According to him "Hindi is like 'carrier food' from the hotel; English is the food made by cook according to one's instructions; and Tamil, food from the mother who knows the family's needs and preferences, and feeds them accordingly". Although this has been hailed by Tamil fanatics it has been ascribed as the prime cause for lack of Hindi knowledge amongst Tamilians.

His son, M.K. Stalin is widely expected to succeed him as leader of the party, causing some political opponents to criticise him for attempting to establish a political dynasty. His defenders counter that Stalin has been in the party for several years and has contributed to its growth. His grand-nephew, Dayanidhi Maran, is currently the Union Minister of Communications & Information Technology.

K Kelappan : K. Kelappan was born in a small village of Calicut District in Kerala on August 24, 1889. In the Days of his college life at Calicut and Madras he acquired an abiding interest in social service and higher values of life. He began his career as a teacher at Changanachery and was the founder President of Nair Service Society. Thereafter, he joined studies in Law at Bombay.

When Mahatma Gandhi gave his call for boycott of the British, Kelappan gave up his studies and decided to dedicate his life in the service of his Motherland. He lead an eventful life fighting the evils present in Indian society on the one hand and fighting the British on the other. He blossomed forth as an ideal Satyagrahi. He was an energetic revolutionary, social reformer and crusader for justice to the downtrodden.

During the Malabar rebellion he faced a group of rebels who came to loot the Ponnani Treasury and persuaded them to retreat by appealing to their good sense. He gave the lead to the Payyannur and Calicut salt Satyagraha and was chosen as the first Satyagrahi from Kerala in the individual satyagraha movement launched by Gandhiji. He played a dominant role in the famous Vaikom Satyagraha and was the hero of Guruvayoor Satyagraha in 1932. It was at Gandhiji's request that he ended his fast at Guruvayoor. He went to jail several times during the freedom struggle. He worked hard for eradication of untouchability and worked for upliftment of Harijans. He set up many Harijan hostels and schools in Kerala. He was in the forefront of Swadeshi Movement and did his best to build up a base of Khadi and Village industries.

After the independence of the country he gave up party politics and joined Sarvodaya Movement. He was the President of almost all major Gandhian organisations like Kerala Sarvodaya Sangh, Kerala Gandhi Samarak Nidhi, Kerala Sarvodaya Mandal and Gandhi Peace Foundation, Calicut. A part from above he was an educationist as well as an accomplished and forceful journalist. He helped in starting 'Mathrubhoomi' and was its editor for a number of years. He worked for unification of Kerala into a new linguistic state. He never aspired for power or position. His whole life was a saga of selfless service to the nation. Since the people of Kerala came to understand Gandhiji and his programmes essentially through Kelappan, he was popularly known as Kerala Gandhi. His life of service ended on October 7, 1971.

K M Beenamol : K Mathews Beenamol, popularly known as K M Beenamol is an international athlete from India. Beenamol became the second Indian to reach an Olympics semi-final since P.T. Usha. Until she won an electrifying first heat at the Sydney Olympics 2000, Beenamol was largely unknown. She won the gold medal in women's 800m. at Busan Asian Games(2002).

Beenamol also made history with her brother athlete K. M. Binu when they became the first Indian siblings to win medals in a major international competition. Binu won a surprise silver medal in men's 800m race. She was a joint winner of India's highest sporting honour, the Rajiv Gandhi Khel Ratna award in the year 2002-2003 along with

Anjali Ved Pathak Bhagwat. In 2004, she was awarded the Padma Shri.

K M Munshi : Kanhaiyalal Maneklal Munshi (1887 to 1971) was an Indian freedom fighter from the state of Gujarat. A lawyer by profession, he then turned to literature and politics. Munshi was born on 30th December, 1887 in the town of Bharuch in Gujarat. He got his education in Vadodara, where he excelled in academics. He later practised in Bombay High Court.

Munshi was an active participant in the Indian Independence Movement ever since the advent of Mahatma Gandhi. He joined the Swaraj Party but returned to the Indian National Congress with the launch of the Salt Satyagraha in 1930. He was arrested several times, including during the Quit India Movement of 1942. A great admirer of Sardar Vallabhbhai Patel, Munshi served in the Central Legislative Assembly in the 1930s.

After the independence of India, Munshi went as the diplomatic envoy and trade agent to the princely state of Hyderabad, where he served until its accession in 1948. He was also part of the ad hoc Flag Committee that selected the Flag of India in August 1947, and one of the members of the committee which drafted the Constitution of India under the chairmanship of Dr. B. R. Ambedkar

Munshi founded the Bharatiya Vidya Bhavan in 1938 in Bombay. Bhavan's is one of the leading educational and cultural institution in India. Munshi separated from the Nehru-dominated Congress Party and joined the newly formed Swatantrata Party led by Chakravarti Rajgopalachari, which was right-wing in its politics and pro-business, pro-free market economy and private property rights. The party enjoyed limited success, and had died out. However later KM Munshi joined the Jan Sangh. He and Purushottam Das Tandon were among those who strongly opposed propagation and conversion in the constituent assembly. He served as the Governor of Indian State of Uttar Pradesh from 1952 to 1957.

Besides being a politician and educationist, K.M. Munshi was also an environmentalist. He initiated the Van Mahotsav in 1950, when he was Union Minister of Agriculture and Food, to increase the area under forest cover. Since then Van Mahotsav a week long festival of tree plantation is organised every year in the month of July all across the country and lakhs of trees are planted.

Munshi was also litterateur with a wide range of interests. He has enriched genres like the novel, short story, biography, autobiography,etc. He is specially known for his historical novels in Gujarati. His trilogy Patanni Prabhuta (The Greatness of Patan), Gujaratno Nath (The Ruler of Gujarat) and Rajadhiraj (The Emperor) is considered significant in the literature of Gujarat. His other works include Jay Somnath, Krishnavatara and Bhagavan Parasurama.

Knnbi-Geet : Kunnbi-geet is a folk song of Goa, prevalent among the hardy labourers called Kunnbis which are sung to the accompaniment of the ghumatt and the drum and the clang of cymbals. These Kunnbis are found concentrated in the Chandor-Kouddi hamlet of Chandor in an exclusive ward of their own called Kunbeam-Vaddo now being called by them as Miream-Jirem. The theme of their songs varies from romantic love to bitter resentment and satire couched in suggestive language against their landlords (Bhakar) who have usurped their lands and are exploiting them. The Kunnbis sing songs at different times, like at different stages of cultivation of rice. It is done at the time of Nondnni (weeding), Mollnni (threshing), Luvnni (harvesting). Winnowing does not find expression in songs. There are also songs with reference to the rain and its bounty.

Kobadak River : Kobadak river is the pre-Dravidian term 'Kabadak' was transformed into 'Kapotaksha' (Kapotaksa) (the 'pigeon-eyed') in Sanskrit. The river Ichamati branched into two streams at Darshana in Kushtia district. One flowing southeast is known as the Bhairab. At the south of Kotchandpur, an offshoot branches out from the Bhairab and flowing south meets with the Shibsa near Paikgachha in Khulna district. This offshoot of the Bhairab is the Kobadak. Once upon a time, the water of this river was clear and transparent like the eyes of a bird. 'Kapot' means pigeon and 'Aksha' means eye.

Kochi : Kochi (often known by the Portuguese name of Cochin) is the largest (pop. 1,355,000 in 2001) city in the state of Kerala, India, and one of the principal seaport in the country. Also known as "Queen of the Arabian Sea", Kochi is located in the district of Ernakulam, about 220 km north of the state capital Thiruvananthapuram. Old Kochi loosely refers to a group of islands and peninsula including Willingdon Island, Fort Kochi, Mattancherry, etc. Today Kochi includes Ernakulam city, old parts of Kochi, Kumbalangi, and outlying islands. For many centuries up to and during the British Raj, the city of Cochin was the seat of the eponymous princely state. The history of that state is detailed at Kingdom of Kochi.

The city derives its name from the Malayalam word "Kochazhi" meaning small lagoon. This was changed to Cochin by Europeans for easy pronunciation. The city reverted to its original name "Kochi" in 1996. The city is still widely referred to as "Cochin".

Kodachadri : Kodachadri is a mountain peak (altitude - 1343 m above sea level) in the Western Ghats in South India (Karnataka State). The name is a corruption of the Sanskrit word "Kutakachalam." Kodachadri forms a picturesque background to the famous temple of Mookambika in Kollur. Situated in the middle of the

Mookambika National Park, it is home to several endemic and endangered species of flora and fauna. Tha rain forests loom in a perpetual layer of mist around the peak.

Kodagu : Kodagu (also called Coorg, especially in English) is a district of Karnataka state, India. It occupies about 4100 sq. km. in the Western Ghats of southwestern Karnataka. It is bordered by Dakshina Kannada to the northwest, Hassan district to the north, Mysore District to the east, Kannur District of Kerala state to the southwest and Wayanad district of Kerala to the south. The district town is Madikeri. Kodagu in Kannada and Coorg in English are derived from the local version Kodavu and the people Kodava. The name Kodavu is supposed to have been derived from Kodimalenad meaning higher forest land. Puranic version says, that the land of initial settlement was called Krodadesa which later became Kodavu. The word Kodava means the people blessed by Godmother Kaveri ('Kod' means give, bless and 'avva' means mother Kaveri) is supported by the puranic version.

Kodaikanal : Kodaikanal (also known as Kodai) is a hill station on the southern tip of the upper Palani Hills in Dindigul District of the state of Tamil Nadu in southern India. Kodai is also a minor tourist attraction, and many of the locals make their living through tourist services. Kodaikanal is sometimes referred to as "Princess of Hill stations".

Kodaikanal is located at a latitude of 10°7' N to 10°20' N and a longitude of 77°16' E to 77°45' E. Kodaikanal is situated at an altitude of about 2,133 m. Kodaikanal is a popular tourist destination, having many natural attractions such as waterfalls, a beautiful lake, and many scenic mountain view points. There is a beautiful site known as Coaker's Walk with magnificent views down to the plains. There is also a huge park with lots of eucalyptus trees and banyan trees known as Bryant Park. Views from Kodai are dominated by Mount Perumal, an extinct volcano.

Kodandera Madappa Cariappa : Field Marshal Kodandera Madappa Cariappa (28 January 1899—15 May 1993) was the first Indian Chief of Staff and led the Indian forces on the Western Front during the Indo-Pakistan War of 1947. He is among only two Indian military officers to hold the highest ceremonial rank of Field Marshal (the other being Field Marshal Sam Manekshaw). His distinguished military career spanned almost three decades, at the highest point of which, he was appointed as the Commander-in-Chief of the Indian Military in 1949. Cariappa settled down amidst greenery and nature, in his own Roshanara at Madikeri after his retirement from public service.

He loved the environment and the flora and fauna around him. He lived a life of simplicity and dignity, which was the hallmark of a man. He spent a lot of his leisure time educating people about cleanliness, pollution control and other essential issues. On 15 May 1993, Field Marshal Cariappa breathed his last in Bangalore at an age of 94.

Kodava Takk : Kodava Takk (literally Kodava language), is the original language of the south Karnataka district of Kodagu. The language is often called Coorgi or Coorg language in English. The number of speakers is estimated at around 300,000. It is the primary language of Kodavas, but a large portion of other communities and tribes in Kodagu also use Kodava Thakk. It belongs to the Dravidian languages family, and is related to and influenced by Kannada, Tamil and Malayalam. Kodava Takk also has words which do not sound similar to words in other Indian languages. Kodava Takk has no written script and usually Kannada script is used to write it.

Kodungallur : Kodungallur (anglicised name: Cranganore) and known in ancient times as Shinkli, Muchiri (anglicised to Muziris), Muyirikkodu,

Muchiripattinam was a famous and prosperous sea-port at the mouth of the Periyar (also known as Choorni Nadi) river in the southern Indian state of Kerala. It is located about 38 km from the present day city of Kochi at 10°13′N 76°13′E.

The name Muchiri (Malayalam for broken lips) denotes the three branches of the Periyar river that open into the Arabian Sea at the town. Kodungallur was a critical trade link in Indian Ancient Maritime History. It was known as Muziris to Pliny the Elder (N.H. 6.26) who describes it as primum emporium Indiae. The port was familiar to the author of the Periplus of the Erythraean Sea which described it as being situated on river Pseudostomos (Greek for "false mouth"—a precise translation of the Malayalam description of the mouth of the Periyar, Alimukam) two miles from its mouth.

The ancient Greek explorer, Hippalus landed at this port after discovering the patterns of the Indian monsoon trade winds on his way from the East coast of Africa. The evidence of the Peutinger Table suggests that there was a temple to the Roman emperor Augustus. The Greeks, the Romans (known locally as the Yavanas), and the Jews all have come to this place at different times in its ancient history. Roman gold and silver coins bearing impressions of Roman Emperors Tiberius and Nero were discovered in the village of Parur near the town during 2000.

A second-century papyrus from Egypt concerning the transshipment of goods originating in Muziris from the Red Sea to Alexandria attests the continued importance of the port in the Indian Ocean commerce a century after Pliny and the Periplus. Thomas the Apostle of Jesus with his followers landed in Cranganore in the year AD 52 and preached the gospel. It thus became the earliest Nasrani Syrian Christian centre of Malabar with monuments built in the memory of Thomas still existing. The existence of a thriving Christian Community here attracted the attention of others and the Bishops who came from Persia chose this place for their residence. The bones of the right hand of St Thomas were placed in 1953 as a memento.

Malik Ibn Dinar and 20 others who were the followers of Prophet Muhammad, the founder of Islam, first landed here when they came to India. Islam received royal patronage in some states here, and later spread to other parts of India. Kodungallur was also the capital of Cheraman Perumal, that is known as the famous cherama Palli the last Chera ruler, in the 7th century AD. After this, This place was ruled by Perumpadapu Swaroopam till India's Independence.

Kohat : Kohat is a town in central North West Frontier Province in Pakistan. Kohat is the capital of Kohat District. The town contains a British-era fort with a pool, a Pashtun bazaar, the tomb of the Sufi teacher Haji Bahadar Ali Abdullah Shah, a mosque and a school. The Narrow Gauge Railway runs through the town. To the north of Kohat lies the Kohat Pass.

Kohat Pass : Kohat Pass is a mountain pass in the North-West Frontier Province of Pakistan, connecting Kohat with Peshawar, crossing the Khigana Mountain. As the current road to the pass is steep and too narrow for large vehicles, an alternate tunnel is being constructed.

Kohima : Kohima is a hilly town which serves as the capital of India's north eastern border state of Nagaland. It shares its borders with Burma. It lies in Kohima District and is the second largest urban hub in Nagaland after Dimapur-Chumukedima.Kohima is also one of the three Nagaland towns with Municipal council status alongwith Dimapur and Mokokchung. In 1944 during World War II the Battle of Kohima along with the simultaneous Battle of Imphal was the turning point in the Burma Campaign.

For the first time in South-East Asia the Japanese lost the initiative to the Allies which they then retained until the end of the war.

Koh-i-Noor : The Koh-i-Noor, Koh-i-Nur, or Kohinoor is a 105 carat diamond that originated in the Indian subcontinent and belonged to various rulers at different points in its history, very often passing from one to another by force or deceit. In 1851 the diamond was given, in controversial circumstances, to Queen Victoria and taken to Britain. It is currently in the consort's crown made for Queen Elizabeth, consort of crown King George VI of the United Kingdom, and part of the Crown Jewels of the United Kingdom. Like all significant jewels, the Koh-i-Noor diamond has its share of legends. This particular stone is reputed to bring misfortune or death to any male who wears or owns it—a claim which its history has, so far, not disproven. Conversely, it is reputed to bring good luck to women owners. It is, by legend, worth the amount of wealth generated around the whole world in seven days.

Kohlu : Kohlu district is in the center of Balochistan province of Pakistan. Kohlu was notified as a district on 6th February 1974 after it was separated from Sibi district. At that time it comprised 5 tehsils : Kohlu, Mawand, Kahan, Sui and Dera Bugti. In July 1983, Sui and Dera Bugti tehsils were transferred from Kohlu district to form Dera Bugti district. In this way Kohlu district was left with three subdivisions-cum-tehsils; namely Kohlu, Mawand and Kahan. Kohlu tehsil is divided into 2 qanungo circles, Urayani and Kote Shehr.

Kokborok : Kokborok is the native language of the Tripuri community in the northeast Indian state of Tripura. The word Kokborok is composed of two words, kok which means "language" and borok which literally means "man" but is used to denote the Tripuri people. Thus Kokborok means "the language of man" or "the language of the Borok people". There is a community of Kokborok speakers in neighbouring Bangladesh.

Kolaghat : Kolaghat is situated on the banks of the Rupnarayan River in the Midnapore West district of West Bengal, and is famous for its Hilsa (Ilish) fishes. It is home to one of the largest thermal power plants in India. This is run by West Bengal Power Development Corporation Limited (WBPDCL) of the West Bengal Government. The riverside has become a popular picnic spot and is often crowded with people, particularly during the Christmas and New Year holidays. The Hilsa fish harvested from the Rupnarayan River has become quite famous in Bengali cuisine.

Kolar : Kolar is a district in Karnataka state of India. Kolar town is the district headquarters. Among other things, this district is famous for the large quantities of gold that are available for extraction in the Kolar gold mines. Kolar is popularly known as the golden land of India, for it is at the famous Kolar Gold Fields of this district that gold mining was first undertaken during modern times.

Kolatam : Kolatam is a play with sticks in Andhra Pradesh. This is known as Hallisaka and Dandarasaka in Sanskrit. In olden days females used to play Kolatam in temple halls as a devotional offering. Now the Kolatam played by males is a folk art form. A troupe consists of twenty to forty members or the least eight members. There are even numbers of players and a leader in every troupe. The troupe leader is called Pennuddi or Kolanna Pantulu or Garuva. He controls and leads the troupe. A pair of two players is called Uddi in which one is called Rama and the other is Lakshmana. All the players form a big circle in the beginning and change into two circles one in another. The leader along with the Mridangam, flute, harmonium and cymbal players, stand in the middle of the inner circle. Each player holds two sticks one in each hand with coloured strings or bells tied to their ends.

As soon as the leader signals, pairs in the circle starts moving with a prayer to Lord Ganesha. The leader then cries out the rhythm Etlugada and begins a song. The songs are in different rhymes and beats. They may be prayers, duets, descriptions or narratives delineating Bhakti, Sringara, Karuna and Virarasa.

The variety in steps is called Kopulu. There are 50 kinds of kopulu as maximum and minimum number ranges from six to twelve. When the troupe leader sings the first line of the song the players sing the second line and strike the sticks moving or jumping forward and backward in the circles. The leader whistles and changes the speed to a high crescendo. This is called 'Usi'. The players accordingly move with fast steps maintaining the speed for some time and stop with Muktayimpu. The troupe leader then takes up another Kopu and the Kolatam continues with different style.

There is a special type of Kolatam called 'Jada Kolatam' or 'Veni Kolatam'. This is more popular in Karnataka. The troupe consisting of 12 to 18 players holding coloured strings or ropes tied above to a pole or branch of a tree form into a circle. The circle's movements inside and outside are so well timed and executed that the ropes hanging from the top become plaited to form a Jada or veni. When the troupe dances anticlockwise the ropes are unwound again, colourful ribbons on platforms during ceremonial occasions.

Kolhapur : Kolhapur is a beautiful city, situated in the south west corner of Maharashtra, India. The population of Kolhapur is around 419,000. The main languages are Marathi, Hindi, and English. It is popular for its Mahalaksmi temple. It is situated on the banks of the river

Panchganga. Many hills and forts like Panhala fort and Jothiba temple hill surround the city. The city is also famous for training wrestlers. There is national stadium for a form of wrestling known as Khasbag. It is also famous for making leather footware, popularly known as Kolhapuri Chappals and sugar products.

Kolkali : It is a group dance form of the farming community in Kerala.

Kolkata : Kolkata, formerly known as Calcutta is the capital of the Indian state of West Bengal and is situated on the east bank of river Hooghly. The urban agglomeration of Kolkata is India's second largest with a population of more than 13 million. It was the capital of British India until 1911 when the capital was shifted to New Delhi. Once one of the most important cities of the British Empire, the city lost out on much of its past glory and economic importance in the years following Indian independence, though it is now undergoing a process of economic uplift and revival. Today, it is a vibrant city with its own distinct social and political culture. Kolkata is noted for its revolutionary history, from the pre-independence era to the Naxalite movements. Kolkata was the home of luminaries like Rabindranath Tagore, Amartya Sen, Mother Teresa, and Satyajit Ray, and is often referred to as the "cultural capital of India" as well as "the city of processions" and "the city of joy".

The name Kolkata appears to have been derived from Ḳalikata, one of the three villages in the area before the arrival of the British. It seems likely that both Calcutta and Kolkata were derived from "Kalikata" with the former being an anglicised version. In an act that was largely seen as a political move, a decision was taken by the state government to change the name of Calcutta to Kolkata, which consequently resulted in the passage of the law legalising the name on July 30, 2001.

Kollam : Kollam, (known to the Portuguese as Quilon), is a city in the state of Kerala, India. It is also the headquarters of a district by the same name, one among the 14 districts in the state of Kerala, India. It is bound on the south by Thiruvananthapuram district, on the north by Pathanamthitta and Alappuzha, on the east by Tamil Nadu and on the west by the Arabian Sea. It has one of the largest fresh water lakes. It is a very beautiful place to visit. The district is very famous for cashew processing and coir manufacturing. About thirty per cent of this district is covered by the Ashtamudi Lake, thereby making it a gateway to the Kerala Backwaters. India's most popular English magazine India Today has rated Kollam as the best district in the country in terms of law and order and social harmony. The second tallest light house in India stands tall at Tangasseri in Kollam. Tourist spots such as Thenmala, Jetayu para, and Kuttalam falls are popular attractions.

During the rule of the Travancore kingdom in southern Kerala, Kollam was the focal point of their trade. The metre gauge railway administered by Indian Railways terminates at Kollam, making the Kollam Railway station a junction station. The district is well connected to other parts of Kerala and India through the National Highways 47, 206, and 101 and by the railway network. The Apostle Thomas founded one of his "seven and a half churches" in Kollam. From these seven and a half churches, including the one in Kollam, have multiplied thousands of churches, hospitals, orphanages and other Christian charities that cover India today. The Mata Amritanandamayi Math is situated in Amritapuri in this district, about 30 km from the Kollam town.

Kollam District : Kollam district, earlier called Quilon district, is one of the 14 districts of Kerala state, India. The district is representative of all the natural attributes of Kerala states, and is endowed with a long coastal region, a major sea port on the Arabian Sea, plains and the mountains, lakes, lagoons and Kerala Backwaters, forests and the farm land, and rivers and streams. The area had mercantile relationship with Phoenicians and the Romans.

Kolleru Lake : Kolleru Lake is a large freshwater lake in India's Andhra Pradesh state. It is located between the deltas of the Krishna and Godavari rivers, in Krishna and West Godavari districts. The lake serves as a natural flood-balancing reservoir for the two rivers. The lake is fed directly by the seasonal Budameru and Tammileru rivers, and is connected to the Krishna and Godavari systems by 30 inflowing drains and channels. The lake also serves as an important habitat for up to 50,000 resident and migratory birds, including the Grey or Spot-Billed Pelican (Pelecanus philippensis). The lake was declared a wildlife sanctuary in November 1999 under India's Wildlife Protection Act, and designated a wetland of international importance in November 2002 under the international Ramsar Convention.

Satellite images taken on February 9, 2001 by the Indian remote sensing satellite IRS-1D and analysed by Dr. K Nageswara Rao from Andhra University found that approximately 42 per cent of the 245 km² lake was occupied by aquaculture, while agriculture had encroached on another 8.5 percent. The area under aquaculture consisted of 1050 fishponds within the lake and 38 dried-up fish ponds, which together covered an area of 103 km². The agricultural encroachments were mostly rice paddies. No clear water could be found in the satellite image. The rest of the lake was being diminished by water diversions or was infested with weeds like elephant grass and water hyacinth. This lake is under troubles from poachers now.

Kolleru Lake Bird Sanctuary : Kolleru lake in Andhra Pradesh is a virtual paradise for nature lovers. It is the largest fresh water lake in Asia. Rich in flora and fauna, it attracts migratory birds from Australia, Siberia, Egypt and Philippines.

Kollur : Kollur is a tiny hamlet situated at Kundapur, about 140 km away from Mangalore. Lying at the foot of the Western Ghats, Kollur is famous for the Mookambika temple, a Hindu pilgrim centre. It is believed that Sri Adi Shankaracharya had a vision of Sri Mookambika Devi and he installed the diety here.

Konark : Konark (or Konarak) is a small town in the state of Orissa, India, on the Bay of Bengal, sixty-five kilometres from Bhubaneswar. This is the site of the 13th-century Sun Temple (also known as the Black Pagoda), built in black granite by King Narasimhadeva I (AD 1236-1264) of the Ganga dynasty. The temple is one of the most important Brahman sanctuaries, and is a world heritage site. It takes the form of the chariot of Surya (Arka), the sun god, and is heavily decorated with stone carving. The entire complex was designed in the form of a huge chariot drawn by seven spirited horses on twelve pairs of exquisitely decorated wheels. The entrance is guarded by two lions, which are shown crushing a war elephant each. Each elephant in turn lies on top a human body.

The temple symbolises the majestic stride of the Sun god. At the entrance of the temple is a Nata Mandir. This is where the temple dancers used to perform dances in homage to the Sun-god. All around the temple, there are various floral and geometric patterns. There are also human, divine and semi-divine figures in sensuous poses. The poses contains couples in various amorous poses, and are derived from the Kama Sutra. The temple is now partly in ruins, and a collection of its sculptures is housed in the Sun Temple Museum, which is run by the Archaeological Survey of India. Konark is also home to an annual dance festival, held every December, devoted to classical Indian dance forms, including the traditional classical dance of Orissa, odissi. Konark beach is a popular tourist destination, though the waters are deceptively calm. Its main attraction lies in its views of the temple.

Koneru Humpy : Koneru Humpy (born 31 March 1987) is a chess grandmaster from India. Her April 2005 FIDE Elo rating is 2508, placing her at number five in the world for women.

In 2001 Humpy won the World Junior Girls Chess Championship.

Konkan : The Konkan, also called the Konkan Coast or Karavali is the name given to a stretch of rugged and beautiful section of the western coastline of India from Ratnagiri to Mangalore. The sapta-Konkan is a slightly larger region described in the Skanda-purana. Konkan is also one of six divisions of the state of Maharashtra. Residents of Konkan and their descendants are called Konkanis. The name may also refer specifically to the Konkani people, an ethnic group of the region; most of them speak the Konkani language, which is related to Marathi. The Sanskrit term Konkanashta, meaning "Native of Konkan", is used to refer to the Chitpawan, a Brahmin caste of the region.

Konkan Railway : The Konkan Railway (Railway Symbol:KR) is a zone of the Indian Railways which operates along the Konkan coast of India. Due to the uneven terrain of the region, railway lines were not laid for many years. National leaders such as Madhu Dandavate who hailed from Konkan played a major role in the conception of Konkan Railway. It was constituted as a separately incorporated railway, with its headquarters at CBD Belapur in Navi Mumbai and E. Sreedharan as its first Chairman and Managing Director. By May 1999, the

Konkan Railway had laid a 760km broad gauge route from Roha to Mangalore along the western coast of India (the Konkan region).

KR does not have divisions like the other Indian Railway, however, it has two regions with headquarters at Ratnagiri in Maharashtra and Karwar in Karnataka. The Ratnagiri region extends from Roha to Sawantwadi, while the Karwar region extends from Pernem to Thokur (the latter being where Southern Railway begins, a few stations north of Mangalore). The route is a single-line track, and is not electrified yet. It has been designed for high-speed traffic (160 km/h). It is open to goods and passenger traffic. The route, which runs parallel to the Arabian Sea coastline, offers some of the most spectacular views of any Indian rail journeys.

Konkani : Konkani is an Indo-Aryan language, although it includes a wealth of words derived from various Dravidian languages. It started as a vernacular of Sanskrit, with inevitable corruption of the words. It has been relatively free of influence of any other language except a little of Portuguese (in the last few centuries) and some Kannada (supposedly during the Kadamba period of 12-14th centuries). It is sometimes said to be a dialect of Marathi. But, history has established that even when the Konkani language had reached maturity, the Marathi language was not even born. There is an inscription written in Konkani dated 1187 A.D. whereas even the earliest Marathi manuscripts are of the 16th century. However, many people only recognized Konkani as an independent language since the 19th century.

Konkani People : The Konkani people are an Indian ethnic group. According to some, the word derives from "kum", meaning 'Mother Earth' and "Kana", meaning 'dust' or 'atom'. The Konkani within the Indian state of Goa have been principally a farming community through most of their history, though now moving increasingly towards tourism. The Konkani people in other states are mainly a business community. Their current centre is in Goa and are thought by some to have settled there around the 11th century CE. Outside of Goa, Konkani people are also settled along the Konkan coast with concentrated population in Mangalore, south coastal Maharashtra, north coastal Kerala and northern Karnataka.

The Konkani families are known to be large and extended. Most of the families have names like Kamath, Nayak,Bhat, Shanbhag,Puranik,Pai, Shenoy, Baliga, Acharya and Prabhu. Some of these names are derivatives of their profession or are conferred upon them by their Swami or religious head of the community. The Kamaths, Pais and the Shanbhags are known for their restaurants and hotels which are spread across the country.

Koodalmanikyam Temple : Koodalmanikyam Temple is the only Hindu temple in India where Bharatha (Lord Sangameshwar), the brother of Sree Rama is worshiped. This beautiful ancient temple is situated in Irinjalakuda a small town in Trissur district of Kerala state, south India. The speciality of this temple is that there is only one place of worship, even Ganapathy is not be found inside the temple. Usually all big temples in India will have more than one deity inside the temple, especially Sree Ganapathy. The temple is surrounded by four vast ponds. The pond inside the compound is believed to be sanctified by Kulipini Maharshi (Sage) who had held a great yaga here. The pond is known as Kulipini Theertham.

Seventeen elephants are engaged for the ceremonial rounds which happens once in a year for ten days, to the accomplishment of Panchari Melam. The head gears ('Netti pattam' in Malayalam language) of seven elephants are made of pure gold and rest of pure silver is another uniqueness of this temple.

Kootu : Kootu is a Tamil dish, common in Tamil Nadu and South India. It is fundamentally a vegetable stew, often cooked with coconut. As a rule it is not sour, since it does not use tamarind and usually does not use tomatoes. It is eaten along with rice that has been mixed with sambar. Its North Indian equivalent would be a curry, but it is never called that because curry in Tamil Nadu refers only to a dry curry, while anything in a gravy is classified as a kootu or kurma, depending on the spices used.The main ingredients of a kootu are lentils or Dal as they are called in India.

Korangi : Korangi is one of the neighborhoods of Landhi Town in Karachi, Sindh, Pakistan. There are several ethnic groups in Landhi Town including Urdu speakers, Punjabis, Sindhis, Kashmiris, Seraikis, Pakhtuns, Balochs, Memons, Bohras, Ismailis. Over 99% of the population is Muslim. The population of Landhi Town is estimated to be nearly one million.

Koraput : Koraput is a city in Koraput District, Orissa, India. This small town consists of 50 thousand population. Jeypore a historical city witnessing King Bikram Dev's Dynasty. National Aluminium Co.has its buxite mines nearby at Damanjodi. Three Hill Temples - A famous Lord Jagannath Temple, Lord Shiva Temple and Swamy Vivekananda Temple at three diferrent hilltops in three diferrent dimention of the town. Blessed with huge natural resources, beautiful natural landscapes, hills, waterfalls(at Kollab), lakes, the place Koraput is a place of pilgrimage and tourist interest. Boating at Chandan Pokhari (The Sandal Pond) attracts tourists to have magnificent experience. Koraput is well linked to Visakhapatnam (by road and rail), Rayagada, Howrah(by rail and road)and to the state capital Bhubaneswar(by rail and road). High Standard Lodging and Boading facilities are also provided by Lord Jagannath Temple Trust to outstation tourists.

Koraput : Koraput is a tribal dominated district of Orissa, India, and known for rich and diverse types of mineral deposits. It is located along the Eastern Ghats. This district abounds in meadows, forests, waterfalls, terraced valleys and darting springs. This land of abundance is home to Orissa's vast tribal population. A real paradise for the nature-lover, Koraput offers an additional benefit to the visitor of first hand meeting with its ancient civilization. In October, 1992, Koraput district was bifurcated, resulting in the creation of Malkangiri district.

Korba : Korba (population 315,965 (2001 census) is a center of Korba District in the newly formed state of Chhattisgarh, India (Nov.1, 2000). It is situated at the confluence of the Hasdeo and Ahiran rivers. Located at 22 20' North latitude and 82 42' East longitude, with a height of 304.8 meter above sea level. It is the major source of electricity in Chhattisgarh.

Korba city enjoys varied climates and weathers. Korba and Champa are well known for "Kosa", a precious cloth, producing the best quality in the world. Being light in weight and having shiny glaze, it is use to make Kurtas, Sarees, Shirts, Salwar-Suits and other garments for party as well as casual wears. Korba is connected to Champa, the nearest railway junction, on the Howrah-Nagpur-Mumbai, South Eastern Railway Zone. It is directly connected to Bilaspur the Divisional Head Quarter by rail and road through Katghora-Pali-Ratanpur. The nearest air-port is at Raipur, which is about 200 KM from Korba.

Koriya : Koriya is the administrative center of Koriya District in the north-east of the state of Chhattisgarh in India. The District came into existence on 25th May 1998 in Madhya Pradesh State. Its parent District was Surguja. After the formation of New State of Chhattisgarh on 1st November 2000, the District falls under the Chhattisgarh

State. The District has derived its Name from the Korea State, the former princely State Korea.The town of Koriya is about 369 km away from Raipur, the capital of Chhattisgarh.

Kosala : Kosala was an ancient Indian Aryan kingdom, corresponding roughly in area with the region of Oudh. Its capital was Ayodhya. In sixth century BCE, Kosala formed one of the sixteen powerful kingdoms (Mahajanapadas) of Buddhist traditions, but was weakened by a series of wars with the neighbouring kingdom of Magadha and finally (4th cent. B.C.) was absorbed by it. Kosala was the setting of much Sanskrit epic literature including the Ramayana. Buddha and Mahavira, founder of Jainism, taught in the kingdom.

Kot Bala : Kot Bala is loacted in Lasbela District, Balochistan, Pakistan. The Indus Civilization site of Kot Bala is located in the interior of the Sonmiani Bay, along the coast of Lasbela coast. It was partly excavated by Professor G. Dales of Berkeley University in the seventies and never published in detail. This site is of great importance for its location close to the Arabian Sea. It is supposed to be one of the main harbors from which the Indus traders sailed their ships to the coasts of the Arabian Peninsula.

Kot Diji : The ancient site at Kot Diji was the forerunner of the Indus Civilization. The people of this site lived about 3000 BC. The remains consist of two parts; the citadel area on high ground, and outer area. Located about 22 kilometres south of Khairpur in the province of Sindh, Pakistan. The site is situated at the foot of the hills where a fort was built by Talpur ruler Mir Suhrab (1803-30). This fort built on the ridge of a steep narrow hill is well preserved.

Kota : Kota (formerly Kotah) is a city in the northern Indian state of Rajasthan. Situated on the Chambal River, the city is the trade center for an area in which cotton, millet, wheat, coriander and oilseeds are grown; industries include cotton and oilseed milling, textile weaving, distilling, dairying, and the manufacture of metal handcrafts. The rail junction, a road hub, lies 4.8 km (3 mi) to the north.

The Crosthwaite Institute is located in Kota, as are old and new palaces of the Maharao (the maharaja). The city was formerly the capital of the princely state of Kota, formed in 1572. Population (1991) 537,371. Kota is also famous for its distinctive style of painting. Kota is well known for its saris, stone products and a vibrant education sector.

Kota Barrage : The Kota Barrage is part of the irrigation canal system on the Chambal River. Barrage operates 18 gates to control flow of flood and canal water downstream, and serves as bridge between parts of Kota on both side of the river. This beautiful setting is ideal for outings and evening strolls. Massive flow/froth of water during opening of gates in monsoon season — and accompanying vibration of bridge — are particular attraction among locals. Though in past, mis- or non-communication about the discharge of water to residents near river bank has resulted in lost of lives of persons engaged in swimming or washing activities downstream. Other Places worth visiting nearby include Kansua temple with a four faced Shiva Lingam, Bhitria Kund, Adhar Shila, Budh Singh Bafna Haveli and Yatayat Park

Kotappakonda Temple Fair : Kotappakonda in Narasaraopet taluk of Guntur district is a temple of Koteseswara Swamy, a chief place of worship. On the Mahashivarathri day, a big fair is held and lakhs of people participate in it. Sweet meats, clothes, bangles, toys, bamboo articles, and also goats, cows and other domestic animals are sold in this fair. Devotees who come here take a vow get their heads shaved. Many of them come to the hill from their villages with decorated and lighted prabhas to redeem their vows. These prabhas number about five hundred at the fair. Some of them are nearly thirty—five metres high and are expense.

Kotli : Kotli is a district of Azad Kashmir,, which in turn is part of the Pakistani-administered part of the former princely state of Jammu and Kashmir. There are two theories about the origin of the name "Kotli". One school of thought claims that in ancient times Prince Raja Shahswar Khan built a small residence here and called it "Kot", which became "Kotli". Another theory states that the name is derived from the Sanskrit word Kotli which means to reside or take up residence. At one stage the area was inhabited by the Mangran and Solhan peoples, and was called Kotli Solwhan. Kotli is well known for its mosques, and is often referred to as Madina-al-Masajed ("city of mosques").

Kottakkal : Kottakkal is 12 km south-west of Malappuram District in Kerala, south India. This place is famed for its pioneering ayurvedic institute known as Kottakkal Arya Vaidya Sala. Kottakkal Arya Vaidya Sala was founded in 1902 by Vaidyaratnam P.S. Warrier. This is one among the best ayurvedic clinics in Kerala and people from all over the world come here for treatment.

Kottayam : Kottayam is a city in the state of Kerala in southern India, located at 9.36 N and 76.17 E. It is the administrative headquarters of Kottayam District. Kottayam is the first town in India to have achieved 100% literacy, in 1989.

Kottayam District : Kottayam is one of the 14 districts in the state of Kerala, India. The district has its headquarters at Kottayam town, located at 9.36 N and 76.17 E. Bordered by the lofty and mighty Western Ghats on the east and the Vembanad Lake and paddy fields of Kuttanad on the west, Kottayam is a land of unique characteristics. Panoramic backwater stretches, lush paddy fields, highlands, hills and hillocks, extensive rubber plantations, places associated with many legends and a totally literate people have given Kottayam District the enviable title: The land of letters, legends, latex and lakes. Kottayam town is the first town in India to have achieved 100% literacy.

Kottayam literally means the interior of a fort—Kotta + Akam. Rulers of Munjanad and Thekkumkur had their headquarters at Thazhathangadi in the present Kottayam town. Marthanda Varma of Travancore attacked Thekkumkur and destroyed the palace and the Thaliyil Fort. The remnants of the palaces and forts are still seen here. The present Kottayam district was previously a part of the erstwhile princely state of Travancore. Earlier, the Travancore state consisted of two revenue divisions viz. the southern and northern divisions, under the administrative control of a 'Diwan Peshkar' for each. Later in 1868 two more divisions Quilon (Kollam) and Kottayam were constituted. The fifth division Devikulam came next but only for a short period, which in course of time, was added to Kottayam. At the time of the integration of the State of Travancore and Cochin (Kochi) in 1949, these revenue divisions were renamed as districts and the Diwan peshkars gave way to District Collectors, paving the way for the birth of the Kottayam District in July 1949.

Kovalam : Kovalam is 12kms to the south of Thiruvananthapuram and is one of the finest beaches in India. It has been developed into an integrated seaside resort. The beach complex has many hotels, cottages, yoga centres etc. Vizhinjam About 2kms south of Kovalam, it is believed to be an ancient port. The Dutch and Portugese had commercial establishments here. It is being developed as a modern fishing harbour.

Kozhencherry : Kozhencherry is a small town in Pathanamthitta district of Central Travancore region (South Central Kerala) in Kerala state, south India. Kozhencherry is one of the five Taluks in Pathanamthitta district. Pathanamthitta town is the capital of Kozhencherry Taluk. The other taluks are Tiruvalla, Mallapally, Ranni, and Adoor. Kozhencherry is a major trading and business centre in Central Travancore. Maramon is a small town on the banks of Pampa River, opposite Kozhencherry town. The river-bed of the Pampa here witnesses the annual Maramon Convention, the largest Christian gathering in Asia.

Kozhikode : Also known as Calicut, is the third largest city in the southern state of Kerala, India. It is the capital of Kozhikode District, and was formerly the capital of an independent kingdom, and later of the erstwhile Malabar District. This city is famous as the place where Zheng He of China first visited, and later Vasco da Gama in 1498. The name of the fibre calico is derived from the name of this city. It is also the pepper capital of the world.

Kozhikode District : Kozhikode District is a district of Kerala state, situated on the southwest coast of India. The town of Kozhikode, formerly known as Calicut, is the district headquarters. Present-day Kozhikode District was among territories ceded to the British East India Company by Tipu Sultan of Mysore in 1792, at the conclusion of the Third Anglo-Mysore War. The newly-acquired British possessions on the Malabar Coast were organized into Malabar District, which included the present-day districts of Kannur, Kozhikode, Malappuram, and Palakkad, and Wayanad. Calicut served as the administrative headquarters of the district. Malabar District was part of the Madras Presidency, a province of British India.

After India's Independence in 1947, Madras Presidency became Madras State, which was divided along linguistic lines by the States Reorganisation Act in 1956. On 1 November 1956, Malabar District was combined with the erstwhile state of Travancore-Cochin and Kasaragod District to form the state of Kerala. Malabar District was considered too large for effective administration, so it was divided into the districts of Kozhikode, Kannur, and Palakkad on 1 January 1957. The district had five taluks, Vadakara, Koyilandy, Kozhikode, Ernad and Tirur. On 16 June 1969 Ernad and Tirur Taluks became part of newly-created Malappuram District. South Wayanad, which forms the southern portion of present-day Wayanad District, was added to Kozhikode for a time, but in 1980 became part of newly-created Wayanad District.

K P Kesava Menon : K. P. Kesava Menon was a well known patriot and active volunteer of the freedom fight against the British.

Born in 1886 in Tharoor village of Palakkad as the grand son of the Raja(Ruler) of palghat. He graduated in Arts from Madras(todays Chennai) University and Bar-at-law from Middle Temple.He joined the Indian National Congress in 1915 and served as the secretary of the Malabar branch of the Home Rule Leeague after setting up practice in Calicut.

Kesava Menon was a member of the Home Rule League under Annie Besant which proceeded to London to present a memoranda to the Secretary of State in 1917. He was the founder of Mathrubhumi daily, a popular news paper which have the second place in cirulation in Kerala.

KPS Gill : KPS Gill began his career as a police officer in the north-eastern state of Assam, quickly earning a reputation as a tough officer. He became a household name across the country as Punjab police chief in the early 1990s, when he was credited with crushing a separatist revolt in the Sikh-majority state.

Widely praised as a one-man army and widely feared by criminals across the country, Mr Gill was dubbed "Super Cop" after his success in Punjab. Years after retiring from government job, Mr Gill's anti-terrorism skills are back in great demand. He publishes the Faultlines journal and runs the Institute for Conflict Management, as well as advising governments and institutions on security related issues. He was asked by the government of Sri Lanka last year for similar advice. Mr Gill has also written a book, "The Knights of Falsehood", which explores the abuse of religious institutions by the politics of terrorism in Punjab.

Krait : The kraits are 12 species of venomous snakes in the genus Bungarus in the Elapidae family. They are found in the Indian subcontinent and southeast Asia. There are 15 various subspecies.

Krait have neurotoxic venom many times more potent than cobra venom. The bite of the krait is very serious and causes respiratory failure in the victim. Before effective antivenin was developed, there was a 75 percent mortality rate among victims. The bite has been described as extremely painful; fortunately, kraits are not usually aggressive. All kraits are nocturnal. The snake is more docile during the daylight hours, becoming more aggressive during the night. However, they are rather timid and will often hide their heads within their coiled bodies for protection. When in this posture, they will sometimes whip their tail around as a type of distraction.

Krantikari Samyavadi Party : Krantikari Samyavadi Party (Revolutionary Communist Party) is an Indian political party in the state of Bihar. KSP was formed as a splinter-group from Communist Party of India. KSP wanted to continue cooperation with Laloo Prasad Yadav's Rashtriya Janata Dal. In the state assembly elections 2000 KSP won two seats (supported by Laloo). In total the party had put up seven candidates. The relation with RJD was later broken.

Krishak Praja Party : Krishak Praja Party is a political party in Bagladesh with considerable influence for a short period in the late 1930s and early 40s. Founded in 1936 the Krishak Praja Party was a spin-off of the Nikhil Banga Praja Samiti (All Bengal Tenants' Association). Because of the India Act of 1919, political groups and associations were formed and reformed among the Muslim elite in rapid succession. Accommodating Muslim leaders of different political persuasions, the Nikhil Banga Praja Samiti was formed in 1929 with Sir Abdur Rahim as its president and with five vice presidents, of whom Ak Fazlul Huq was the first. The effects of the depression of the 1930s led to the formation of Praja Samitis in most east Bengal districts. Fazlul Huq chose to devote his life to praja politics and came out of the elitist Nikhil Banga Praja Samiti.

The decline of the KPP began immediately after its spectacular electoral victory. Fazlul Huq, the KPP leader, formed a coalition ministry with the support and participation of the Muslim League and some other smaller groups and independent members. As the Chief Minister, Fazlul Huq seemed to have concentrated his attention more on power politics than on proping up his party. Of the eleven ministers in his cabinet, only two, including him, were from the KPP and the rest were from the Muslim League and other factions.

Disgruntled KPP members led by Shamsuddin Ahmed, the secretary of the party, openly defied Huq and sat as a separate group in the Assembly. The rebel group convened a general meeting of the party at Gaibandha on 11 September 1937 and adopted a resolution expelling Huq and members loyal to him from the party. In retaliation, Huq also expelled the rebels. In holding on to power in the face of virulent Congress opposition, Fazlul Huq joined the Muslim League at its Lucknow Session on 15 October 1937. Under the pressure of the League, Syed Nausher Ali, the KPP member in the cabinet besides Huq, was forced to resign on 22 June 1938. Huq remained the lone KPP member on the cabinet. His participation in the Muslim League virtually made him an inactive person both for his KPP faction as well as for the Bengal Muslim League of which he happened to be the president.

Krishna District : Krishna District is a district of India's Andhra Pradesh state. It is named after the Krishna River which flows through the district. Machilipatnam is the administrative headquarters of the district. The district is bounded by Khammam District to the north, West Godavari District to the east, the Bay of Bengal to the south, Guntur District to the southwest, and Nalgonda District to the northwest. Vijayawada is the most populated and well known city of this district. Krishna district is also considered as the hub for pre-university education in Andhra Pradesh.

Krishna has considerable historic significance. Historic places in the district include Bandar Port, Kondapalli Killa, Gudivada, Ghantasala and Gandhi Hill. Religiously significant places include the Kanaka Durga Temple, Gunadala Matha Shrine, and the Penuganchi Prolu Temple. It is the birth place of significant personalities in this part of the world, including N. T. Rama Rao, Akkineni Nageswara Rao, Ghantasala Venkateswara Rao, Pingali Venkaiah, Ayyadevara Kaleswarao, K. L. Rao, Duggirala Gopala Krishna, Kaikala Satyanarayana and Viswanatha Satyanarayana.

Krishna River : The Krishna River is one of the longest rivers of India (about 1300 km in length). It originates at Mahabaleswar in Maharashtra, passes through Sangli and meets the sea in the Bay of Bengal at Hamasaladeevi in Andhra Pradesh. The Krishna River flows through the states of Maharashtra, Karnataka and Andhra Pradesh. The traditional source of the river is a spout from the mouth of a statue of a cow in the ancient temple of Mahadev in Mahabaleshwar. Its most important tributary is the Tungabhadra River, which itself is formed by the Tunga and Bhadra rivers that originate in the Western Ghats. Other tributaries include the Koyna, Bhima, Mallaprabha, Ghataprabha, Yerla, Warna, Dindi, Musi and Dudhganga rivers. Two big dams have been constructed on the river, one at Srisailam called Srisailam Dam and the other at Nagarjuna Hill. The latter called Nagarjuna Sagar Dam is considered to be the largest earth dam in the world with a natural reservoir spanning tens of square kilometres.

Temples like Ganapati Temple of Sangli, Sangameshwar Shiva Temple at Haripur and Ramling Temple are located on the banks of river Krishna near Sangli. Out of these, Ganapati Temple of Sangli is one of the most beautiful temples of Lord Ganesha. Popular pilgrim spots like Audumber and Narsobawadi are located on the banks of river Krishna near Sangli in Maharashtra state.

Three tributaries meet Krishna river near Sangli. Warana river meets Krishna river near Sangli at Haripur. This spot is also known as Sangameshwar. Panchaganga river meets Krishna river at Narsobawadi near Sangli. These places are considered among the holiest in Hindu mythology. It is said that Lord Dattatraya spent some of his days at Audumber on the banks of river Krishna.

Krishnadevaraya : Sri Krishnadevaraya, was a Vijaynagar emperor who presided over the empire at its zenith and ruled from 1509 until his death in 1529. He is regarded as a hero of people of Telugu and Kannada descent in South India and considered to be one of the great kings of India. Much of our information about his reign comes from the accounts of Portuguese travelers Domingos Paes and Nuniz. Within six months of his coronation, he defeated Sultan Mahmud of Bidar and his ally, Yusuf Adil Khan. In 1510, he attacked in the north, besieged Raichur and moved to Gulburga and Bidar. Once Krishnadevaraya secured the north, he overthrew the rebels of Ummattur and a new province of Vijayanagar was created with Seringapatnam as its capital. He subdued a local ruler, Prataparudra, and seized lands up to the Krishna river. In 1516-1517, he pushed beyond the Godavari river. He defeated the Gajapatis of Orissa who had land in northern Andhra in five campaigns.

The complicated alliances of the empire and the five Deccan sultanates meant that he was continually at war; in one of these campaigns, he defeated Golconda and captured its commander Madurul-Mulk, crushed Bijapur and its sultan Ismail Adil Shah and restored Bahmani sultanate to Muhammad Shah. He established friendly relations with the Portuguese, who set up the Portuguese Dominion of India in Goa in 1510. The Emperor obtained guns and Arabian horses from the Portuguese merchants. He also utilized Portuguese expertise in improving water supply to Vijayanagaram City.

The highlight of his conquests occurred on May 19, 1520 where he secured the fortress of Raichur from Ismail Adil Shah of Bijapur after a difficult siege during which 16,000 Vijaynagari soldiers were killed. During the campaign against Raichur, we are told that 703,000 foot soldiers, 32,600 cavalry and 551 elephants were used. Finally, in his last battle, he razed to the ground the fortress of Gulburga, the early capital of the Bahmani sultanate. His empire extended over wide areas of the present day Andhra Pradesh and Karnataka.

Krishna Deva Raya respected all sects of Hinduism, although he personally leaned in favour of Vaishnavism, and lavished on the Tirupati temple numerous objects of priceless value, ranging from diamond studded crowns to golden swords. Additionally, he is known to have commissioned the making of statutes of himself and his two wives at the temple complex

Krishnarayalu's reign was the golden age of Telugu literature. Eight poets known as Astadiggajalu(eight elephants in the eight cardinal points such as North, South etc.) were part of his court (known as Bhuvanavijayamu). According to the Vaishnavite religion there are eight elephants in eight corners in space and hold the earth in its place. Similarly these eight poets were the eight pillars of his literary assembly. These Astadiggajas were: Allasani Peddana, Nandi Thimmana, Madayyagari Mallana, Dhurjati, Ayyalaraju Ramambhadrudu, Pingali Surana, Ramarajabhushanudu, and Tenali Ramakrishnudu.

Krishnadhan Banerjee: Krishnadhan Banerjee (1846-1904) was a Bengali musician and musicologist, born in Kolkata. Krishnadhan Banerjee was one of the three musicologists who introduced new trends in Bangla music, the other two being kshetramohan goswami and Shaurindramohan Thakur.

Krishnagar : Actually called Krishnanagar, Krishnagar is a town in the Indian state of West Bengal, and the headquarters of Nadia district and is located in the eastern part of India. The town is well connected by road to different parts of the state, and also has a railway junction. The major agricultural products of the area include rice, jute, and sugarcane, and industrial activities include sugar milling and ceramic manufacturing.

Krishnajanmabhoomi : Krishnajanmabhoomi, which means 'the birth-place of Krishna', is a temple built on the birthplace of Krishna (an avatar of God Vishnu) in Mathura, India. It is believed that Lord Krishna was born here in a cell of a prison, which once stood there, and in which his parents (Vasudeva and Devaki) were kept in bondage by the tyrannical king of Mathura, Kamsa.

In relatively modern time, a temple called Keshavdas was built on the spot where Krishna was born. The temple was built by Rao Veer Singh Bundela, who was a prominent Hindu nobleman at the Mughal court of Jehangir (1605-27). In late 17th century, during the reign of Aurangzeb (1618-1707), a mosque, was constructed after destroying parts of the existing Krishna temple strucutre. With the decline of the Mughal Empire, and by the early 19th century, the East India Company had emerged as the de facto ruler of large parts of undivided India, and exercised jurisdiction over the region.

Before India's independence, Madan Mohan Malaviya, endeavored during 1940s to build a temple over the spot where Krishna was believed to have been born. In 1953, an organization named the Krishna Janmabhoomi Sansthan was formed, and with the monetary assistance received from different sources, construction of a temple was commenced. The temple was opened to public in 1984.

Krishnamachari Srikkanth : Krishnamachari "Kris" Srikkanth (born 21 December 1959 in Chennai, India) is a former Indian cricket player. He made his one-day international debut against England in Ahmedabad in 1981, followed two days later by his Test debut against England at Mumbai. Srikkanth made his debut at the age of 21 as an opener of the Indian team to partner Sunil Gavaskar. Srikkanth redefined batting with his power hitting and he gave so wonderful starts to the team against even the toughest of oppositions. He was gifted with good eye and super quick reflexes.

Srikkanth was a stylish opening batsman with a keen eye and sharp reflexes, allowing him to play aggressive attacking strokes with power and precision. Although somewhat rash in execution, which led to his downfall at times, his swashbuckling style and free scoring like Virender Sehwag were a favourite with Indian crowds, making him a popular player. As he matured, he tempered his aggression somewhat and became a mainstay of the Indian cricket team. He was an integral member of the Indian squad when they won the 1983 Prudential World Cup and 1985 Benson & Hedges World Championship Cup. He was made the captain of the Indian team in 1989. After retirement he took up the mantle of coaching the India 'A' team and was a quite successful stint. Now he is a broadcaster and commentator with a sports channel.

Krishnan Sasikiran : Krishnan Sasikiran (born January 7, 1981) is an Indian chess player. Among Indians, he is third only to Vishwanathan Anand and Pentala Harikrishna in FIDE rating. "Sasi" as he is sometimes called, comes from Chennai in Tamil Nadu in south-eastern India. He became an International Chess Grandmaster at the 2000 Commonwealth Championship.

In 2001, he won the prestigious Hastings International Chess tournament. In 2003, he won the 4th Asian Individual Championship as well as the Politiken Cup in Copenhagen. Sasikiran tied Jan Timman for first place in the 2005 Sigeman Tournament in Copenhagen/Malmö Denmark. In the October 2004 FIDE rating list, Sasikiran was ranked number 35 in the world with an Elo rating of 2668.

Krittibas : Krittibas is a Bengali poetry magazine that first appeared in Kolkata in 1953. It played a highly influential role in the Kolkata literary scene in the decades after Indian independence, and provided a platform for young, experimental poets, many of whom went on to become luminaries of modern Bengali poetry.

Kriya Yoga : Kriya Yoga is a system of Indian yoga that was revived in modern times by Lahiri Mahasaya. Paramahansa Yogananda brought it into widespread public awareness through his book Autobiography of a Yogi. The system consists of a number of yogic techniques that purportedly hasten the practitioner's spiritual evolution and help to bring about a profound state of tranquility and god-communion within one's own self.

According to Paramahansa Yogananda, in his Autobiography of a Yogi, Kriya Yoga was well-known in ancient India, but was eventually lost, due to "priestly secrecy and man's indifference". In 1861 however, the immortal yogi Mahavatar Babaji initiated Lahiri Mahasaya into Kriya Yoga. Lahiri Mahasaya then revived the practice, and it soon spread throughout India. Yogananda, a disciple of Swami Sri Yukteswar Giri who was himself a disciple of Lahiri Mahasaya, then brought Kriya Yoga to the United States and Europe during the 20th century. Since that time it has spread throughout the world through various Guru lineages, most of which claim descent from Lahiri Mahasaya.

Lahiri Mahasaya's most well known disciples were Swami Sri Yukteswar Giri, Panchanon Bhattacharya, Swami Pranabananda, Swami Kebalananda, Swami Keshabananda, and Bhupendranath Sanyal (Sanyal Mahasaya).

K R Narayanan : Kocheril Raman Narayanan (b. at Uzhavoor in Kottayam, Kerala, 4 February 1921; d. in New Delhi, 9 November 2005), known as K. R. Narayanan, was the tenth President of the Indian Republic. He is the only Dalit (and also, the only Malayali) to have held the Presidency. Shri Kocheril Raman Narayanan assumed office as President of India on July 25, 1997. Shri

Narayanan was born on October 27, 1920 in the village of Uzhavoor in Kottayam district, Kerala.

Shri Narayanan received his education from the University of Travancore where he obtained an M.A. degree in English Literature standing first in the University. Later, he obtained B.Sc. (Econ.) degree from the London School of Economics with First Class Honours specialising in Political Science. Shri Narayanan started his career as a Lecturer in the University of Travancore (1943). Later he took to journalism and worked with The Hindu, Madras (now Chennai) and Times of India, Bombay (now Mumbai - 1944-45). While a student in London, he served as the London Correspondent of "Social Welfare", a weekly from Bombay edited by Shri K.M. Munshi (1945-48).

Shri Narayanan joined the Indian Foreign Service in 1949 and served in Indian Embassies in Rangoon, Tokyo, London, Canberra and Hanoi and held different positions in the Ministry of External Affairs. In between he taught Economic Administration at Delhi School of Economics from 1954-55 and was also the Joint Director of the Orientation Centre for Foreign Technicians.Shri Narayanan also served as India's Ambassador to Thailand (1967-69), Turkey (1973-75), the People's Republic of China (1976-78) and Secretary, Ministry of External Affairs (1976).

After retirement from the Foreign Service in 1978, Shri Narayanan was appointed as Vice-Chancellor of Jawaharlal Nehru University, New Delhi in January 1979 and held the post till October 1980. Shri Narayanan was sent as a political appointee to be India's Ambassador to the United States of America from 1980-84. After completing his term as Indian Ambassador to USA, Shri Narayanan entered politics and won three successive General Elections in 1984,1989 and 1991 from his Parliament Constituency of Ottapalam in Kerala. He was Member of Parliament from

1985 to 1992. During this period he was Union Minister of State for Planning (1985), External Affairs (1985-86) and Science and Technology, Atomic Energy, Space, Electronics and Ocean Development and Vice-President, Council of Scientific and Industrial Research (1986-89). He was elected Vice-President of India and served in this position from 21st August, 1992 till he assumed the office of the President of India in July 1997. He was ex-officio Chairman of the Rajya Sabha during this period. He has been associated with several institutions in diverse capacities. He was President, Indian Council for Cultural Relations; President, Indian Institute of Public Administration; President, Ramakrishna Mission Institute of Cultures, Calcutta; Patron of the International Award for Young People - India.

Shri Narayanan has also served as Chairman of (i) The Jury of the Jawaharlal Nehru Award for International Understanding; (ii) The International Jury for the Indira Gandhi Prize for Peace, Disarmament and Development; (iii) The Advisory Committee for the Rajiv Gandhi Sadbhavana Award; (iv) The Jury for International Gandhi Award for Leprosy; (v) The Jury for Indira Gandhi Paryavaran Puraskar; (vi) The Jury for Dr. B.R. Ambedkar Award for Social Understanding and Upliftment of Weaker Sections; (vii) The Jury for Dr. B.R. Ambedkar International Award for Social Change; (viii) The Jury for G.D. Birla Awards for Humanism, India's Heritage and Culture and Rural Upliftment; and (ix) The Jury for Communal Harmony Awards.

K S Chitra : Born in Thiruvananthapuram the capital of Kerala state, K.S.Chitra, with her melodious voice, has built a formidable reputation as a playback singer for South Indian as well as Hindi films. She has to her credit, over 11,000 songs in languages like Tamil, Telugu, Malayalam, Hindi, Bengali and Oriya.

From her young age she learned the basics in music from her father, late Krishnan Nair who was a singer and composer of repute. The gifted singer learned music at the graduate and post-graduate levels and completed her B A in music with the third rank from the university. She went on to complete her MA in music from Kerala University, for which she was chosen under the aegis of the National Talent Search Scholarship programme and was trained by Professor K.Omanakutty.

Ms Chitra got a chance in films when Prof. K.Omanakutty introduced her to her brother Mr. M.G.Radhakrishnan, a famous music director in Malayalam film industry. Her first songs were for the films like 'Attahaasam', 'Snehapoorvam Meera', and 'Njaan Ekananu' and from then on there was no looking back. Her expressive melodious voice got her plenty of offers and she was soon making a mark in Malayalam films to the extent that she has today monopolised Malayalam film music. Ilayaraja gave her the big break into Tamil films through his film 'Nee Thaanaa Antha Kuyil' but it was with 'Sindhu Bhairavi' she became a known name in Tamil industry which also won her the National Award for best playback singer. Ms Chitra's foray into Hindi film music was with the song 'Saathiya, ye tune kya kiya' in the film 'Love'. Some of the Hindi films that she has given hit songs are 'Pyaar Tune Kya Kiya', 'Aks', 'Ashoka', 'Rangeela' etc. She is one singer who has successfully broken the North-South divide and blazed a trail of glory in both worlds.

She has won the National Award for the best playback singer many times. The Kerala government has heaped upon her the best playback singer award more than 12 times and she has the unique distinction of being the first female singer in the history of South Indian film playback singing to be honoured by all the four southern state governments as the best playback singer.

Chitra who has a strong base in classical music has an ability to pick up even the most difficult pitch with ease. Ms Chitra has many albums especially devotional music to her credit. She has also tried her hand in pop music and made an album with the 'Voodoo Rapper'. Her hugely successful albums include 'Piya Basanti'; her collaboration with sarangi exponent Ustad Sultan Khan, 'Sunset Point', where she worked with Gulzar and Bhupinder. She has had the opportunities to work with famous music directors like Salil Choudhary, Anu Malik, Nadeem-Shravan and world renowned music maestro A R Rahman. But she remains her simple down to earth self with the trademark pleasant smile. This immensely talented singer continues to impress her numerous fans with memorable songs.

Kshatriya : According to the Hindu code of Manu, a Kshatriya is a member of the military or kingly order and are generally considered the Arya. The priest king Manu the law giver has over 50 sons. Since Manu himself is king and brahmin, his children are all highborn. However, due to differences in jobs, end up as different jatis and caste. Those sons who studied the Vedas became known as brahmins, those sons who took up kingship became the Aryans. The word "Aryan" itself is related to the Aristocracy and initially only related to the kings and nobles and later applied to the priests and businessmen.

Ksheerarama : Ksheerarama is one of the Pancharama Kshetras which is located in Palakollu near Narsapuram in West Godavari District of Andhra Pradesh in South India. Lord Shiva is known as Ksheera Ramalingeswara Swamy here. The Sivalinga at this place is installed and established by Lord Vishnu.

Kshudiram Basu: Kshudiram Basu (1889-1908) is a revolutionary and martyr. Born at Habibpur village of Midnapur district, he was brought up by his eldest sister as he lost his mother Lakshmipriya Devi at the age of six and his father Trailokyanath Basu a year later.

Having his primary education at the village school he joined Hamilton School at Tamluk and later Midnapur Collegiate School in 1903, where he read upto class VIII. Though meritorious, he took less interest in studies and was drawn more towards juvenile pranks and adventures.

K S Lal : K.S. Lal is an Indian historian. He wrote many historical books, mainly on medieval India. Many of his books, such as History of the Khaljis and Twilight of the Sultanate, are regarded as standard works. He obtained his Master's degree in 1941 at the University of Allahabad. In 1945 he obtained his D.phil. with a dissertation on the history of the Khaljis. This dissertation formed the basis for his book History of the Khaljis. From 1945 to 1963 he taught at Government Colleges in Madhya Pradesh. After 1963, he was a professor at the University of Delhi in Medieval Indian history.

K S Narasimhaswamy : Dr. K. S. Narasimhaswamy (KSN, affectionately known as K. S. Na) (January 26, 1915—December 27, 2003) was a famous poet who wrote in the Kannada language. Born in Kikkeri, Mandya district, he studied in Mysore and Central College in Bangalore, India. His romantic love poems, inspired by Robert Burns (whose work he translated to Kannada as Robert Burns Premageetegallu), were unique to the language at a time when most Kannada poetry dealt with nature and the natural world. He is considered to be part of the Navodaya movement in Kannada literature. By virtue of his innovative 'simple Kannada' poetry, KSN was able to bring Kannadic poetry to a broad audience. KSN received many awards and recognitions, including the prestigious 'Pampa' award for Kannada literature (given by the Government of Karnataka) for his poetry collection 'Dundu Mallige' in 1997.

Kuadam : Kuadam (also known as Kua or more popularly Kapadapuram) was the capital of the ancient Pandian kingdom of the Meen'Koodal epoch (the second Sangam academy). The grand old poet and saint Nakkeerar and the Iraiyanaar porul'urai mentions that Kuadam was the capital from c.5400 BCE to c.1750 BCE for about 3650 years.

Around 1750 BCE, the last great deluge flooded forever Kuadam and the remaining part of the Kumari kaandam (correlates with the Biblical record of "the flood" around 2050 BCE). Kuadam was to the north of the ancient Paqruli river about 700 kaadham south of the Kumari river delta.

Kuakata : Kuakata is a scenic sea beach in south-western Bangladesh. It is about 320 Kilometres south of Dhaka, the capital, and about 70 Kilometres from the Patuakhali District headquarters. Kuakata is famous for being the only sea beach in Bangladesh where both sunrise and sunset can be seen.

Kuchipudi : Kuchipudi, one of the art forms of the South had its origin in Andhra Pradesh. It presents scenes from Hindu Epics and mythological tales through dance-dramas combining music, dance and acting. The lyrics used in Kuchipudi are usually in Telugu, though Sanskrit verses are also not uncommon. While Kuchipudi, like Bharata Natyam comprises pure dance, mime and histrionics, it is the use of speech as well that distinguishes its presentation as dance drama.

Kuchipudi dance-dramas, each present a particular episode or a series of episodes. A solo recital, on the other hand, typically consists of such items as the 'Sabdam', 'Bhama kalapam' which is the main item, 'Padams' and 'Tarangams'. In 'Bhama kalapam', the dancer has enormous scope for the dramatisation of characters. The main character is Satyabhama, a beautiful but arrogant queen who goes through the process of discovering the path of true love and devotion. In the 'Tarangam', the dancer frequently perform a balancing feat, her feet poised on the edge of a brass plate as she moves around.

Kuchipudi, a representation of a fine combination of Natya, Nritta and Nritya was earlier never a solo affair and required a number of actors. It was presented in the open air on an improvised stage by men and boys who were given a vigorous training in abhinaya, music, dancing and singing. Earlier the female roles were played by boys and young men of comely appearance. The Sutradhar or the director of the stage played the key role. He was the conductor, dancer, singer, musician, comedian, all rolled into one. The play began with the orchestral music which included Mridanga, Madala and a pair of cymbals, followed by an invocation to a deity and appearance of Ganesha, the elephant headed god to bless the performance. Then came the dancers offering worship to the Flagstaff or Flag of Indra. The Sutradhara then announced the theme of the play, introduced the characters in his sing-song voice and appealed the audience to witness the show with attention. This marked the end of the prelude and the beginning of the play proper. Each character entered the stage dancing and singing the merits of the character he or she was impersonating, which is known as 'Daruvus'. The play progressed at a leisurely pace and relaxed tempo punctuated with dances both abstract and expressional. It contained some very complicated items of original footwork such as tracing out an outline of a lion or an elephant with the feet on the floor or dancing with the feet on the edges of a circular brass tray or with a water pot delicately and precariously balanced on the head.

Today Kuchipudi is considerably a different style of dance form than it originally used to be. In most of the cases it is now a solo performance done by female dancers. The Sutradhara has become a phenomenon of the past and the Vachika abhinaya, that is, expressional numbers are sung by the danseuses herself instead by the vocalists in the background on the stage as was the traditional practice. The element of devotion to gods has also been done away with and it has become purely a secular affair with predominance of 'sringar' or erotic flavour. Besides the drama component has also been totally reduced. The main expressional number is from Jaideva's Ashtapadi, the Ramayana, the Puranas, Tirtha Narayana's Krishna Lila Tarangini or Tyagaraja's compositions, but now the dancer combines into herself the roles of the singer who sings the 'daruvu', the actor who speaks the lines and the dancer who mimes and dances to interpret the text. Elements not indigenous to the dance drama such as sculpture like stances and freezes based on perfect iconographic forms motifs and shapes have also been incorporated into Kuchipudi dance recitals to make it more competitive with other dance forms.

Kud : It is basically a ritual dance performed in honour of Lok Devatas in Himachal. This dance style is performed mostly during nights. It is spontaneous dance and people of all ages and sexes participate in this folk dance form. Instruments used during this dance are Narshingha, chhaina, flute, drums etc. It is the rhythm of music which contrils the movement of participants. This dance continues for the whole night. Number of participants ranges from 20 to 30 members.

Kudargarh : Kudargarh is a famous Hindu pilgrim centre situated in Surguja district of the state of Chhattisgarh in India. Major point of attraction here is Maa Bagheshwari Devi Temple, dedicated to Goddess Kudargarhi, perched on top of a hill. It is 98 km from district headquarter Ambikapur connected by all weather road. Best time of visit is during Chaitra Navaratra (in the month of April). History of the temple is obscure. According to Dalton, the temple was built by Baland Kings. Balands were the original rulers of Korea state in 17th century.

Kudremukh National Park : The Kudremukh or Horse Face Range is situated 95 Kms southwest of Chickmagalur town. The broad hills which overlook the Arabian Sea are chained to one another with deep valleys and steep precipices and is so named because of the unique shape of the Kudremukh peak which has the highest elevation at 1892 metres. The park named after the peak, extends over three districts, Dakshin Kannada (South Kanara), Chickmaglur and parts of Udupi and stretches between Narasimha Parvatha (in Sringeri Taluk) in the north to the Jamalabad Fort (in Belthangady Taluk) in the south. The park is divided into four ranges Kudremukh, Kerekatte, Kalsa, Shimoga.

Kukis : The Kukis have numerous types of culture and tradition since their forefathers' times. They are unique, interesting, and impressive. Rice is the staple food of this people. They domesticated a number of animals, which some of them are very useful and helpful to their masters. Of these animals, Sel (mithun) is the most prized possession, while a dog is considered as a faithful animal. It is know that the Kukis were in possession of some documents, inscribed on leather, known as 'Savun Lekhajo'l' (scroll). These scrolls were lost in the passage of time and along with this, the Kukis also lost their script. Therefore, there is no known Kuki script. Today, the Roman script forms the basis for Kuki literature. Although the existence of formal learning institutions is not available, the Kukis were not unfamiliar with astronomy and astrology. They were able to study the stars and the phases of the moon and could forecast for themselves certain aspects of nature, particularly rainfall, drought and the seasons.

Kulfi : Kulfi is South Asian (Indian, Bangladesh, Pakistani, etc.) ice cream made with boiled milk typically from water buffalo. It comes in many flavors, including malai, mango, elaichi (cardamom), and kesar (saffron). Kulfi differs from western ice cream in that it is richer in taste and creamier in texture. As well, where western ice creams are whipped with air or overrun, kulfi contains no air; it's a solid dense frozen milk. It is made by boiling milk until it is reduced to half. Then sugar is added and the mixture is boiled for another ten minutes. Then flavorings, dried fruits, cardamom, etc. are added. The mixture is then put in moulds and frozen. One can eat kulfi plain as is or it can be garnished with ground cardamom, saffron, or pistachio nuts. As well, Kulfi is also served with Falooda noodles vermicelli noodles.

Kulli culture : The Kulli culture was a prehistoric culture in Southern Baluchistan, Pakistan (Gedrosia), ca. 2500 - 2000 B.C.E. The culture is named after an archaeological site discovered by Sir Aurel Stein. Several settlement sites are known but very few excavated. Some of them have the size of small towns and are similar to those of the Indus Valley Civilization. The house are built of local stone. Agriculture was the economical base of this people. At several places dams were found, providing evidence for a highly developed water management. The pottery and other artifacts are similar to those of the Indus Valley Civilization and it not sure whether the Kulli culture is a local variation of the Indus Valley Civilization or an own culture complex.

Kullu : Kullu is a town in the Kullu District,Himachal Pradesh in India. It is located on the banks of the Beas River in the Kullu Valley about ten kilometres north of the airport at Buntar. The Kullu Valley, also known as the "Valley of Gods", is well known for the seven day festival of Dussehra, a celebration of the mythical Lord Rama's victory over the evil king Ravana. The festival takes place in the months of October or November depending upon the Hindu calendar. Kullu Valley is also infamous for "malana cream" marijuana which is grown in the remote village of Malana. The economy of the town largely depends on tourism, horticulture (apples, plums, pears, and almonds) and the weaving of shawls.

Kulpahar : Kulpahar is an ancient town situated on the National Highway 76 connecting Pindwara in Rajasthan and Allahabad. This town holds relics of temples and tanks of the Chandela Dynasty. Kulpahar is a town in Mahoba District of the Indian state of Uttar Pradesh, in the Bundelkhand region. Before 11 Feb 1995 Kulpahar was a Tehsil of Hamirpur District. On 11 Feb 1995 Mahoba District carved out of Hamirpur and Kulpahar is now a part of the Mahoba District. Kulpahar is the largest Subdivision of Uttar Pradesh. Kulpahar is known for its closeness to Khajuraho and other historic places like Mahoba, Charkhari, Kalinjar, Orchha, and Jhansi. The town is connected with indian railways, national highways and state highways.

Kulpahar was the capital of a princely state of the same name in British India. Kulpahar was founded in 1700 by Senapati, a Bundela Rajput who was the son of Raja Jagat Raj of Jaitpur and grandson of Maharaja Chhatrasal. Kulpahar was captured by the British in 1804, and became a princely state in the Bundelkhand Agency of the Central India Agency. The chief resided at the town of Nowgong in Madhya Pradesh. The fort of Kulpahar, situated on a steep hill, towers more than 800 ft (244 m) above the sea level, and contains the ruins of elaborately carved sculptures.

Kumaon : Kumaon is one of the two regions and administrative divisions of Uttaranchal, a hilly (and mountainous) state of northern India, the other being

Garhwal. It includes the districts of Almora, Bageshwar, Champawat, Nainital, Pithoragarh, and Udham Singh Nagar. It is bounded on the north by Tibet, on the east by Nepal, on the south by Uttar Pradesh state, and on the west by Garhwal region. The people of Kumaon are known as Kumaonis. It is home to a famous Indian Army regiment, the Kumaon Regiment. Important towns of Kumaon are Haldwani, Nainital, Rudrapur, Almora, Pithoragarh and Ranikhet. Nainital is the administrative centre of Kumaon Division.

It consists of a large Himalayan tract, together with two submontane strips called the Terai and the Bhabhar. The submontane strips were up to 1850 an almost impenetrable forest, given up to wild animals; but after 1850 the numerous clearings attracted a large population from the hills, who cultivated the rich soil during the hot and cold seasons, returning to the hills in the rains. The rest of Kumaon is a maze of mountains, part of the Himalaya range, some of which are among the loftiest known. In a tract not more than 225 km in length and 65 km in breadth there are over thirty peaks rising to elevations exceeding 5500 m. The rivers rise chiefly in the southern slope of the Tibetan watershed north of the loftiest peaks, amongst which they make their way down valleys' of rapid declivity and extraordinary depth.

Kumaon Regiment : Kumaon Regiment is one of the crack troops of the Indian Army. It has received 2 Param Vir Chakras, 3 Ashok Chakras, 10 Maha Vir Chakras, 6 Kirti Chakras, 2 Uttam Yudh Seva Medals, 78 Vir Chakras, 1 Vir Chakra & Bar and 23 Shaurya Chakras, apart from numerous other honors and awards. The regiment is headquartered at Ranikhet (Uttaranchal). It has the unique distinction of producing three Army Chiefs (General S.M. Srinagesh (4th Kumaon), General K.S. Thimayya (4th Kumaon) and General T.N. Raina (14th Kumaon)).

Kumaoni : Variously used to signify the people or the local dialect of Kumaon Division of Uttaranchal, a region in the Indian Himalayas.

Kumar Gandharva : Kumar Gandharva (real name Shivaputra Siddramayya Komkali) (April 8, 1924 – January 1992) was a famous Hindustani classical singer, famous for his unique vocal style, refusal to be bound by the tradition of any gharana and his innovative genius. He was a great music intellectual. Shivaputra was born in Dharwad (Karnataka, India). As a child, he was stricken with tuberculosis, and left with only one functioning lung. This of course greatly affected his singing – he was to be known for powerful short phrases and his very high voice. He may not have reached the same heights of popularity as contemporaries like Bhimsen Joshi, but Kumar (a title given to child prodigies) Gandharva (god of music in Hindu mythology) always enjoyed the love and support of dedicated and connoisseur enthusiasts. His singing was also true to the Indian Classical Music tradition of dialogue with the listners, of impromptu creation and interactivity.

Kumarji also experimented with other forms of singing such as Bhajans (Devotional songs), folk songs et cetera. His nirgun (literally "without existential attributes") Bhajans are a great treasure trove for all spiritual people, atheists included. He would experiment with both ragas and presentation, often going from fast to slow compositions in the same raga, something rarely done by any other North Indian musician. One of the most inventive singers in recent years, he is remembered for his great legacy of innovation, questioning tradition without rejecting it wholesale, resulting in music in touch with the roots of Indian culture yet groundbreaking in its own right.

Kumar Purnima : In Orissa, festival is celebrated on the full moon day of the lunar month of Ashwina bring untold pleasure to the unmarried boys and girls in. The worship of moon God is held at home as Janha Mamu (Moon, the maternal uncle.) brings them various delicacies and new clothes.

Kumar River : Kumar river is an old river originates from the Mathabhanga at Hatboalia in Chuadanga district. Rennell depicted this river in his atlas prepared in 1764. The river was not much active at that time. Though the river overflows in monsoon, it turns almost dry in the lean period. The river was locally called as Kalobeel (Black coloured Beel).

The Kumar flows southeast from its origin keeping its course parallel to the Nabaganga. Near Magura, the river meets with the Nabaganga and the joint flow keeping the name Nabaganga flows further south. Once upon a time, the Kumar received its major flow from the Kaliganga, Chhaku, Hanu, Muchikhali etc on its course. These are all offshoots of the gorai. The origin of the Kumar has been disconnected from the Nabaganga after commissioning of the Ganges-kobadak Irrigation Project. As a result, the Kumar is now turned into a narrow channel. The only source of the river is excess water from the G-K project and local rainwater.

Kumar Sanu : Kumar Sanu alias Kedarnath Bhattacharya is a Calcutta born Mumbai based leading playback singer of Bollywood. He has modelled his singing style on that of the legendary Kishore Kumar. He had his first success in the film Aashiqui released in 1990. Since then has lent his voice to more than 7000 songs. He is a winner of 5 Filmfare Awards (India's equivalent of the Oscars), won back-to-back between 1990-1995. He is also credited with the rare feat of recording 28 songs in a single day, which is a world record.

Kumar Shanu, as he liked to be called, has reduced his immense recording schedule in recent times and is no longer the main male playback singer in Bollywood that he once was. He sung for the film Barsaat and the soundtrack has become a success. He has also turned his trade at making music for Indian films and also recently as a producer for a new Bollywood film, Utthaan.

Kumara Vyasa : Kumara Vyasa is one of the most famous poets in the Kannada language, spoken in the state of Karnataka, India. Kumara Vyasa's original name was Naranappa, and Kumara Vyasa is really his penname. The name is meaningful, since his magnum opus is a translation of the Sanskrit Mahabharata, written by the famous poet Vyasa. His lifetime work, the Karnata Bharata KathaManjari is a sublime adaptation of the first ten Parvas (chapters) of the Mahabharata. Kumara Vyasa has been highly influential in the further development of Kannada literature.

Kumarakom : The village of Kumarakom is a cluster of little islands on the Vembanad Lake in Kerala, a state in India. Geographically, it is located at 9.35 North and 76.26 East. Kumarakom's soil is extremely fertile due to the proximity of a water source, the Vembanad Lake which has resulted in the growth of a wide variety of flora in Kumarakom, especially the mangrove and coconut trees. Furthermore Vembanad Lake is home to several types of marine life exclusively the 'Karimeen' (Pearl Spotted Fish), the 'Chemeen' (Prawns) and the 'Konju' (Tiger Prawns).

Kumarakom is also a habitat to several migratory birds which are attracted by the availability of a safe nesting area provided by the trees and a close source of food and water which is delivered by the Vembanad Lake. The authorities have successfully attempted to protect the birds and their habitat through the construction of a bird sanctuary which spans 14 acres (57,000 m^2).The Bird Sanctuary is now a major tourist attraction and has been bought under the jurisdiction of KTDC (Kerala Tourism Development Corporation).

Kumarakom is not entirely a tourist dependent town but also derives a reasonable income from agriculture. The area is populated by mangrove forests, paddy fields and coconut groves. This rich agricultural environment is mainly irrigated using interspersed waterways and canals. Furthermore Kumarakom's perfectly balanced tropical climate poses an advantage to the growth of plants and trees.

Kumaran Asan : N. Kumaran Asan (also known as Mahakavi Kumaran Asan, the name prefix Mahakavi meaning great poet and the suffix Asan meaning scholar or teacher) was a Malayalam poet, philosopher and social reformer. Kumaran Asan was one of the famous triumvirate poets of Kerala in the first half of the 20th century.

Kumaran Asan initiated a revolution in Malayalam poetry in the first quarter of the 20th century, transforming it from metaphysical to lyrical. Deep moral and spiritual commitment is evident in Asan's poetry. His works are eloquent testimony of his poetic concentration and dramatic contextualization. in Malayalam literature. His elegy Prarodanam mourns the death of his contemporary and friend A.R. Rajaraja Varma, the famous Grammarian.

Asan's Khanda Kavyas (small poems) like Nalini, Leela, Karuna and Chandaalabhikshuki, were popular. In Chintaavishtayaaya Seetha (Seetha Lost in Thought) he displays his poetic artistry, while in Duravastha, he patiently and skillfully tears down the barriers created by feudalism, orthodoxy and casteism and consummates the dictum of the Guru, "One Caste, One Religion, One God for man".

Kumararama : Kumararama is one of the Pancharama Kshetras which is located in Samarlakota in East Godavari District of Andhra Pradesh in South India. Lord Shiva is known as Kumara Bhimeswara Swamy here. The consort of Lord Kumara Bhimeswara Swamy is Bala Tripurasundari. The Sivalinga at this place is installed and established by Lord Kumaraswamy. Maha Shivaratri, Karthika Masam and Sarannavarathri are the main festivals celebrated at this temple.

Kumari Kandam : Kumari Kandam is a legendary sunken landmass to the south of Kanyakumari, at the tip of South India. Kumari Kandam has often been compared and identified with Lemuria in modern times. According to Tamil Tradition, the Dravidians originally came from a submerged island, Kumari kandam, to the South of India. According to the legend, there were two main rivers in Kumari Kandam, the Pagruliyaru and Kumari River. There were also mountains. The second Tamil Sangam, Idai Sangam, was said to have been held on the now submerged land. The 'kadal kol' (land swallowed by sea) may not be totally fictitious. Several earthquake-caused tsunamis, mistaken for sinking, may have destroyed the island over a period of time.

Kumbakonam : Kumbakonam is a town in the Thanjavur district of Tamil Nadu state in southern India. Kumbakonam is sometimes called temple town because of the large number of temples within the town and the nearby areas. The festival of Mahamaham is celebrated every 12 years at the Mahamaham tank in Kumbakonam. According to legend, Kumbakonam is the location where the kumbha (pot) in which Brahma placed the seed of creation during the great deluge came to rest. Kumbakonam is thus said to be the location from which life in the current cycle of creation first came forth. It is said that the town was once the capital of the Cholas in the 7th century.

Of the many temples in Kumbakonam, the most striking is the Lord Sarangapani Temple, a Vaishnavite temple. This twelve storied 147 feet high temple was built by the Nayak Kings during 15th century. The Ramaswamy Temple which depicts the paintings of Ramayanam is another important Vaishanavite temple in Kumbakonam. The greatness of Ramaswamy Temple is said to be the only temple where Lord Rama, Goddess Sita are in the same platform and Lord Hanuman is playing the veena instead of reading the Ramayana. The entire deity is said to be made from Saligrama Monolith which is truly astounding.

Kumbh Mela : The largest religious gathering on Earth. Around 70 million people (followers of Hinduism) from around the world participated in Kumbh Mela at one of the Hindu Holy city Allahabad (India). Kumbh Mela (the Urn Festival) is a Hindu pilgrimage that occurs four times every twelve years and rotates between four locations: Prayag, Haridwar, Ujjain and Nashik. Each twelve-year cycle includes one Maha Kumbh Mela (Great Kumbh Mela) at Prayag, which is attended by millions of people, making it the largest gathering anywhere in the world.

The precise dates of the Kumbh Mela are astrologically determined, based upon the positions of the Sun, the Moon and Jupiter. At Prayag, the Maha Kumbh Mela is held in the month of Magha (January/February in the Gregorian calendar). The highest spiritual merit is attached to bathing on the new moon day, when Jupiter is in Taurus and both the Sun and Moon are in Capricorn. At Haridwar, the Kumbh Mela is held in the months of Phalgun and Chaitra (February/March/April), when the Sun passes to Aries, the Moon is in Sagittarius and Jupiter is in Aquarius. In Ujjain, the festival is held in the month of Vaishakha (May), when other planets are in Libra, the Sun and Moon are in Aries and Jupiter is in Leo. At Nashik, the Kumbh Mela takes place in the month of Shravana (July), when the Sun and Moon are in Cancer and Jupiter is in Scorpio.

The observance of Kumbh Mela is based upon the following legend: Thousands of years ago, in the Vedic period, gods and demons made a temporary agreement to work together churning amrita manthanam (the nectar of immortality) from the Ksheera Sagara (primordial ocean of milk), and to share the nectar equally. However, when the Kumbh (urn) containing the amrita appeared, the demons ran away with it and were chased by the gods. For twelve days and twelve nights (equivalent to twelve human years) the gods and demons fought in the sky for possession of this pot of amrita. It is said that during the battle, drops of amrita fell at four places: Prayag, Haridwar, Ujjain and Nashik. Thus, the Kumbh Mela is observed at these four locations where the nectar fell.

Kumbh Mela is attended by millions of people on a single day. The major event of this festival is a ritual bath at the banks of the rivers in each town. Other activities include religious discussions, devotional singing, mass feeding of holy men and women and the poor, and religious assemblies where doctrines are debated and standardized. Kumbh Mela (especially the Maha Kumbh Mela) is the most sacred of all the Hindu pilgrimages. Thousands of holy men and women (monks, saints and sadhus) attend, and the auspiciousness of the festival is in part attributable to this.

Kumbhalgarh : Kumbhalgarh is a fortress in Rajsamand District of Rajasthan state in western India. The fort has perimeter walls that extend 36 kilometres in length. Claimed to be the longest in the world after "The Great Wall of China". Over 360 temples are within the fort. 300 ancient Jain and the rest Hindu. The vista from the palace top typically extends tens of kilometers into the Aravalli Range. The Kumbhalgarh Wildlife Sanctuary surrounds the fortress, covering an area of 578 km^2. The sanctuary extends across the Aravalli Range, covering parts of

Rajsamand, Udaipur, and Pali districts, ranging from 500 to 1300 meters elevation.

Kumbhamkali (Kumbhamthullal) : Kumbhamkali or Kumbhamthullal (pot dance) is a folk ritual dance of devotees carrying pots on the head.

Kummattikali : It is a temple folk art and an awe-inspiring mask dance.

Kummi : In this dance, which is performed by the womenfolk of Tamil Nadu, the dancers gather in a circle and clap their hands as they dance.

Kumrahar : This archeological site is located 5kms from Patna railway station on the Kanjarbagh Road. Excavations here have revealed relics of over a thousand years of four ruling periods from 600BC to 600AD. The remains found here is a huge Mauryan hall supported by 80 sandstone pillars dating back to 300BC.

Kunal : Kunal (3rd Century B.C) was the son of Emperor Ashoka and Queen Padmavati. Legend has it that Kunal was renowned for his beautiful eyes. Tishyaraksha, Ashoka's youngest wife gained Ashoka's confidence and plotted to have him blinded and killed, but the official executioners spared Kunal and he became a wandering singer accompanied by his favourite wife Kanchanmala. In Pataliputra, Ashoka hears Kunal's song, and realizes that Kunal's misfortune may have been a punishment for some past sin of the emperor himself and condemns Tishyaraksha to death, restoring Kunal to the court. Kunal was succeded by his son, Samprati. A semi-fictionalized portrayal of Kunal's life was produced as a motion picture under the title Veer Kunal (1925).

Kundalini : Kundalini is derived from a Sanskrit word meaning either "coiled up" or "coiling like a snake."

There are a number of other translations of the term usually emphasizing a more serpent nature to the word—e.g. 'serpent power'. The caduceus symbol of coiling snakes is thought to be an ancient symbolic representation of Kundalini physiology. The concept of Kundalini comes from Yogic philosophy of ancient India and refers to the mothering intelligence behind yogic awakening and spiritual maturation. It might be regarded by yogis as a sort of deity, hence the occasional capitalization of the term. Within a western frame of understanding it is often associated with the practice of contemplative or religious practices that might induce an altered state of consciousness, either brought about spontaneously, through a type of yoga, through psychedelic drugs, or through a near-death experience.

Kundan Lal Saigal : Kundan Lal Saigal or K L Saigal, the famous singer was born on April 11,1904 in Jammu and Kashmir. Even at a young age he had a special talent for singing folk songs beautifully. He was very much influenced by his mother who used to sing Punjabi religious bhajans. He also had talent in acting. Saigal's initial performance was at the age of 12 in the Darbar of Maharaja Prathap Singh. Later he left home and took up various jobs in order to earn a living.

His visit to Kolkatta in 1932 for an official matter, was a turning point in his life. There he met the famous film cum music director R.C.Boral and he gave a chance for Saigal. He stepped into the film field by singing R.C.Boral's songs in the film 'Pooran Bagath'. The songs of this film attracted the music lovers in India. He got chances to sing and act in the films of New Theaters. He became popular as an actor after releasing the film 'Devdas'. His association with the famous film producer and director Chandulal Shah in 1941 gave him a chance to enter the Hindi film world. Some of Saigals' famous songs are 'soja rajakumari soja' and 'jab dil hi toot gayaa', 'karoom kya asniraz bari' (dushman), 'main kya janoo kya jadoo hai (zindhagi) etc. He died on January 18,1947 at the age of 43.

Kundar River : Kundar River is located in Balochistan, Pakistan. The meltwater from the Sulaiman Mountains forms Kundar River and it flows through Balochistan and drains into Gomal River. The two principal drainage channels of the Zhob district are the Zhob River and the Kundar River, both flow into the Gomal River. The general direction of the rivers is from Southwest to northeast. The Zhob River rises at Tsari Mehtarazai pass, the watershed a distance of about 400 kilometers. The broad plain of the Zhob River is occupied by the alluvial formation. The Kundar River rises from the central and highest point of the TobaKakar range, a few kilometers northeast of the Sakir. It constitutes boundary between Pakistan and Afghanistan territory for a considerable length. The other subsidiary rivers or streams are the Baskan, Chukhan, Sri Toi, Sawar, Surab, etc.

Kunhar River : Kunhar River is located in Kaghan Valley, North-West Frontier Province, Pakistan. The Kunhar River, swollen by glacier melt, meanders its way through the Naran Valley and Trout is plentiful.

Kuninda Kingdom : The Kingdom of Kuninda (or Kulinda in ancient literature) was an ancient central Himalayan kingdom from around the 2nd century BCE to the 3rd century, located in the modern state of Uttaranchal in northern India. The history of the kingdom is documented from around the 2nd century BCE. They are mentioned in Indian epics and puranas. The Mahabharata relates they were defeated by Arjuna. One of the first kings of the Kuninda was Amoghbhuti, who ruled in the valley of the Jamuna, Beas and Sutlaj rivers (in today's Punjab in northern India).

The Greek historian Ptolemy linked the origin of the Kuninda to the country where the rivers Ganges, Yamuna, and Beas originate. One the Edicts of Ashoka on a pillar is also present at Kalsi, in the region of Garhwal, indicating the spread of Buddhism to the region from the 4th century BCE. The Kuninda kingdom disappeared around the 3rd century, and from the 4th century, it seems the region shifted to Shaivite beliefs.

Kunitha : Karnataka region has immense treasure house of ritualistic dances, all denoted by the generic term Kunitha. In Puja Kunitha, there is a wooden structure with a deity on the head. Devare Thatte Kunitha, Yell-ammana Kunitha, Suggikunitha and others take their name from the deity or the symbol or instrument which is balanced on the head, or held in the hand of the dancer. The Dollu Kunitha is a popular drum dance of Karnataka.

Kunjali Marakkar : Mohammed Kunjali Marakkar was the Muslim naval chief of the Samoothiri Raja Manavikraman (Samoothiri was anglicized as Zamorin) a title of the Hindu kings of Kozhikode (anglicized Calicut, also known as Kolikottu), in present day state of Kerala, India during the 16th century.

Kunjali Marakkar was the first of the four Kunjalis who played a part in the Raja's naval wars with the Portuguese, who arrived in India in 1498. The Marakkars are credited with organizing the first naval defence of the Indian coast, to be later succeeded in the 18th century by the Maratha Sarkhel Kanhoji Angre.

Kunjarani Devi : Nameirakpam Kunjarani Devi (b.1968) was an Indian sportswoman in weightlifting. She competed in the 48 kg category towards the later part of her career.

Kunjarani Devi was a recipient of Arjuna award in 1990 and shared the Rajiv Gandhi Khel Ratna award with

Leander Paes for the year 1996-1997. She has more than 50 international medals to her credit.

Kuppam : Kuppam is a town in Andhra Pradesh that is 105 km from Bangalore and 250 km from Chennai by rail. It is famous for its granite quarries, so much so that a granite variety is named after the town, viz. Kuppam Green. Kuppam shot to fame after the ex AP Chief Minister and the TDP supremo N. Chandra Babu Naidu won the elections from this constituency.

Kural : The Kural is one of the most important forms of classical Tamil poetry. It is a very short poetic form, exactly in 2 lines, the first line consisting of 4 metrical feet or sIr and the second line consisting of 3 metrical feet. It should also conform to the grammar for Venpa. Thirukkural, one of the greatest philosophical works in Tamil language by Thiruvalluvar, is a typical example.

Kuravanji : Kuravanji is a type of dance-drama distinctive to the Tamils. As an entertainment its emphasis is balanced between the classical and folk arts. There are hundreds of Kuravanjis in Tamil. The earliest patron of this art was King Rajaraja Chola. He constructed a platform in the big temple at Thanjavur for holding Kuravanji performances during the annual festival; it goes by the name Kuravanji Medai. In each Kuravanji, the heroine, a dancing girl falls in love with the local presiding deity or the ruler of the land. She appears to the god of love to grant her wish and describes the divine being's state procession, the natural wealth of the area, its fertility. Fortune telling by reading the palm is also one of the features of Kuravanji.

Till some decades ago, the Kuravanji's were regularly performed in temples and the artistes kept themselves trim and in form. With the passing of the legislation prohibiting dancing by devadasis in temples, the practice of performing

Kuravanjis was given up. The rustic tunes sung by the kurathi waxing eloquent on the prosperity and greatness of her mountainous abode, have a naive simplicity about them. Compositions like the 'Thirukkutrala Kuravanji' are noted for their poetic value. The Viralimalai Kuravanji is noted for its musical value. In the Azhagar Kuravanji and the Thirumalai Andavar Kuravanji music and literature are equally balanced.

Kurnool : Kurnool is a city in Andhra Pradesh state of southern India. It is the administrative seat of the district of the same name. During the 18th century Kurnool formed the jagir of a semi-independent Pathan Nawab, whose descendant was dispossessed by the British government for treason in 1838. The Nawab's former territory became a district of Madras Presidency, with Kurnool as its capital. The district surrounded the princely state of Banganapalle. After India's independence in 1947, Kurnool became part of the state of Madras, created out of the former Madras presidency, and Banganapalle was added to the district.

The eleven northern districts of Madras state became the new state of Andhra in 1953, and Kurnool served as the state's first capital. In 1956 Andhra Pradesh was formed by combining the Andhra State and Telangana region, formerly part of Hyderabad state. Hyderabad was made the capital of new enlarged state of Andhra Pradesh. Kurnool is the only city in India that is located in between two rivers: Tungabhadra and Hundri. The historic Konda Reddy Fort is located in the heart of Kurnool. This has an underground hidden pathway (swarang) of about 25 km to Allampur (a neighbouring town).

Kurta : A kurta (or sometimes kurti, for women) is a traditional piece of clothing worn in northern India, Pakistan, and Afghanistan. It is a loose shirt falling either just above or somewhere below the knees of the wearer, and is worn by both men and women.

Kurtha can be worn with either a paijaamaa (men), salwar (women), or chudidaar (a unisex tight-fitting trouser). They are typically worn in more formal occasions, especially in the case of men, who in South Asia have largely moved to Western clothes as everyday wear.

Kurtas are usually custom-made by South Asian tailors, who work with the fabric their customers bring them. South Asians overseas, and Westerners, can buy them at South Asian clothing stores or order them from web retailers. In 2004 and 2005, a modified kurta has become fashionable and appeared in the collections of designers such as Versace, and has also graced the racks of stores like JCPenney and Wal-Mart. These kurtas are typically much shorter than the traditional garments, made with a lighter material more often resembling that of a kameez. They are often worn with jeans, both in India and Pakistan and throughout the rest of the fashion world.

Kurukshetra : Kurukshetra is the name of a district in the present-day Indian state of Haryana. The name literally means "Land of the Kurus" after the famous Kuru vansha (clan), but is also sometimes referred to as Dharam Kshetra meaning the "Land of Righteousness". It purports to be the site of the Kurukshetra war, described in the Hindu epic the Mahabharata. Nevertheless, this place holds inestimable importance in Hinduism as this is where the Bhagavad Gita ("The Song Celestial") was recited to Arjuna amidst the battle field, just before the great war of Mahabharata.

A few kilometeres from Kurukshetra is the village, Amin where there are remnants of a fort and it is said to be Abhimanyu's fort. The places to visit are Braham Sarovar, Sannihit Sarovar, Krishna Museum, Science

Panorama, Jyotisar, Bhishma Kund at Naraktari, Sthaneshwar Mahadev, Kamal Nabhi, Bhadrakali Mandir, Birla Mandir, Chhati Path Shahi Gurudwara Sheikh-Chilli ka makbara, and Pehowa. Every year lakhs of people come to take holy bath at Braham Sarovar on the occasion of "Somavati Amavasya" (Sacred Solar Eclipse). Also located in Kurukshetra are the Kurukshetra University and National Institute of Technology, Kurukshetra (formerly known as Regional Engineering College).

Kurukshetra University : The Kurukshetra University was established in 1956 as a unitary residential university and its foundation stone was laid by late Dr. Rajendra Prasad, the first President of India. Located in the holy city of Kurukshetra (Haryana), land of the historical battle of Mahabharata and the great message of Bhagawad Gita, its campus is situated on the western bank of Brahm Sarover (the holy tank) and extends over an area of over 400 acres.

Kurukshetra War : The Kurukshetra war was perhaps one of the most important battles fought in ancient India and forms an essential component of the Hindu epic Mahabharata. According to various archaeological, astronomical and literary evidence, the Kurukshetra war took place around 3067 BCE in the modern day state of Haryana in India.

According to Mahabharata, Kurukshetra, literally Land of the Kurus, was the battleground on which this war, known as the Kurukshetra war, was fought. Kurukshetra was also known as Dharamkshetra meaning a land of Dharma because of the pious ruler of this region. Legend has it that this site was chosen for the war because even a sin committed on this land was forgiven on account of good deeds of the king ruling this land.

The two sides to the war were the Pandavas and the Kauravas. Earlier during the Mahabharata, the Kauravas cheated the Pandavas at a dice game, forcing their Pandava cousins to go into exile for thirteen years, being twelve years of forest exile, and one year of anonymous exile. If the Pandavas were caught during the year of anonymity, they would have to go to twelve years of exile again. Even after the exile, the eldest of the Kaurava brothers, Duryodhana, refused to return the kingdom to the Pandavas. In order to regain the kingdom, the Pandavas fought the war.

Kurwai : Kurwai is a town in Vidisha District of the state of Madhya Pradesh in central India. Kurwai was formerly a Muslim princely state of British India. The state was 368 sq km in area and in 1892 boasted a population of 24,631. The state, which came under British sovereignty in the early nineteenth century, was founded in 1730 by Mohammed Dalair Khan, an Afghan rising through merit in the Mughal army. His descendants ruled the state until June 15, 1948, when the last ruling Nawab acceded to the Indian Government. Kurwai became part of the newly-created state of Madhya Bharat, and was added to Vidisha District. Madhya Bharat was merged into Madhya Pradesh on November 1, 1956.

Sarwar Ali Khan, son of the last Nawab of Kurwai, married Abida Sultan of Bhopal, eldest daughter and heiress presumptive of the Nawab of Bhopal. They had one son named Shahryar Khan. Abida Sultan gave up her right to the throne of Bhopal and opted for the Muslim nation Pakistan in 1950, eventually entering that country's Foreign service. Abida Sultan arrived in the newly created Pakistan when she was 37 and a mother of a young son. She was to spend the greater part of her life in Pakistan. She died in 2002. Shaharyar Khan was to become the Foreign Secretary of Pakistan and then the Chairman of the Pakistan Cricket Board.

Kushan Empire : The Kushan Empire (c. 1st–3rd centuries) was a state that at its height, about 105–250, stretched from Tajikistan to the Caspian Sea to Afghanistan and down into the Ganges river valley in northern India. The empire was created by the Kushan tribe of the Yuezhi, a people from modern Xinjiang, China, possibly related to the Tocharians. They had diplomatic contacts with Rome, Sassanian Persia and China, and for several centuries were at the center of exchange between the East and the West.

The Kushans are believed to have been predominantly Zoroastrian and later Buddhist as well. However, from the time of Wima Takto, many Kushans started adopting some aspects of Indian culture like the other nomadic groups who had invaded India. The first great Kushan emperor Wima Kadphises may have embraced Saivism, as surmised by coins minted during the period. The following Kushan emperors represented a wide variety of faiths including Zoroastrianism, Buddhism, and possibly Saivism.

The rule of the Kushans linked the seagoing trade of the Indian Ocean with the commerce of the Silk Road through the long-civilized Indus Valley. At the height of the dynasty, the Kushans loosely oversaw a territory that extended to the Aral Sea through present-day Uzbekistan, Afghanistan, and Pakistan into northern India. The rule of Kanishka I, the second great Kushan emperor, fifth Kushan king, who flourished for at least 28 years from c. 127, was administered from two capitals: Purushapura (now Peshawar in northern Pakistan) and Mathura, in northern India.

Kanishka is renowned in Buddhist tradition for having convened a great Buddhist council in Kashmir. This council is attributed with having marked the official beginning of the pantheistic Mahayana Buddhism and its schism with Nikaya Buddhism. Kanishka also had the original Gandhari vernacular, or Prakrit, Mahayana Buddhist texts translated into the language of Sanskrit. Along with the Indian king Ashoka, the Indo-Greek king Menander I (Milinda), and Harsha Vardhana, Kanishka is considered by Buddhism as one of its greatest benefactors.

The art and culture of Gandhara, at the crossroads of the Kushan hegemony, are the best known expressions of Kushan influences to Westerners. Several direct depictions of Kushans are known from Gandhara, where they are represented with a tunic, belt and trousers and play the role of devotees to the Buddha, as well as the Bodhisattva and future Buddha Maitreya. From the 3rd century the Kushan empire began to fragment.

Kushinagar : Kushinagar or Kusinagar is a Buddhist pilgrimage site located next to Kasia, a rural town in Kushinagar District of the state of Uttar Pradesh in northern India 52 km from Gorakhpur, In ancient times, it was known as Kushavati (Jatakas). Kushinagar was a celebrated center of the Malla kingdom of ancient India. Later, it would be known as Kushinara, one of four holy sites for Buddhists. At this location, near the Hiranyavati River, Gautama Buddha attained Parinirvana, and was cremated. Many of the ruined stupas and viharas here date back to 3rd century BCE - 5th century CE when prosperity was at its peak. The Mauryan emperor Ashoka is known to have contributed to significant construction at this site.

Prior to its rediscovery in the 19th century, there was a silence of more than half a millennium at Kasia. Due possibily to violent invasions, Kushinagar lost its vitality and eventually was neglected. The notable Buddha Temple, when rediscovered, was covered in a 40 foot high mound of bricks surrounded by a dense thorny forest. After E. Buchanan, an officer of the East India Company, arrived in Kasia in the course of his survey-work, H. H. Wilson, in 1854, made the suggestion that ancient Kushinagar and

Kasia were the same. Work resumed around 1861-1862 when General Alexander Cunningham, an archaeological surveyor, would prove the site to be that of Gautama Buddha's passing. A British officer named Mr. A.C.L. Carlleyle followed suit. Excavations began in the late 1800s and many important remnants of the main site such as the Matha Kuar and Ramabhar stupa were unveiled.

Today, Kushinagar is a much-frequented pilgrimage site for foreign tourists and temples have been constructed by Chinese, Sri Lankan, Thai, and Japanese Buddhists alongside the ruins of monasteries and stupas. For Buddhists, this is one of four pilgrimage sites related to the life of Gautama Buddha, the other three being Lumbini, Bodh Gaya, and Sarnath.

Kushiyara River : Kushiyara river is one of the Trans-boundary rivers of Bangladesh. The Barak of India originates from the northern hills of Assam in India and then it flows further creating the border between Nagaland and Manipur states. The river enters Bangladesh along 24 53 north latitudes and 92 32 east longitudes after flowing westward from Milchar in Kachar district (India). The Barak separates into two branches at Amalshid in the northeast border of Zakiganj upazila of Sylhet district. The northwest arm is the Surma and the southwestern arm is the Kushiyara. The Kushiyara rejoins with the Surma at Markuli in Ajmiriganj upazila and flows south upto Bhairab Bazar receiving the name Kalni. The Kalni meets with the Dhanu, a branch of the Surma and renamed as the Meghna. In the upstream from Markuli, partly the course of the Kushiyara is known as the Bibiyana.

Kushtia : Kushtia, Kushtia district or Kushtia Zilla is the name of a district in the Khulna administrative division of western Bangladesh. Kushtia has existed since the inception of Bangladesh. Kushtia was once a part of the Nodia district (West Bengal) of undivided India. A municipality was established in Kushtia in 1869. Hamilton's Gazetteer has the mention of Kushtia (Kustee) town and of the fact that the local people called the town Kushtay (Kushte).

Kushtia, however, is not an ancient township. A river port was developed in the district during the reign of Emperor Shahjahan. Although the British East India Company made extensive use of the port, it was not until indigo planters and traders settled that the township began to grow. A railway connection with Kolkata, capital of British India, made in 1860, made the town an alluring location for mills and factories, including the Jagneshwar Engineering Works (1896), Renwick and Company (1904), and the Mohini Mills (1919).

During the Partition of India, Kushtia was made a separate district, consisting of Kushtia Sôdor, Chuadanga and Meherpur subdivisions, in 1947. The town once again became attractive for development with the establishment of the Ganges-Kobadak Project headquarters and a number of government offices in 1954.

Kut : Observed on the 1st of November every year this is an autumnal festival of the different tribes of Kuki-Chin-Mizo groups of Manipur. The festival has been variously described at different places amongst different tribes as Chavang-Kut or Khodou, etc. The festival is celebrated as a symbol of gratitude to God, the giver of an abundant harvest.

Kutch : Kutch is a district of Gujarat state in western India. Covering an area of 45,612 km2, it is the largest district in the state of Gujarat and the second largest in India. According to some theorists, the name "Kutch" is a reference to the shape of the area, which when viewed from space, resembles a tortoise. The word for "tortoise" is Kaachbo in the Kutchi and Gujarati languages.

Kutch Festival : The 3-day organised package in February which combines the journey into the lovely destinations with evenings filled with the choicest food, dance, music and craft from Kutch is an unforgettable experience.

Kuthiottam : It is a song and dance ritual exclusive to the Devi temples of South Kerala.

Kutralam Falls : Kutralam Falls is a group of waterfalls in southern India. The falls are locate 160 kilometers from Madurai and 59 kilometers from Tirunelveli at an elevation of about 167 meters on the Western Ghat in Tirunelveli District. Kutralam has nine waterfalls; Peraruvi (Main Falls), Chitra Aruvi, Shenbaghadevi Falls, Then Aruvi (Honey Falls), Aintharuvi (Five Falls), Puli Aruvi (Tiger Falls), Pazhaya Courtrallam (Old Falls), Puthu Aruvi (New Falls), Pazhathotta Aruvi (Fruit Garden Falls). Kutralam has the nickname the Spa of the South India.

Kuttanad : Kuttanad in Kerala, India is the lowest region of India, with 500 square kilometres of the region below sea level. Its elevation ranges from 0.6 m above to 2.2 metres below sea level. Most of the area is covered with water throughout the year. Kuttanad is one of the few places in the world where farming is carried out below sea level. The region has a population of 1.8 million and comes under the Alappuzha district. Four major Kerala rivers, the Pampa, Meenachil, the Achankovil and the Manimala flow into Kuttanad. Despite being surrounded by water, there are acute potable water shortages, with water supplied only twice a week. Crops grown in Kuttanad include rice, bananas, casava and yams.

Kutubdia : Kutubdia is an island in the Bay of Bengal, off the coast near Chakaria, Cox's Bazar District, Bangladesh. The island forms the Kutubdia upazila or sub-district. A police station at Kutubdia was established in

1917. The island was upgraded into an upazila in 1983. Kutubdia is divided into 6 unions, 9 mouzas and 29 villages. The only town of the island is Kutubdia town, with an area of 9.82 square kilometres.

Kuvempu : Kuvempu is the pen name of a well-known Kannada writer/poet of the 20th century; Kuppalli VenkaTappa PuTTappa (1904—1994).He is the recipient of the highest award for literary work in India: Jnanpith Award. He was first among the Kannada writers to receive this honour.

Kuvempu's work RamayanaDharshanam, the rewriting of the great ancient Indian epic Ramayana, in contemporary Kannada, is regarded as the work that gave a fresh glimplses of the era of Mahakayva (Great Epics) in a contemporary form and charm. He is immortalised by some of his phrases and in particular far his contribution to the Universal Humanism or in his own terms "Vishwamanavata Vaada".